I Must Be About My Father's Business

Volume VII

Deeper Life
Spiritual Growth Cycle

Relationship, Transformation and Dominion
Working in the Love of God

James A. Twentier

Order this book online at www.trafford.com
or email orders@trafford.com

Most Trafford titles are also available at major online book retailers.

Print information available on the last page.

ISBN: 978-1-4907-6767-3 (sc)
ISBN: 978-1-4907-6766-6 (e)

North America & international
toll-free: 1 888 232 4444 (USA & Canada)
fax: 812 355 4082

Table of Contents and Course Curriculum

Table of Contents and Course Curriculum

Table of Contents and Course Curriculum

Appendices

Note: The 13 lessons described in the "Table of Contents" above, serve as the foundational curriculum for teaching in Global Missions Bible Schools. Each student is given an E-copy of this book and the other seven volumes in the series, "I Must Be About My Father's Business."

Introduction

The primary purpose and scope of the lesson series in this book are directed and driven by the greatest need and challenge for the born-again believer in these momentous days of the endtime. And that is to attain the spiritual maturity required to operate in the apostolic power, dominion and authority demonstrated in the book of Acts. Only this course of action will combat and overcome the evil and vicious spirit of the Antichrist, rapidly rising in the world today, and empower us to effectively reap the end-time harvest.

The key spiritual growth <u>cycle</u> concepts discussed in this book include: Relationship, Transformation and Dominion, all working in the (agape) love of God.

The term "**cycle**" is used here with "spiritual growth" because it emphasizes the need for repeated actions that bring greater and increased levels and depths of relationship, transformation, dominion and love required for apostolic ministry. The following charts, displayed in subsequent chapters, demonstrate and emphasize this concept:

Chapter	Chart	Chart Name	Repeated Cycles of:
1	E-1	The Ecosystem of the Kingdom	Relationship, transformation and dominion working in the love of God
2	R-1	Complete Relationship With God	Communication, love and trust
3	T-9	Spiritual Growth (Rending the Veil of Self)	The infilling of Holy Ghost and the work of the Holy Ghost. Less of self and more of God.
	T-12	Spiritual Maturity Cycle	Impartation (power of the Holy Ghost), engagement (in the battle), and transformation
4	D-2	Dominion in the Supernatural	Love, obedience, burden, sacrifice, anointing, charity, and the Gifts of the Spirit
	D-6	Impartation Plus Encounter Releases Supernatural Power	Impartation, Encounter and Power
5	S-4	Soul Winning Cycle	Building a relationship with God, operating as a son of man and operating as a son of God
6	L-4	Our Love for God is Measured by Our Love for Our Brother	God's love to us, our love to our brother and our love to God
7	H-1	Perfect Love, the Foundation for Humility and Unity Required for Another Pentecost	Love, humility, unity and revival
8	P-5	Levels of Prayer, Burden and Anointing	Increased levels of prayer, burden and anointing

Spiritual Growth – A Continuous Cycle of Change

The initial conversion experience can be viewed as a **straight line** with four sequential steps that can happen in one day:

**(1) Believing + (2) Repentance + (3) Baptism in Jesus name
+ (4) Receiving the Gift of the Holy Ghost = Conversion**

But spiritual growth must be viewed as a **circle,** a lifetime process with **repeated cycles of continuous change and growth**. As disciples of Jesus Christ, we are called to a life of constant renewal, revival, change and growth as we assume more of the nature and character of the Master Teacher. This is discussed in detail in Chapter 4, "Transformation of the Inner Man."

Old Testament: The story of King Joash and the prophet Elisha depicts God's demand for repeated cycles of action to demonstrate our zeal and fervor in partnering with Him for victory in the battle:

Now Elisha was fallen sick of his sickness whereof he died. And Joash the king of Israel came down unto him, and wept over him . . . And Elisha said unto him, Take bow and arrows . . . And he said to the king of Israel, Put thine hand upon the bow. And he put his hand upon it: and Elisha put his hands upon the king's hands. Then Elisha said, Shoot. And he shot. And he said, The arrow of the Lord's deliverance, and the arrow of deliverance from Syria: for thou shalt smite the Syrians in Aphek, till thou have consumed them. And he said, Take the arrows. And he took them. And he said unto the king of Israel, Smite upon the ground. And he smote thrice, and stayed. And the man of God was wroth with him, and said, Thou shouldest have smitten five or six times; then hadst thou smitten Syria till thou hadst consumed it: whereas now thou shalt smite Syria but thrice (2 Kings 13:14-19).

God's part: The king, no doubt, knew how to use a bow better than the prophet did. But the arrow to be shot needed to have the power and direction of the divine. Therefore Elisha put his hands upon the king's hands, to signify that in all of his battles against the Syrians he must look to God for direction and strength. He must acknowledge that his own hands were not sufficient to defeat the enemy, and his dependence upon divine aid. The trembling hands of a dying prophet, signified the presence and power of God -- giving this arrow a supernatural force that dwarfed that of the king in his full strength.

Man's part: Having prophesied the victory over the Syrians, the prophet tested the king's intensity and zeal to carry out his part in claiming and securing total victory. Elisha was angered at the half-hearted actions of King Joash, because he did not sense the greatness of the opportunity and the abundant favor of God to grant total victory over the enemy. The prophecy of total victory was changed to one of only partial victory over the Syrians.

-- From The Pulpit Commentary

Elisha was angered at the lukewarmness of Joash, and his lack of faith and zeal. He himself, from his higher standpoint, saw the greatness of the opportunity, the abundance of favor which God was ready to grant, and the way in which God's favor was stinted and narrowed by Joash's want of receptiveness. Had the king been equal to the occasion, a full end might at once have been made of Syria, and Israel might have been enabled to brace herself for the still more perilous struggle with Assyria, in which she ultimately succumbed. If he had been earnestly desirous of victory, and had faith in the symbolical action as divinely directed, he would have kept on smiting till the prophet told him it was enough. He abstained because he was wanting in the proper zeal for obtaining the full promises of God.[1]

After more than 2,800 years, two timeless truths, depicted in the text of this narrative, are still applicable to us today:

(1) We must always depend on God's hand on our lives for divine ability to bring victory over the enemy.

(2) God requires a constant and zealous pursuit of Him through increased and repeated cycles of actions to obtain His full promises.

New Testament: Jesus emphasized, in the story of the "talents", His demand for fervor and increased levels of growth and effectiveness working in His Kingdom. To the servants who doubled what had been given them, five and two talents respectively, the Lord commended them: *"Well done, thou good and faithful servant: thou hast been faithful over a few things, I will make thee ruler over many things: enter thou into the joy of thy Lord" (Matt. 25:20-23).*

To the servant who received one talent, hid it and did not multiply it, the Lord angrily condemned him to eternal damnation: *"His Lord answered and said unto him, Thou wicked and slothful servant . . . Thou oughtest therefore to have put my money to the exchangers, and then at my coming I should have received mine own with usury. . . Cast ye the unprofitable servant into outer darkness: there shall be weeping and gnashing of teeth" (Matt. 25:24-30).*

Challenges of the Battle and Harvest

Today the challenges of the battle and harvest seem an insurmountable task unmatched in the history of mankind:

- Satan is leading a revival of wickedness with more sin, abuse, sickness and perversion than any prior generation.

- There is an ever increasing population on the earth to reach with the gospel. As of 2015, the population is increasing by 202,400 people each day; 73,926,600 each year.

- The affluence and prosperity of our society is fighting against the mission and vision of the church.

- This spirit of the Antichrist is rapidly increasing in the world and challenging the church on every front:
    - The Supreme Court has just redefined the biblical definition of marriage and changed the laws of the U.S. to support same sex marriage.
    - The LGBT agenda is being pushed at every level from the Supreme Court and the president in the White house, to the city government and local school districts. Speaking out against sin defined in the Bible is a hate crime in some countries and will soon be in the U.S.
    - Lawlessness, with rebellion and hatred toward lawmen, is rising at an unprecedented rate in our country. Examples of this include: city officials illegally refusing to obey federal law to detain and deport illegal immigrants that have committed felonies, organizations formed that disrespect, demonize and encourage the killing of police officers, who are commissioned to keep us safe.
    - Terrorism in every part of the world with airplanes being blown out of the sky, suicide bombers, major attacks on innocent people in public places, etc. – wars and rumors of wars threatening the start of a global conflict (World War III).

The church has never worked in a harvest nor fought in a battle like that of today. We are working in the endtime -- in the late evening shadows of 6,000 years of man's day. We are standing on the brink of eternity with the task of reaching a generation that is further from God than any prior one. Many voices of the enemy are screaming that restoration, of the first century church apostolic power and authority with continuous miracles and signs, is impossible today. This seemingly impossible task, to reach the lost of this godless, hopeless generation, with time running out, sets the stage for God to do a new thing -- a supernatural thing.

Our great omnipotent, omniscient, omnipresent God is calling every born-again believer to partner with Him at the supernatural level as a son of God -- fighting in His battle and working in His harvest with dominion and authority over satan and sickness:

"And as ye go, preach, saying, The kingdom of heaven is at hand. Heal the sick, cleanse the lepers, raise the dead, cast out devils: freely ye have received, freely give" (Matt. 10:7-8).

"And these signs shall follow them that believe; In my name shall they cast out devils; . . . they shall lay hands on the sick, and they shall recover" (Mark 16:17-18).

The Importance of the Father's Business
The Father's business is unlike any other business. His business is the one enterprise that surpasses and supersedes all others. There is no comparison to another, because His Kingdom is on a different plane, a different planet, and a different universe. His Kingdom is eternal. The Kingdom of God, of which every believer is a part, holds a place in time and history and importance that every other kingdom, past, present, and future pales in comparison.

Introduction

Business corporations set goals and continuously measure results to track their progress and growth. Jesus said in *Luke 16:8,* ***"For the children of this world are in their generation wiser than the children of light".*** Let it not be said that the men of this world, whose ends and aims are bounded by the horizon of this world, are more skillful and zealous in their temporal endeavors than we as children of God in our noble toiling in the Father's business -- the things of the eternal.

As a son of God, we have inherited His business. An heir not only inherits the wealth and assets of the father, but he also inherits the father's business. It is God's will for us to inherit more than His benefits, but also to inherit His business. The Father's eternal purpose for us, as sons of God, is to fulfill and complete His mission -- His business. He took our place in His death at Calvary and it is His will for us to take His place in this world to complete His mission and His work that He started while on earth.

The first recorded words of Jesus are very significant and are etched on the pages of time as a message to all of mankind -- ***"I must be about my Father's business."*** These immortal words defined Jesus, as a twelve year old boy (Son of man), as He began to understand His identity and purpose as Son of God.

When we become aware of who we are as sons of God, we should likewise declare: **"I must be about my Father's business."** As we pursue the Father's business, we will have favor with God and be assured: *"Thou art my beloved son in whom I am well pleased."* As we minister to the needs of the lost, God will give us favor with man and confirmation to them: *"This is my beloved son in whom I am well pleased."*

It is God's will for us to spend the last few remaining days of the Church Age completing His mission, His business, and His work that He exampled and defined for us in His brief ministry on earth. Jesus defined His business as the battle against the evil powers of satan and reaping the harvest of lost souls:

> **The Battle (Sword):** *"For this purpose the Son of God was manifest that he might destroy the works of the devil"* (1 John 3:9). If we are to be a part of this, we must put on the whole armor and sharpen our sword for the final battle.

> **The Harvest (Sickle):** *"For the Son of man is come to seek and save that which was lost"* (Luke 19:10). *"Pray ye the Lord of the harvest, that he would send forth labourers into the harvest"* (Matthew 9:3 – Jesus' only prayer request).

- **To experience the results of the first century church in the book of Acts, there must be visionaries and innovators whose greatest joy and priority is the Father's business.**

The book of Acts contains 28 chapters, but it has no amen -- no ending. Many other chapters have been added over the past 2,000 years. In these closing days of the Church Age, just before the second coming of Jesus Christ, the last chapter is being recorded.

Will we be content to just read history or will we be a part of the visionaries whose actions are recorded in the final frame? To be a part of this, we must press with our prayers, fasting and actions of ministry until the doors of evangelism and miracles are blown wide open and the book of Acts power flows unrestricted to those hopelessly bound in prisons of sickness, sin and abuse.

We must determine that we will not stand at the Judgment having done less in our Father's Kingdom than we did in our kingdom for our employers and our personal interests. When the day is done and we stand on the other side looking back, let us have the testimony of Apostle Paul: *"I have fought a good fight; I have kept the faith; I have finished my course"* -- I have given my life in the Father's business.

Elevating the Father's Business to the Top Priority

Something in the heart of many Jewish people is not complete outside the Promised Land. Likewise, with the Kingdom of God, His church should occupy the highest position and priority in our lives. It must be our greatest joy **-- our chief joy.**

King David, the man after God's own heart, penned an eternal truth that remains after three millennia: **To please God we must make Jerusalem, Zion (His Kingdom, His Church) our chief joy.** He is referring to a time when the Israelites were prisoners of war in Babylon. They were captives far away from their homeland seemingly with no possibility of returning.

Psalms 137:1, 5-6
1 By the rivers of Babylon, there we sat down, yea, we wept, when we remembered Zion.
5 If I forget thee, O Jerusalem, let my right hand forget her cunning.
6 If I do not remember thee, let my tongue cleave to the roof of my mouth; if I prefer not Jerusalem above my chief joy.

5 If I forget you, O Jerusalem, let my right hand forget its skill [with the harp].
6 Let my tongue cleave to the roof of my mouth if I remember you not, if I prefer not Jerusalem above my chief joy! AMP

-- From Barnes' Notes

[If I prefer not Jerusalem] literally, "If I do not cause to ascend." That is, if I do not exalt Jerusalem in my estimation above everything that gives me pleasure; if I do not find my supreme happiness in that.

[Above my chief joy] Margin, as in Hebrew, the head of my joy. The chief thing which gives me joy; as the head is the chief, or is supreme over the body. There are other sources of joy which are not in any way inconsistent with the kingdom of God: the joy of friendship; of domestic life; of honorable pursuits of the esteem of people. So of music, the arts, gardens, literature, science, hobbies and careers. But when one interferes with the other, or is inconsistent with the other, the joy of the world is to be

12

sacrificed to the joy of God's kingdom. When the joy of God's kingdom is sacrificed for the joy of the world, it proves that there is no true righteousness in the soul. The kingdom of God must always be supreme.[2]

- **Jerusalem or Zion to us in the New Testament church is the Kingdom of God and it must always be our first priority -- our chief joy.**

- **Only strong Christians will experience the completed work of restoration. To be strong Christians, we must be joyful because, *"The joy of the Lord is our strength"* (Neh. 8:10).**

- **When the work and will of God become our chief joy, it will occupy the highest priority in our lives -- positioning us to partner with Him in the supernatural.**

Deeper Life Spiritual Growth Cycle Lesson Series

The lesson series in this book provides a high level summary of some of the key foundational principles discussed in the other seven books in the progressive series, "**I Must Be About My Father's Business**":

Volume	Book Name	Spanish Translated
I	God's Purpose for Man -- Relationship and Dominion	*
II	Dominion -- Doing God's Will and Work	*
III	Spiritual Growth -- Dominion Over Sin and Self	*
IV	Unlimited Partnership With a Supernatural God	*
V	Revival and Evangelism -- Passion for God / Compassion for the Lost	*
VI	Perfect Love -- The Highest Law and Strongest Force	
VIII	Addendum Volume PowerPoint Charts that support all the volumes	*

Refer to Appendix 3 for the major subjects addressed in this book cross referenced to the other seven books in the series, "**I Must Be About My Father's Business.**"

This book (Volume VII) was designed to provide enough detail to teach more than the 13 lessons outlined here. However, if more information is desired on any of these subjects, hard copies and E-copies are available for each of these books. For a brief summary of each book and how to obtain copies, refer to Appendices 4 and 8 and websites: My-Fathers-Business.net (English) and Negocios-de-mi-Padre.net (Spanish).

I Must Be About My Father's Business
Seven Volume Progressive Series

The message of "Perfect Love" in Volume 6 is essential for the principles in the other five volumes to work effectively. The Addendum Volume contains the 8.5 X 11 copies of the PowerPoint Charts that support the themes presented in the above six volumes.

1. The Ecosystem of God's Kingdom - Overview

Every living thing is defined and sustained by three functions: **input, process and output**. Even a computer program is defined by these three basic processes. Likewise, the spiritual growth and maturity of a Christian revolves around these three processes or themes redefined as: **Relationship, Transformation and Dominion.** Refer to Chart E-1 on the following page.

Relationship involves God and man sharing a mutual interaction of love, communication and trust. Refer to Chapter 2 for a high-level overview.

Transformation involves continuous change. It involves emptying of self to be filled with more of God: less of my will and more of God's will, less of my mind and more of God's mind, less of my limited human love and more of God's perfect agape love. It involves dominion over self (the soul: will, mind and emotions) -- *"He must increase and I must decrease."* Refer to Chapter 3 for a high-level overview.

Dominion involves God sharing His authority and power with man, as a son of God, to fulfill His will and work on earth as he is **directed and driven by God's perfect love**. This involves engagement in the harvest field and battlefield with dominion over satan and sickness. Refer to Chapter 4 for a high-level overview.

Every concept in the Bible that pertains to Christian living and service relates to one or more of these three key subjects or themes. These three biblical concepts should be repeated in a continuous cycle in our lives as we mature and become more like our heavenly Father. These three inter-related concepts work together in the **ecosystem of God's Kingdom** to bring spiritual maturity and fulfillment of God's purpose and will for our lives. Refer to Charts E-5 and E-6, at the end of this chapter for the definition of the term "ecosystem."

Agape Love (God's Perfect Love)

There is one key overarching theme that is woven into these three processes that is superior to every theme or subject in the Bible. And that is the perfect **L-O-V-E** of God -- the highest law and strongest force in the Kingdom of God. The perfect love of God is the life flow in the body of Christ. It is the currency of God's Kingdom.

Just as oxygen is the key element in our natural ecosystem for us to live, God's perfect love is the key element in God's ecosystem for the spiritual man to survive and thrive. Love is the only motive accepted by God for working in His Kingdom: *"Though I have all spiritual gifts . . . give all my goods to the poor . . . give my body to be burned, and have not love, it is nothing" (1 Cor. 13:1-3).*

It must be the foundation for every Christian concept and action for there to be anything accomplished that is effective and lasting. Only love will produce the humility required for the one mind and one accord unity evident at the birth of the church on the Day of Pentecost. Refer to Chart E-7 at the end of this chapter and Chapter 6 for a high-level overview of perfect love.

Chart E-1

The Ecosystem of God's Kingdom

Just as oxygen is the key element in our natural ecosystem for us to live, PERFECT LOVE is the key element in God's ecosystem for the spiritual man to grow and be productive. It is the key element and driving force in a growing relationship with God, transformation of the inner man and dominion in the harvest field and battlefield.

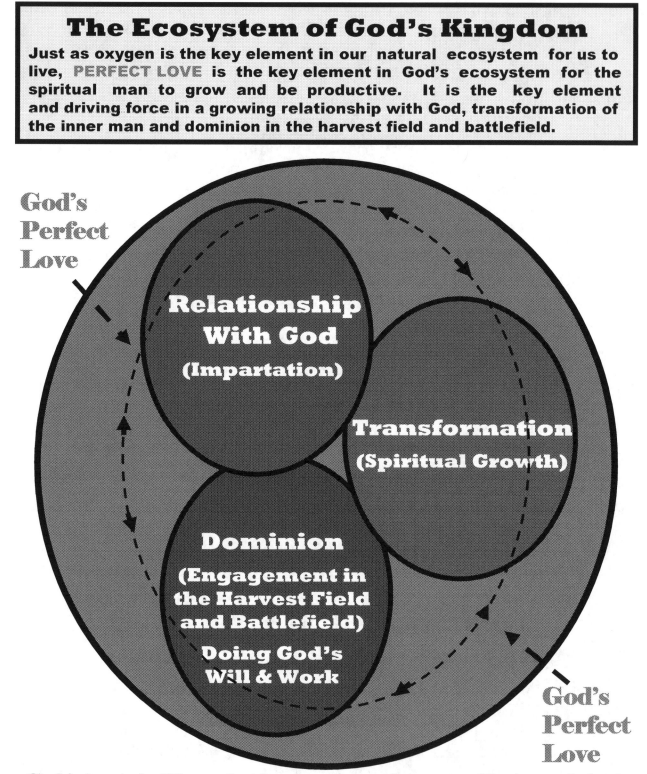

God's Perfect Love

Relationship With God
(Impartation)

Transformation
(Spiritual Growth)

Dominion
(Engagement in the Harvest Field and Battlefield)
Doing God's Will & Work

God's Perfect Love

God is love -- in His perfect love we live and move and have our being!

Isaiah's Three Dimensional Vision

Isaiah's vision recorded in Chapter 6 illustrates the three significant elements in the ecosystem of God's Kingdom: Relationship, Transformation and Dominion.

(1) An upward vision of God (need for a renewed **relationship**).

(2) An inward vision of himself (need for repentance and **transformation**).

(3) An outward vision of the world (answering God's call to minister to the needs of the world - **dominion**).

Refer to Chart E-4 at the end of this chapter.

After King Uzziah's death, Isaiah went to the house of God. Isaiah Chapter 6 describes his life-changing vision and encounter with God:

Relationship with God:

1 In the year that King Uzziah died I saw also the Lord sitting upon a throne, high and lifted up, and his train filled the temple.
2 Above it stood the seraphims: each one had six wings; with twain he covered his face, and with twain he covered his feet, and with twain he did fly.
3 And one cried unto another, and said, Holy, holy, holy, is the LORD of hosts: the whole earth is full of his glory.
4 And the posts of the door moved at the voice of him that cried, and the house was filled with smoke.

Repentance and Transformation:

*5 Then said I, **Woe is me! For I am undone**; because I am a man of unclean lips, and I dwell in the midst of a people of unclean lips: for mine eyes have seen the King, the LORD of hosts.*
6 Then flew one of the seraphims unto me, having a live coal in his hand, which he had taken with the tongs from off the altar:
*7 And he laid it upon my mouth, and said, **Lo**, this hath touched thy lips; **and thine iniquity is taken away**, and thy sin purged.*

Dominion (doing God's Will and Work):

*8 Also I heard the voice of the Lord, saying, Whom shall I send, and **who will go for us**? Then said I, **Here am I; send me.***

Isaiah was a man called of God, a prophet, and a priest who performed priesthood duties in the temple. As the son of Amos, he knew all about the sacred place, having performed those functions numerous times. He served through the reign of four monarchs. But of all the kings whom he served, King Uzziah was to him the greatest.

King Uzziah was second only to King David in military might. He had invented very powerful weapons of war and cannons that could shoot stones from the walls of the cities. He was a great military warrior and served as the monarch of Israel for many years. When his name was spoken the nations of the world trembled because of his military strength. During his reign, the nation of Judah developed into a strong commercial and military state. Yet during this time period Judah witnessed a spiritual decline.

Isaiah felt extremely secure under the leadership, friendship and protection of this king, because his name was revered throughout the world. But Isaiah's relationship with Jehovah was incomplete, because he relied on the arm of flesh. It appears that he began trusting too much in a powerful earthly king and not enough in the heavenly King.

When it comes to the Kingdom of God and our relationship with God, it is very dangerous to depend on human strength. It will displease God, affect our trust in Him and weaken the leading of His Spirit in our lives. God desires a relationship with His children of complete trust and confidence in His wisdom, power and ability.

Isa. 31:1
Woe to them that go down to Egypt for help; and stay on horses, and trust in chariots, because they are many; and in horsemen, because they are very strong; but they look not unto the Holy One of Israel, neither seek the LORD!

Jer. 17:5
Thus saith the LORD; Cursed be the man that trusteth in man, and maketh flesh his arm, and whose heart departeth from the LORD.

A Vision, like Isaiah's is one that we all must experience from time to time.

Upward vision: He saw the Lord in His holiness and glory. He saw his need to renew his **relationship** with God. It was a vision of heighth -- the Lord high and lifted up. It was a vision of God's holiness. A Holy God with the angels crying: "Holy, Holy".

Inward vision: He saw himself and his need for repentance, and **transformation**. It was a vision of depth. He saw the recesses of his own heart that needed to be cleansed and changed. It was a vision of helplessness: "I am undone" (my needs). Any time we draw near to God and feel His awesome holiness, we have to fall at His feet like Isaiah and repent.

Outward vision: He saw the world, the needs of others and a calling to step into the **dominion** role to do God's will and work. It was a vision of breadth that revealed a world with needs that must be met. It was a vision that revealed the desire of God's heart – for someone to deliver His message to the world. It was God calling for help -- *"Whom shall I send, and who will go for us?"* (God's needs).

Woe, was a word of confession for a need to be cleansed. **Lo,** was a word of remission for sins forgiven. **Go** was a word of commission to take God's message to the world. Twenty five hundred years later, "Go" is still the most important word of Jesus recorded in His Great Commission to every born-again believer. And may our answer be that of Isaiah: *"Here am I; send me."*

Hudson Taylor stated that: "The Great Commission is not an option to be considered; it is a command to be obeyed!"

This all-consuming priority of Jesus is emphasized in His Great Commission recorded in the first five books of the New Testament:

- Matthew: *"Go make disciples of every nation."*

- Mark: *"Go into all the world and preach the good news to all creation."*

- Luke: *"Repentance and remission of sin should be preached in every nation."*

- John: *"As my Father hath sent me, even so send I you."*

- Acts: *"Ye shall be witnesses unto me both in Jerusalem, and in all Judea, and in Samaria, and unto the uttermost part of the earth."*

But before Jesus sent them, He told them to tarry in Jerusalem for **revival power** to accomplish the **task of evangelism**: *Behold, I send the promise of my Father upon you: but **tarry** ye in the city of Jerusalem, **until ye be endued with power** from on high (Luke 24:49).*

It is Jesus, the Lord of the harvest, who gave the sequence of the two commands: *"Tarry ye"* and *"Go ye."* **"Tarry ye" -- that is revival.** **"Go ye" -- that is evangelism.** And it must always be in that sequence.

Like Isaiah, a vision of God will first bring an upward look to see anything between us and God -- anything we have relied on more than God. An inward look will bring an awareness of our need to change and be transformed -- producing inward fruit. Then the burden and call of God will bring an outward look to a lost world and our need to step into the **dominion** role of doing God's will and work – producing outward fruit.

- **The greater our inward look and inward revival with inward fruit -- the greater will be our outward look and outward revival with outward fruit.**

Isaiah's Revelation: After Isaiah's vision and life-changing reaction to the call of God, his ministry took a dramatic change and he became one of the greatest prophetic voices of the Old Testament pointing to the coming Messiah. At the beginning of the very next chapter, he gets a glimpse of Jesus, the promised Messiah and writes: *"Therefore the Lord himself shall give you a sign; Behold, a virgin shall conceive, and bear a son, and shall call his name Immanuel"* *(Isa. 7:14).*

After that, we see again and again in his writings, through the telescope of prophecy, an incredible unfolding revelation of the coming Messiah, Jesus Christ. A few of these prophecies include the following:

Isa. 9:6   Unto us a child is born . . . and his name shall be called Wonderful, Counsellor, The mighty God, The everlasting Father, The Prince of Peace.

Isa. 11:2   The Spirit of the Lord will rest upon Him, the Spirit of wisdom and understanding.

Isa. 25:6-12   He will swallow up death in victory.

Isa. 29:18   The deaf shall hear, eyes of the blind shall see.

Isa. 42:6   He will be a light to the Gentiles.

Isa. 50:7   He will be beaten and spat upon.

Isa. 52:14   He will so abused and tortured that from his appearance He would scarcely be recognized.

Isa. 53:1-4   He will be despised, rejected, bear our grief and carry our sorrow.

Isa. 53:5   He will be wounded for our transgressions, bruised for our iniquities and by His stripes we will be healed.

Isa. 53:7   He will be led as a lamb to the slaughter, accused, and will not open His mouth.

Isa. 53:10   He will be made an offering for sin and intercession for the transgressors.

Isa. 60:1-3   Darkness shall cover the earth, but people shall walk in the light of the Lord.

Isa. 61:1-2   Records Jesus' mission statement that He quoted in His first sermon:

The Spirit of the Lord GOD is upon me; because the LORD hath anointed me to preach good tidings unto the meek; he hath sent me to bind up the brokenhearted, to proclaim liberty to the captives, and the opening of the prison to them that are bound; To proclaim the acceptable year of the Lord (Luke 4:18).

- **New levels of relationship with God will always create new levels of revelation and transformation -- resulting in new levels of dominion in doing His will and work.**

Refer to the following pages for the charts related to this chapter.

Chart E-2

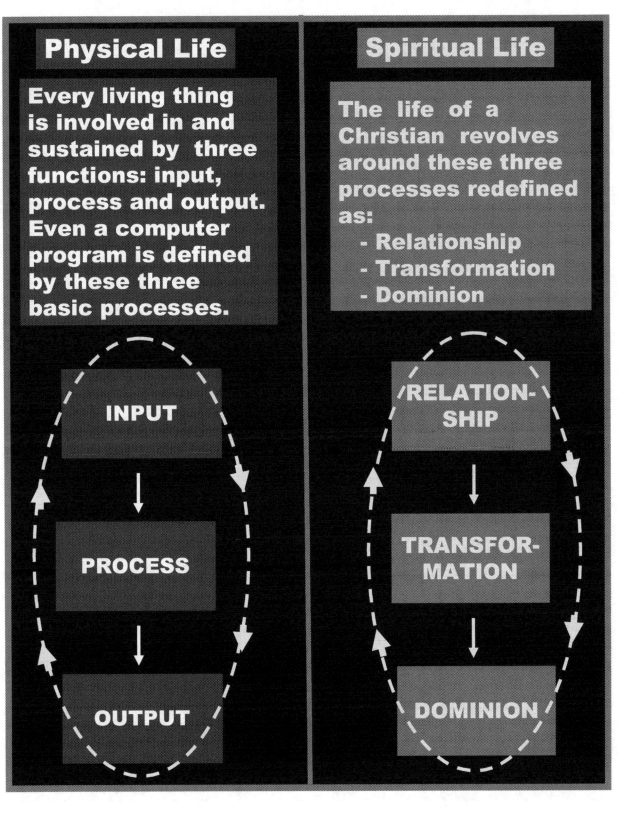

Physical Life

Every living thing is involved in and sustained by three functions: input, process and output. Even a computer program is defined by these three basic processes.

INPUT

PROCESS

OUTPUT

Spiritual Life

The life of a Christian revolves around these three processes redefined as:
- Relationship
- Transformation
- Dominion

RELATION-SHIP

TRANSFOR-MATION

DOMINION

Chart E-3

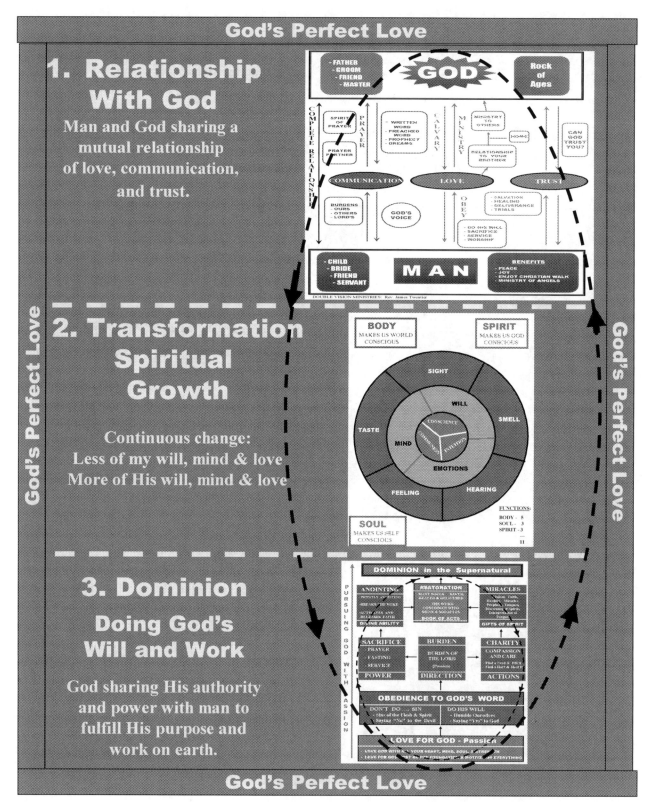

God's Perfect Love

1. Relationship With God

Man and God sharing a mutual relationship of love, communication, and trust.

2. Transformation Spiritual Growth

Continuous change:
Less of my will, mind & love
More of His will, mind & love

3. Dominion

Doing God's Will and Work

God sharing His authority and power with man to fulfill His purpose and work on earth.

God's Perfect Love

Chart E-4

Isaiah's vision illustrates the three significant elements in the Ecosystem of the Kingdom: Relationship, Transformation, Dominion:

- An upward vision of God (need for a renewed Relationship).

- An inward vision of himself (need for Transformation).

- An outward vision of the World (doing God's will, ministering to the needs of the world - Dominion).

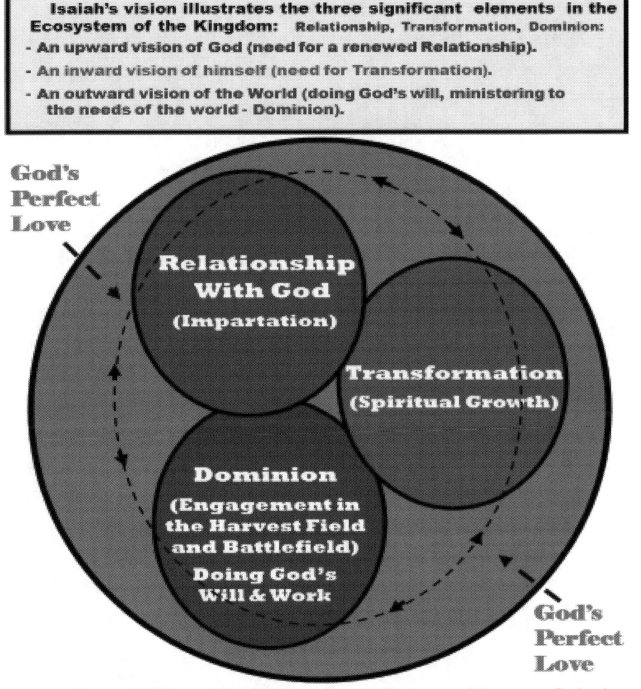

God's Perfect Love

Relationship With God (Impartation)

Transformation (Spiritual Growth)

Dominion (Engagement in the Harvest Field and Battlefield) Doing God's Will & Work

God's Perfect Love

God is love – in His perfect love we live and move and have our being!

Chart E-5 [1]

Natural Ecosystem

The environment (conditions, surroundings, forces and influences) that affect the growth, health and progress of a living thing.

Aquatic Ecosystem

A <u>balanced</u> aquatic ecosystem provides an environment where fish can survive, thrive and reproduce:

- Clean water, free from toxic chemicals
- Proper amounts of oxygen
- Adequate supply of nutrition
- Protection from predators
- Adequate sunlight

Chart E-6

The Ecosystem of God's Kingdom

Spiritual Ecosystem

The environment (Biblical principles, forces and influences) that affects the growth, health, progress, power and actions of a born-again Christian.

Chart E-7

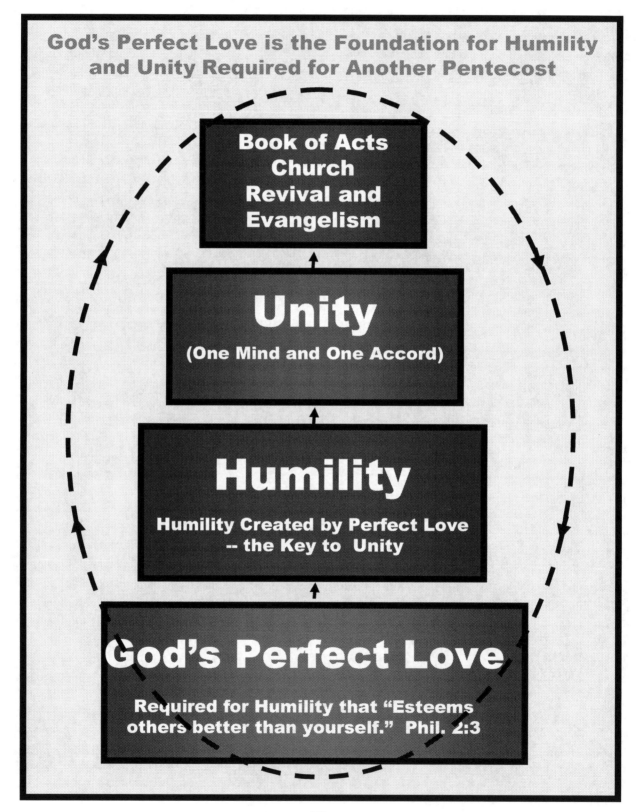

God's Perfect Love is the Foundation for Humility and Unity Required for Another Pentecost

Book of Acts
Church
Revival and
Evangelism

Unity
(One Mind and One Accord)

Humility
Humility Created by Perfect Love
-- the Key to Unity

God's Perfect Love
Required for Humility that "Esteems others better than yourself." Phil. 2:3

2. A Complete Relationship With God

Theme Summary and Key Scripture Text

Relationship
(Man depending on God)

Involves God and man sharing a mutual interaction of **love**, **communication**, and **trust**.

Man's relationship with God is depicted in Scripture as a **son** of God, a **servant** of God, a **friend** of God and the **bride** of Christ.

Levels and Depths of Relationship:

In the Gospels we see four circles and inner circles of relationship of Jesus with His twelve disciples:

- John (inner most circle)
- Peter, James and John (inner circle)
- The other eight disciples
- Judas (outer circle)

Loving God and loving our brother are completely and indivisibly linked, because we are members of one body and our love for God is manifest by our love for our brother.

Our Connection to the Father
(Impartation and Empowerment)

- I stand at the door, and I am constantly knocking. If anyone hears me calling him and opens the door, I will come in and fellowship with him and he with me. (Rev. 3:20) TLB

- I am the vine, ye are the branches: He that abideth in me, and I in him, the same bringeth forth much fruit: for without me ye can do nothing. (John 15:5)

- If you live in Me [abide vitally united to Me] and My words remain in you and continue to live in your hearts, ask whatever you will, and it shall be done for you. (John 15:7)

- May Christ through your faith dwell (abide, make His permanent home) in your hearts! May you be rooted deep in love and founded securely on love. (Eph. 3:17) AMP

- The anointing (the sacred appointment, the unction) which you received from Him abides [permanently] in you . . . But just as His anointing teaches you concerning everything and is true, so you must abide in (live in, never depart from) Him [being rooted in Him, knit to Him]. (1 John 2:27) AMP

- The Lord hath appeared of old unto me, saying, Yea, I have loved thee with an everlasting love: therefore with loving kindness have I drawn thee. (Jer. 31:3)

- For God so loved the world, that he gave his only begotten Son, that whosoever believeth in him should not perish, but have everlasting life. (John 3:16)

- Thou shalt love the Lord thy God with all thy heart, and with all thy soul, and with all thy strength, and with all thy mind; and thy neighbour as thyself. (Luke 10:27, Matt. 22:37, Mark 12:30)

- If we love one another, God dwelleth in us, and his love is perfected in us. (1 John 4:12)

- He who does not love his brother, whom he has seen, cannot love God, whom he has not seen. And this command (charge, order, injunction) we have from Him: that he who loves God shall love his brother [believer] also. (1 John 4:20-21) AMP

Study References

Vol.	Book Name	Primary Study Section / Chapter	Elective Study
I	God's Purpose for Man - Relationship - Dominion	Sec. II / Ch. 1-3	Sec. I / Ch. 1-3, Sec. II / Ch. 3
VI	Perfect Love -- The Highest Law and Strongest Force	Sec. I / Ch. 11, 12	Sec. I / Ch. 4, 5
VIII	Addendum Volume (PowerPoint Charts)	Charts at the end of this chapter	A-1, 3, 6, 8-12

One of a Christian's highest goals should be to develop a close and growing relationship with God. A relationship that is not growing will eventually die. The term, "relationship with God" is so commonly used that it could easily lose its real meaning and value. This lesson will discuss:

- God's plan and desire for a close relationship with man.
- The basic components of a complete and growing relationship with God.

God's desire to have a close and growing relationship with man goes back to the beginning of time, in the Garden of Eden. God prepared a wonderful paradise for Adam and Eve, where He communicated with them every day. Because of sin, their close relationship with God was broken. But God had another plan for a closer relationship with man.

The Three Tabernacles

In these three tabernacles, we see God's progressive plan for a closer relationship with man:
- God dwelling in the tabernacle of Moses.
- Jesus Christ - God tabernacled in human flesh.
- God tabernacled in the born-again believer.

Like the tabernacle of Moses with three parts (outer court, Holy Place, and Most Holy Place), our tabernacle is made up of three parts (body, soul, and spirit). And when we are born again of the water and the Spirit, **we become the tabernacle of God's Spirit** with a dual nature as a son of man and a son of God.

Human Relationships Used to Describe Our Relationship With God

In the Holy Scriptures God used every human relationship to help us understand how He wanted our relationship with Him to be close and growing. These relationships teach us how God sees our relationship with Him -- how He wants to relate to us and how He wants us to relate to Him.

Relationship	God / Man
Father / Child	He is the Father and we are His children
Groom / Bride	He is the Groom, we are His bride
Friend / Friend	He is a Friend that is closer than a brother
Master / Servant	He is our Lord and Master, we are His servants (love slaves)
God / Man	Beyond human relationships

Father / Child Relationship

This is the most frequently used relationship in the Bible to describe the relationship between God and man. In my kingdom I am a son of man. In His Kingdom I am a son of God.

Luke 12:32
Fear not, little flock; for it is your Father's good pleasure to give you the kingdom.

1 John 3:1-3
*1 Behold, what manner of love the Father hath bestowed upon us, that we should be called the **sons of God**: therefore the world knoweth us not, because it knew him not.*
*2 Beloved, now are we the **sons of God**, and it doth not yet appear what we shall be: but we know that, when he shall appear, we shall be like him; for we shall see him as he is.*
3 And every man that hath this hope in him purifieth himself, even as he is pure.

Phil. 2:15
*That ye may be blameless and harmless, the **sons of God**, without rebuke, in the midst of a crooked and perverse nation, among whom ye shine as lights in the world;*

The Father / Child relationship depicts provision for every need we have:

Mark 11: 25 - Forgiveness when we fail.
Ps. 103:13 - Divine sympathy.
Matt. 10:29 - Cares about every detail of our life.
Luke 11:13 - Gives precious and valuable gifts.
Heb. 12:6 - Correction when we sin.
Isaiah 1:2 - Gives us nourishment.
Matt. 6:6 - Rewards us when we pray.
Rom. 5:8 - Unconditional love.

The list of Scriptures is endless that speaks of the Father / Child relationship. This relationship provides unconditional love. In other relationships there is conditional love. If feelings of love are not mutual, the relationship will not survive. But our heavenly Father has given us unconditional love -- *"While we were yet sinners Christ died for us"*. He loved us and sought us before we knew Him.

This relationship should change and progress through the different stages of maturity. The life stages of infant, child, youth, young adult, and mature adult, bring new levels of relationship with the father. A small child loves his parents for what they do for him, not for who they are. Our relationship with our heavenly Father must likewise mature and grow beyond seeing Him only as the provider of our needs.

Apostles Paul and Peter address the spiritual growth of a babe in Christ to a mature Christian:

Heb. 5:12-14
12 For when for the time ye ought to be teachers, ye have need that one teach you again which be the first principles of the oracles of God; and are become such as have need of milk, and not of strong meat.
13 For every one that useth milk is unskilful in the word of righteousness: for he is a babe.
14 But strong meat belongeth to them that are of full age, even those who by reason of use have their senses exercised to discern both good and evil.

1 Peter 2:2
As newborn babes, desire the sincere milk of the word, that ye may grow thereby:

Bride / Groom Relationship
The bride and groom relationship depicts:
- Closeness and intimacy.
- Lifelong commitment.
- Bonding together as one.

At the beginning of this relationship, in the courtship phase, it is often love at first sight -- often one-sided. If it remains one-sided, the relationship cannot develop. God loved us at first sight: *"While we were yet sinners, Christ died for us"*. He courted us and pursued us even when we weren't looking for Him.

It is not a coincidence that you are where you are in your relationship with Him today. He followed you; He set Himself up in your path. He allowed circumstances and even problems in your life for you to feel your need of Him. He courted and wooed you. However, this relationship must continue to grow and mature. It cannot exist on just the initial attraction basis.

Isa. 54:5
For thy Maker is thine husband; the LORD of hosts is his name; and thy Redeemer the Holy One of Israel; the God of the whole earth shall he be called.

Hos. 2:19, 20, 23
19 I will make you my wife forever, showing you righteousness and justice, unfailing love and compassion.
20 I will be faithful to you and make you mine, and you will finally know me as the Lord.
23 I will show love to those I called 'Not loved.' And to those I called 'Not my people,' I will say, 'Now you are my people.' And they will reply, 'You are our God!'" NLT

2 Cor. 11:2
For I am jealous over you with Godly jealousy: for I have espoused you to one husband, that I may present you as a chaste virgin to Christ.

Additional Scriptures: Eph. 5:25-32, Rev. 19:7.

Often, the longer a husband and wife live together in a good relationship, the more they think and act alike. Similarly, it should be likewise with our heavenly Bridegroom. We need to think like Him, *"Let this mind be in you that was in Christ Jesus."* We need to act like Him conducting our life in holiness and righteousness.

Friend / Friend Relationship
The friend relationship depicts:
- Someone in which to confide.
- Someone you choose to be with, no strings attached.
- Someone you choose to be with, every time you get together.
- Someone with whom you are comfortable.

John 15:13-15 (Jesus told His disciples, you are My friends)
13 Greater love hath no man than this, that a man lay down his life for his friends.
14 Ye are my friends, if ye do whatsoever I command you.
15 Henceforth I call you not servants; . . . But I have called you friends.

Ex. 33:11 (Moses talked to God as a friend)
And the LORD spake unto Moses face to face, as a man speaketh unto his friend.

- **There is no greater honor or privilege in the world than to be called the friend of God.**

Abraham was called the friend of God. He had a great relationship with God. There are many examples of God and Abraham talking together. Before God destroyed the city where Lot lived, He said, "I must tell My friend Abraham."

Gen. 18:17
*And the LORD said, **Shall I hide from Abraham** that thing which I do;*

2 Chron. 20:7
*Art not thou our God, who didst drive out the inhabitants of this land before thy people Israel, and gavest it to the seed of **Abraham thy friend for ever**?*

Isa. 41:8
*But thou, Israel, art my servant, Jacob whom I have chosen, the seed of **Abraham my friend**.*

James 2:23
*And the scripture was fulfilled which saith, Abraham believed God, and it was imputed unto him for righteousness: and he was **called the Friend of God**.*

Master / Servant Relationship

The employer / employee relationship in today's business world does not properly depict the master / servant relationship desired by God. Our dedication and allegiance to our Lord and Master should go far beyond what we give to an employer.

The relationship intended here is best described in the Old Testament setting. The slave who had completed his term of service and was free to leave the master's house says, "I love you and I want to stay and voluntarily be your love slave or servant for the rest of my life". A special ceremony was performed with a blood covenant that bound him to the master as a **love slave** forever.

Deut. 15:16-17
16 But if your slave, because he loves you and your family and has a good life with you, says, "I don't want to leave you,"
17 then take an awl and pierce through his earlobe into the doorpost, marking him as your slave forever. MSG

-- From "Jamieson, Fausset, and Brown Commentary"

If they say I will not go away. If they decline to avail themselves of the privilege of release, and chose to remain with their master, then, by a special form of ceremony, they became a party to the transaction, voluntarily sold themselves to their employer, and continued in his service until death.[1]

This relationship depicts a servant carrying out his master's desires and orders based on his love for the master. A dedicated servant never says what he will or will not do. He finds out what the master wants. The good servant is accountable and follows his master's laws and management style. Jesus related a parable of the king who left talents with his servants before departing on a long journey. When he returned, he demanded an accounting of their labor.

The dedicated servant never puts his desires ahead of the master's. He says, "Whatever you want, I am happy to do". In the workplace we tell our employers:

- We are willing to learn new things that are difficult.
- For financial reward, we are willing to do things for which we do not have a natural talent.

Our Lord and Master deserves the same allegiance. Why should we choose what we will do? Why should we rely on our strengths and weaknesses to determine what we will do for Him? He is the King, He is the Master, and we must do His bidding.

All through Scripture, we see God using man without natural ability to accomplish His work. It is good and needed to dedicate our natural talents and giftings to the service of the Master. But God wants to use us beyond our abilities, with His anointing and supernatural ability, to accomplish His will and work -- reaching a lost world.

Basic Foundational Elements of Our Relationship With God		
(Refer to Charts R-1 and R-2 at the end of this chapter)		
Relationship Element	**Man to God**	**God to Man**
Communication	Man Talking to God	God Talking to Man
Love	Man Loving God Man Loving His Brother	God Loving Man
Trust	Man Trusting God	God Trusting Man

These components of the relationship are interrelated. So, what is the sequence or the order of this model? It depends on each individual's level of experience or relationship with God. God initiates the relationship with a sinner and a new convert. It is initially one-sided:

- God loved us, before we loved Him.
- God began speaking to us through various means, before we began talking to Him.
- God began to trust us before we trusted Him. He trusted us and invested in us because He saw what we could become. He had an eternal purpose and will for our lives.

But when we mature as Christians, God expects us to initiate the process and pursue Him:

- *And ye shall seek me, and find me, when ye shall search for me with all your heart.*
- *Blessed are they which do hunger and thirst after righteousness: for they shall be filled.*
- *Grow in grace, and in the knowledge of our Lord and Saviour Jesus Christ.*

There will be some point in our relationship that God will wait on us to pursue Him. And if this doesn't happen, this is the point where the relationship stops growing. If this continues, backsliding will result.

Communication - Talking to God

God speaks to us in many ways but the only way we can communicate with God is through prayer. Prayer fuels and keeps the relationship engine running. All of the aspects of our relationship with God are enabled only by communication with Him. Without prayer the relationship will not grow, resulting in a lukewarm and distant relationship.

Your long term relationship with God will not survive without talking to Him often and for quality periods of time in prayer. To know someone you must spend time talking to them. That is how you understand who someone is, what they stand for, what their goals and values are. This is true in our relationship with God. By talking to God we get to know Him.

Satan will let you do anything but pray. He will let you go to church; he will let you teach Bible lessons; he will let you pay your tithes and be faithful in other ways. But he will challenge you every day at your prayer closet door, because that is the key to a deeper relationship and power with God.

Prayer is the last frontier of a mature Christian. In order to experience new places in the Spirit where we have never been before, there is only one door and one path, and that is through the door of consistent, persistent prayer. Refer to Chapter 8, "Prayer the Power Arm of the Christian and Church."

Communication - God Talking to Us

God's communication to us is much more effective if we have consistently talked to Him. An electronic communication device has a **transmitter** and a **receiver**. Regardless how strong the transmitter is, the receiver must be turned on and tuned in.

Jer. 23:29
Is not my word like as a fire? saith the Lord; and like a hammer that breaketh the rock in pieces?

The transmitter (God's voice) has no weakness -- *"The Word of God is **powerful** and sharper than any two-edged sword"*. But it takes prayer to tune our spiritual receiver to receive God's message. It takes prayer to open our spiritual ears to hear with clarity what God is speaking to us. Eight times in the book of Revelation it is recorded: *"He that hath an ear, let him hear what the Spirit saith unto the churches."*

- **The final authority is the written Word of God. Although God uses other means to talk to His people (the preached Word, Gifts of the Spirit, dreams and His still small voice) no message from God will ever supersede His written Word.**

Love - God's Love to Us

God's love to us can be described in one word -- Calvary. God drove a stake in the ground at Calvary displaying His great love for man. Calvary was the greatest event in all of history.

Nothing was the same after Calvary. The single event of Calvary marked the ending of the dispensation of Law and the beginning of the dispensation of Grace, when man could directly approach God for himself. The message of the sufferings of Jesus, and what was accomplished through His death, burial and resurrection, is the cornerstone of our salvation. Refer to Chapter 6, "Perfect Love – the Highest Law and Strongest Force."

Love – Our Love for God

The more we know God, the more we should be hopelessly in love with Him. He is the Groom, we are His bride. He is the lover of our soul. He is wooing us, His bride, desiring to destroy all the other loves in our lives -- anything that we love more than we love Him.

One of the saddest things on earth is a relationship where the love of one grows cold for the other. In all of the affairs of man, since the beginning of time, there is nothing more tragic as a relationship when one stops loving and the other is still in love. The same is true concerning the love of God for us and our response to that love -- our love for Him. He loves us unconditionally. He has always loved us and He always will.

Jer. 31:3
I have loved thee with an everlasting love: therefore with lovingkindness have I drawn thee.

John 15:13
Greater love hath no man than this, that a man lay down his life for his friends.

Loving God includes loving our brother: Loving God and loving our brother are completely and indivisibly linked, because our love for God *(the invisible)* is manifested by our love for our brother *(the visible)*, as shown by many Scriptures penned by the Apostle John.

1 John 4:20-21
20 If anyone says, I love God, and detests his brother [in Christ], he is a liar; **for he who does not love his brother, whom he has seen, cannot love God, Whom he has not seen.**
21 And this command we have from Him: that he who loves God shall love his brother also.
AMP

Trust - Trusting God

The theme and concept of trusting God is repeatedly demonstrated in God's Word. It is one of the foundational principles of our relationship with God.

Psalms 125:1
They that trust in the LORD shall be as mount Zion, which cannot be removed, but abideth forever.

Prov. 3:5-6
5 Trust in the LORD with all thine heart; and lean not unto thine own understanding.
6 In all thy ways acknowledge him, and he shall direct thy paths.

The biggest conflict in my approach to life and God's approach to my life is -- my way vs. God's way:

My Way	God's Way
I want to plan my life out into the future (my whole life if possible).	God wants me to live one day at a time and depend on Him and trust in Him for tomorrow.
I want to be in control and build on my strengths and feel self-confident.	God wants to be in control, He wants me to depend on His strength, and have my confidence and trust in Him.

Apostle Paul's experiences taught this concept well, *"For when I am weak, then I am strong."* Trials remove us from control and cause us to live and trust Him one day at a time. They make earth seem less desirable and the things of God more desirable. Trial enhances our awareness of our need for Him. God sometimes uses trouble to sharpen our communication to Him in prayer and our trust in Him.

Trust is the highest level of faith. Trusting God is more difficult than just believing that He can do it. Trust goes beyond believing. Trust says, "Lord, I really want this miracle and I believe You for it. However, I want You more; I want Your will more. I relinquish my will -- Thy will be done. You know what is best for me. Whether You deliver me or not, I will still trust and serve You." Trust and submission of our will removes the fear that hinders us from receiving a miracle. It places the outcome in His hands (where it really is anyway).

The small sea creature in the ocean is buffeted around with the wind and waves. But when it clings to the rock, it receives the strength of the rock and is no longer controlled by the wind and waves. When we cling to the Rock of Ages and anchor ourselves to Him, we take on the strength and attributes of the Rock, and are not tossed to and fro by the storms of life.

We have many limitations, but our eternal God has none.

MAN	GOD
We are weak	He is strong – all powerful (omnipotent)
We are one small grain of sand on the shores of time	He covers the entire universe and beyond. He is everywhere (omnipresent)
We are insecure and unstable	He is secure and unmovable
We can do nothing	He can do anything
Our life is but a vapor and temporal	He is eternal and everlasting

Our knowledge and wisdom is inadequate	He has all knowledge, wisdom and understanding (omniscient)
We are unworthy	He is worthy
We are nothing	He is everything

Trust - God Trusting Us

This is a subject that is seldom addressed or discussed: **"Can God trust you?"**

If all of our burdens and difficulties were removed and we had no fear or negative influences; if our jobs were perfect with a seven digit income; if we were happy, peaceful and joyful all of the time, would we live for God just as consistently as when difficulties and struggles drive us to our knees?

Can God trust us with miracles, or would we take some of the credit? If we were used by God in a number of notable miracles of healing, would we make sure someone knew who prayed the prayer of faith? Or would we follow the example of Jesus, recorded many time in the New Testament: *"He straitly charged them that they should not make him known" (Mark 3:12).*

Why did God use Gideon, with no military talent; why did God use David, as a young inexperienced warrior; why did God use the boy with the loaves and fishes to feed the 5,000? **It was because He could trust them!**

Can we afford to be blessed by God? Can God trust us? When we can say, "yes" to this, we are progressing toward a complete relationship with God.

Levels or Depths of Relationship

In the Gospels we see four circles and inner circles of relationship of Jesus with His twelve disciples. Refer to Chart R-4, "Levels of Relationship With Jesus", at the end of this chapter.

In the twelve handpicked disciples we see four levels or circles of relationship:

1. John (Most Inner Circle)

- He sat closest to Jesus at the table: *". . . The disciple whom Jesus loved; which also leaned on his breast at supper" (John 21:20).*

- Five times in Scripture, he is described as, ***"The disciple that Jesus loved."***

- The only disciple who stood by Jesus at the cross.

- The disciple whom Jesus entrusted the care of His mother at the time of His death on the cross.

- The one chosen to witness and record the Revelation of Jesus Christ.

2. Peter, James and John (The Inner Circle)

- Jesus took these three with Him up the mountain to pray, revealing His glory as He was transfigured: *"He took Peter, John and James, and went up into a mountain to pray. And as he prayed, the fashion of his countenance was altered, and his raiment was white and glistering" (Luke 9:28-29).*

- At special times of healing and raising the dead, Jesus took only these three: *"And he suffered no man to follow him, save Peter, and James, and John" (Mark 5:37).*

- At times only these three met with Jesus and He taught them: *"And as he sat upon the Mount of Olives, Peter and James and John and Andrew asked him privately, Tell us, when shall these things be?" (Mark 13:3).*

- In the Garden of Gethsemane Jesus led them a little further than the others: *"And they came to a place which was named Gethsemane: and he saith to his disciples, Sit ye here, while I shall pray. And he taketh with him Peter and James and John, and began to be sore amazed, and to be very heavy" (Mark 14:32-33).*

3. The Other Eight Disciples

- All of these men obeyed Jesus' last commandment to: *"Tarry in Jerusalem until ye be endued with power from on high" (Luke 24:49).*

"Then returned they unto Jerusalem from the mount called Olivet, which is from Jerusalem a Sabbath day's journey. And when they were come in, they went up Into an upper room, where abode both Peter, and James, and John, and Andrew, Philip, and Thomas, Bartholomew, and Matthew, James the son of Alphaeus, and Simon Zelotes, and Judas the brother of James" (Acts 1:12).

- All tarried in the Upper Room and were present when the Holy Ghost was poured out on the Day of Pentecost.

- All became great men, who moved into the innermost circle, their ministry impacting the world -- becoming martyrs for the gospel of Jesus Christ.

4. Judas (Outer Circle)

- He betrayed Jesus.
- The first disciple to die (suicide).
- He lost both his physical and eternal life.

Judas received the highest calling when he was chosen as one of the twelve disciples. He was invited along with all the other disciples into this close-knit group. He was favored by Jesus and was privileged to be a part of His ministry. He ate miraculous bread with Jesus when the loaves were multiplied. But Judas did not respond to this great privilege or the invitation to a close relationship with Jesus. He had selfish priorities and remained on the edge, uncommitted in the outermost circle.

At the Last Supper, Jesus washed Judas' feet and gave him, *"the sop"*, in His last attempt to reach him. Judas rejected this final loving gesture. Immediately satan entered into him; he went out and it was night. He traded the Light of the World for the darkness of an evil kingdom. After he realized his horrific error, he hung himself. A most sobering Scripture describes this tragic event preceding the most exciting event in history -- the birth of the church on the Day of Pentecost:

Acts 1:17, 20
17 For he was numbered with us, and had obtained part of this ministry.
*20 For it is written in the book of Psalms, Let his habitation be desolate, and let no man dwell therein: and **his bishoprick let another take.***

The Closer the Relationship With God -- the Greater the Revelation of God

It is evident that Peter, James and John enjoyed a closer relationship with Jesus during His earthly ministry than did the other disciples. They participated in a unique time of teaching and prayer alone with Jesus. They alone witnessed the revelation of Jesus in His glory as He was transfigured before them -- the brilliant light shining from Him.

Also apparent after John witnessed the Transfiguration, something dramatically changed in his relationship with Jesus. Thereafter, he was referred to as, ***"The disciple whom Jesus loved."*** Certainly Jesus loved all of the disciples, but John's special bond was stronger than the others at that time.

When God chose who would paint the last brush strokes of the New Testament, the one privileged to record the Revelation of Jesus Christ, He selected John, the one closest to Him in relationship. By this time, the other disciples had greatly impacted their world with their dedication to Jesus Christ and died a martyr's death. There was an attempt to kill John by boiling him in a pot of hot oil, but he was miraculously delivered.

By then, John was possibly 80 years old. After all of his love, sacrifice and suffering for Jesus Christ, it seems that he should have spent his last days as a respected apostle living in peace. But God designated one more assignment for John -- one that transported him, as a prisoner to Patmos, a remote, lonely island. But there are no barriers that can prevent or diminish one's relationship with Jesus. John was in the Spirit on the Lord's Day; no one else was around -- just Jesus and John.

Rev. 1:10, 12-16
10 I was in the Spirit on the Lord's Day, and heard behind me a great voice, as of a trumpet,
12 And I turned to see the voice that spake with me.
13 And in the midst of the seven candlesticks one like unto the Son of man, clothed with a garment down to the foot, and girt about the paps with a golden girdle.
14 His head and his hairs were white like wool, as white as snow; and his eyes were as a flame

of fire;

15 And his feet like unto fine brass, as if they burned in a furnace; and his voice as the sound of many waters.

16 And he had in his right hand seven stars: and out of his mouth went a sharp twoedged sword: and his countenance was as the sun shineth in his strength.

John did not see Jesus as he had seen Him in His earthly ministry -- as the lowly Shepherd or the bleeding and suffering Savior. In this revelation, he saw Jesus as the lion of the tribe of Judah in all of His power, glory and majesty; as the King of Kings and Lord of Lords.

- **If we are to experience a greater revelation of Jesus Christ, we must also develop a deeper relationship with Him.**

This special encounter will only occur when we, like John, leave the hustle and bustle of life's distractions and climb the mountain of prayer to be alone with Jesus. This will require a sacrifice of our time, and a change of our priorities and agendas. The setting will be isolation without distractions, where we will have:

  - A new revelation of Jesus in His beauty and glory until He is elevated to the very center of our life, while all other priorities blur into the background.

  - A revelation of ourselves, of who we are now and what He intends for us to be and do in His Kingdom.

  - A revelation of His will compared to ours; His mind compared to ours; His love compared to ours.

When we have experienced this encounter with Jesus, His light will be shining through us, affecting our dark and hurting world. We will be sitting in heavenly places and will be singing the song of the redeemed recorded in the book of Revelation.

  - *"Blessing, and glory, and wisdom, and thanksgiving, and honor, and power, and might, be unto our God forever and ever. Amen."*

  - *"Alleluia, salvation, and glory, and honor, and power, unto the Lord our God."*

  - *"Alleluia: for the Lord God omnipotent reigneth."* (Not only reigning over the universe, but ruling and reigning in our lives).

Four Depths of Water Flowing From the House of God

The Spirit of God is referred to as water many times in Scripture:

Isa. 12:3
Therefore with joy shall ye draw water out of the wells of salvation.

Isa. 44:3
For I will pour water upon him that is thirsty . . . I will pour my spirit upon thy seed.

Isa. 55:1
Ho, every one that thirsteth, come ye to the waters, and he that hath no money . . .

John 4:14
Whosoever drinketh of the water that I shall give him shall never thirst; but the water that I shall give him shall be in him a well of water springing up into everlasting life.

John 7:37, 39
37 Jesus stood and cried, saying, If any man thirst, let him come unto me, and drink.
39 But this spake he of the Spirit, which they that believe on him should receive . . .

Ezekiel 47 addresses four levels of water proceeding from the house of God: water to the ankles, water to the knees, water to the loins, and water over the head to swim in.

Ezek. 47:1, 3-5
1 Afterward he brought me again unto the door of the house; and, behold, waters issued out from under the threshold of the house eastward.
*3 And when the man that had the line in his hand went forth eastward, he measured a thousand cubits, and he brought me through the waters; the **waters were to the ankles**.*
*4 Again he measured a thousand, and brought me through the waters; the **waters were to the knees**. Again he measured a thousand, and brought me through; the **waters were to the loins**.*
*5 Afterward he measured a thousand; and it was a river that I could not pass over: for the waters were risen, **waters to swim in**, a river that could not be passed over.*

Although this text is from the Old Testament, there is a spiritual application for us as we examine the available levels and depths of relationship with God:

1. Water to the Feet

In ankle deep water our walk is affected. The path we take and the places we go are different than on dry land. But a shallow experience can be dangerous, because it is too close to the bank (the world); it is too easy to return to the shore. Ankle deep water depicts an unstable and inconsistent walk; part of the journey is affected by the water (Spirit) and part is affected by the land (world).

2. Water to the Knees

This depth affects our lifestyle in a greater way. It reflects a greater commitment further from the world. It affects our knees; we bend our knees in a more consistent prayer life, walking closer to God.

3. Water to the Loins

This deeper level is where living for God gets exciting. We quit talking about the places we can't go or things we can't do. We didn't give up anything, compared to what He gives us in return. We traded the curse of sin and death for salvation and eternal life. He gave us beauty for ashes (Isa. 61:3).

- **How can we compare giving up things in our kingdom for things in His Kingdom? The eternal and temporal are incomparable. They are not on the same level -- not in the same universe.**

When we are in spiritual waters to the loins it gets in our innermost being. It gets inside of us, and becomes a part of us. We have to do something for Him -- we have to tell somebody. Jeremiah described it like this: *"His word in my heart is like fire that burns in my bones, and I can't hold it in any longer."*

4. Water to Swim In

At this level we are in the deep water where the undertow of the Spirit will cause us to lose control of our life allowing Him to have full control. We know He is **first** and He knows He is **first** in our life. He is the Lord of our life and has **preeminence** in every area.

Col. 1:18
And he is the head of the body, the church: who is the beginning, the firstborn from the dead, that in all things he might have the preeminence (first place).

At this level, we are one with Him. Immersed in His will, we have access to His supernatural power. We are praying and coveting the best gifts to be used to deliver, save and heal others. We are seeking the limitless depths of Christ. We can dive to the 20 foot depth or we can don our spiritual scuba gear and dive to the depths.

We can choose ankle-deep, knee-deep or the limitless depths of God's Kingdom. The only limit is our passion and hunger for God.

In the church of Jesus Christ are circles, inner circles and varying depths of relationship with God that we can attain. We can passively remain in a comfort zone or advance to new levels.

- **It is very important the level or the circle of relationship where we identify ourselves. But more importantly, is the direction we are looking or the direction we are going.**

It is better to be in the outer circle headed toward an inner circle of relationship with Him than to be going the other way. We must be careful where we are looking, because that is where we will soon be going. The late Bishop James Kilgore said many times: "If your heart is not in this, your body will eventually join your heart out there, somewhere away from God and the church."

Outer and Inner Circles of Relationship With God in the Church Today

Summarized here for discussion purposes are three levels of relationship: (1) the **outermost circle**; (2) the **middle**; (3) the **innermost circle**. One or more of the descriptive items under each level may apply to a particular individual:

(1) **The Outermost Circle (The Flesh Ruling):**

- Perimeter area around the church where people do not completely follow the teachings of the Bible.
- Places they go and things they do are inconsistent with the Christian walk.
- Limited daily personal devotion of prayer and the Word.
- Motive for church attendance is to soothe their conscience or to visit their family and friends.
- Seeking a comfortable zone, simultaneously trying to be a part of the church and a part of the world.
- Other things (jobs, entertainment, hobbies, etc.) have replaced God as first in their life.

(2) **The Maintenance Level (The Soul Ruling):**

- Faithful to the house of God in attendance and offerings.
- Personal daily devotion of prayer and the Word.
- Not struggling with sin but with **self** (the **will**, **mind** and **emotions**):
  - Their will vs. God's will.
    - Their mind (ways) vs. God's mind (ways).
      - Their love (emotions) vs. God's agape love toward others (even their enemies).

(3) **The Innermost Circle or Level (The Spirit Ruling):**

- God is placed as the highest priority.
- Seeking God's ways, desiring to do His perfect will.
- Consumed with the purpose and work of God.
- Seeking to be a book of Acts Christian and be led by the Spirit.
- Praying and living in the Spirit.
- Relying on the anointing (divine ability) to operate as a son of God in the supernatural to effectively reach lost souls.
- Willing to endure sacrifice and self-denial to be transformed and do His perfect will.

Our lost and hurting generation will only be delivered by God's supernatural power working through those living in the innermost circle. The Gifts of the Spirit sit like giant tool boxes in the Most Holy Place (inner-most circle), waiting for those desiring to be used as a son of God. Not just a one-time decision, this is a continuous decision to sacrifice and purify at new levels and depths. New levels of relationship with God require new levels of sacrifice and purity.

- **The sacrifices that God requires of those dwelling in the innermost circle makes the ones we made initially to separate from the world appear exceedingly small.**

Refer to the following pages for the **"Relationship"** overview charts.

Chart R-1

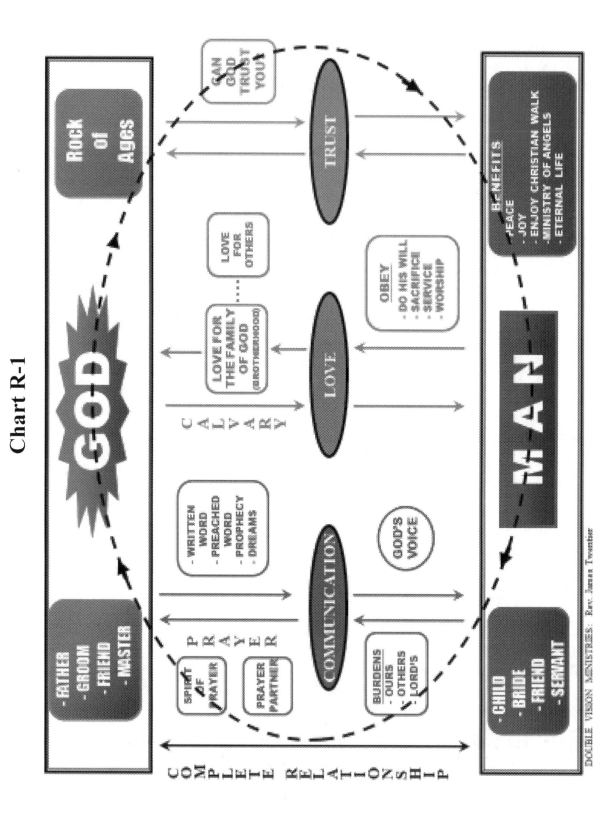

Chart R-2

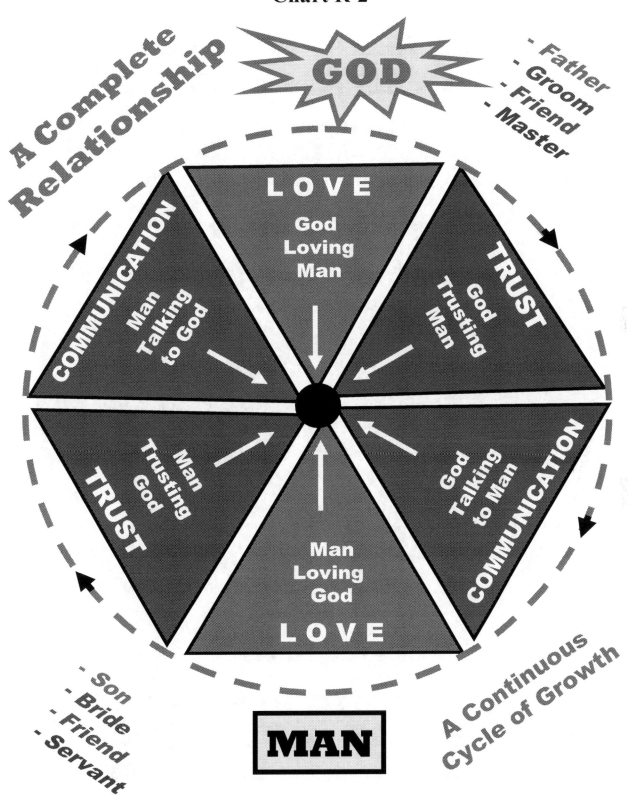

Chart R-3

OUR PRIORITIES AND COMMITMENTS

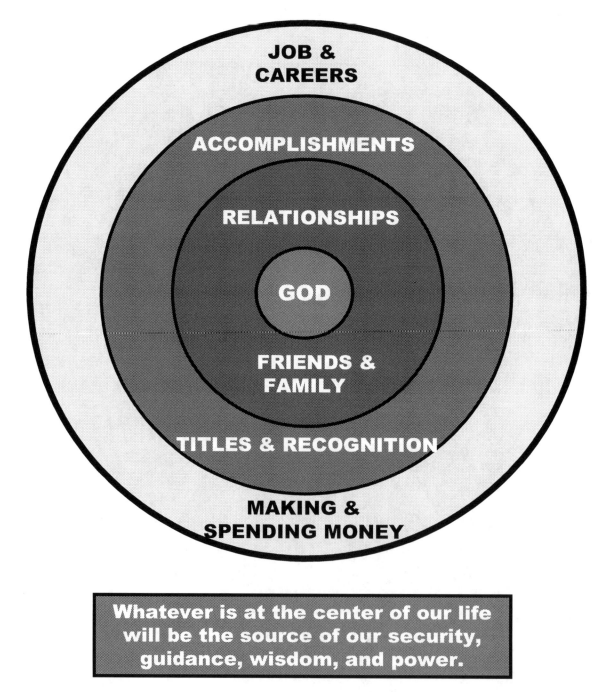

Chart R-4

LEVELS OF RELATIONSHIP WITH JESUS

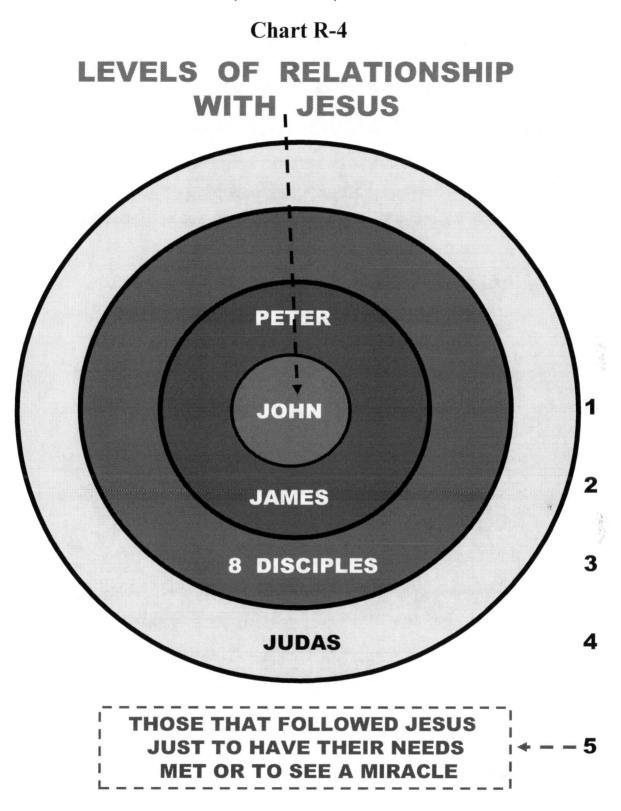

Chart R-5

DEPTH OF RELATIONSHIP

DEPTH OF THE WATERS
THAT FLOWED OUT OF THE HOUSE OF GOD

1. WATER TO THE ANKLES

2. WATER TO THE KNEES

3. WATER TO THE LOINS

4. WATER OVER THE HEAD TO SWIM IN

3. Transformation of the Inner Man

Theme Summary and Key Scripture Text

Transformation

(Becoming like Christ)

- The act or process of being transformed, continuous change
- I must decrease and He must increase: less of my will, mind and emotions; more of God's will, mind and (agape) love.
- Crucified with Christ.
- Changed into His image from glory to glory.
- Becoming more effective in the Father's business.

Spiritual Growth

(Dominion over self (my will, mind and emotions)

- Be ye transformed by the renewing of your **mind**, that ye may prove what is that good, and acceptable, and perfect, **will of God**. (Rom. 12:2)
- Going on to perfection. (Heb. 6:1)
- Abounding more and more in knowledge and discernment. (Phil. 1:9)
- Pressing toward the mark for the prize of the high calling in Christ Jesus. (Phil. 3:14)
- Striving for the mastery, temperate in all things. (1 Cor. 9:25)
- Growing in the grace and knowledge of our Lord and Savior Jesus Christ. (2 Peter 3:18)
- The inward man being renewed day by day. (2 Cor. 4:16)
- Transformed into His likeness in an ever greater degree of glory. (2 Cor. 3:18) GNT
- My little children, of whom I travail in birth again until Christ be formed in you. (Gal. 4:19)
- To be conformed to the image of His Son. (Rom. 8:2)
- That ye might be partakers of the divine nature . . . add to your faith virtue . . . knowledge . . . temperance . . . patience godliness . . . brotherly kindness . . . charity. (2 Peter 1:4-10)

Study References

Vol.	Book Name	Primary Study Section / Chapter	Elective Study
III	Spiritual Growth 　- Dominion Over Sin and Self	Sec. I / Ch. 4, Sec. II	Sec. I / Ch. 1-3, 5
IV	Unlimited Partnership With a Supernatural God	Sec. I / Ch. 4, Sec. II	Sec. I / Ch. 1-3, Sec. III
V	Revival & Evangelism 　- Passion for God 　- Passion for Souls	Sec. I / Ch. 3	
VIII	Addendum Volume (PowerPoint Charts)	Charts at the end of this chapter	C-1 - C-21

If there is continued spiritual growth after the initial salvation experience and grounding in the basic foundational truths of Christian living, it will be because we desire it and pursue it with passion, diligence and purpose. What are our desires?

- Whatever we desire, we will pursue.
- Whatever we pursue, we will obtain.
- Whatever we obtain, we will become.

This lesson addresses actions that are required to become more effective in the Father's business. This encompasses foundational principles of continuous spiritual growth that will prepare individuals to be more fruitful Christians. **The primary emphasis is dominion over self (the soul: will, mind and emotions) and the related deadly sins of the soul.**

God desires for His children to grow and mature and become everything He intended them to be. He desires that we partner with Him in touching the lives of others -- spreading His message of deliverance, salvation and righteousness throughout the whole earth. Seeking first the Kingdom of God means submitting every area of our life to His authority. What we submit to Him, He blesses.

God's complete access to our lives, for His perfect will to be done, must come through the veil of self (our soul: the will, mind and emotions):

- Our mind is what we think.
- Our emotions are what we feel.
- Our will determines what we will do.

It is at Mount Calvary, the mountain of sacrifice, where we are changed into His image as we become the sacrifice. Being crucified with Him brings death to self:

- Death to our will, for His will to be done in our lives.
- Death to our thinking and ways to have the mind and ways of Christ.
- Death to our limited human love to be a partaker and provider of God's perfect love.

Continued Spiritual Growth Requires Discipline

What hinders us from continuing to grow spiritually? What keeps us from pursuing real priorities in our lives? What causes the gap between what we know we should do and what we actually do? The answer is the lack of discipline. Some of the areas of our life to consider for discipline, to insure continued spiritual growth, include the following:

- Discipline in our prayer life.
- Discipline in our reading habits.
- Discipline in our church attendance.
- Discipline in our fasting.

- Discipline in our entertainment.
 - Discipline in our conversation.
  - Discipline in our friendships.
   - Discipline in our accountability.
    - Discipline in our business dealings.
     - Discipline in our career.
      - Discipline in our time.

Discipline is the glad surrender of a life to a higher purpose. It is saying, "no" to many things so that we may say, "yes" to a few excellent pursuits. An excellent example of discipline is athletes training to compete in the Olympic Games. They punish their bodies with grueling exercises to qualify. They refuse good tasting food, for food that will enhance their physical strength and endurance. They sacrifice their entire lives for many years to win a gold medal -- one-half ounce of gold.

May we embrace the discipline described by Apostle Paul in his reference to training for the ancient Olympics: *"All athletes are disciplined in their training. They do it to win a prize that will fade away, but we do it for an eternal prize. I discipline my body like an athlete, training it to do what it should. Otherwise, I fear that after preaching to others I myself might be disqualified" (1 Cor. 9:25, 27). TLB*

Of the five games in the ancient Olympics, Apostle Paul refers to three: running, wrestling, and boxing.

1 Cor. 9:24-27
24 Know ye not that they which **run in a race** *run all, but one receiveth the prize? So run, that ye may obtain.*
25 And every man that **striveth for the mastery** *is temperate in all things. Now they do it to obtain a corruptible crown; but we an incorruptible.*
26 I therefore so run, not as uncertainly; **so fight I**, *not as one that beateth the air:*
27 But I **keep under my body**, *and* **bring it into subjection**: *lest that by any means, when I have preached to others, I myself should be a castaway.*

1. Running - *run in a race*

   stadion - a certain measure of distance; by implication, a stadium or race-course.[1]

   The winner must observe the laws of racing, staying within the boundaries, or be disqualified by the judge.

2. Wrestling - *striveth for the mastery*

   agonizomai - to struggle, literally (to compete for a prize), figuratively (to contend with an adversary), labor fervently.[1]

3. Boxing - *so fight I*, *not as one that beateth the air*

pukteo - to box (with the fist), i.e. contend (as a boxer) at the games.[1]

I **keep under** *my body.*

hupopiazo - to hit under the eye (buffet or disable an antagonist), i.e. (figuratively) to annoy (into compliance), subdue (one's passions).[1]

Transformation of the Complete Man (Body, Soul and Spirit)

After Calvary, God chose to dwell in the tabernacle of man. Like the tabernacle of Moses, the tabernacle of man has three rooms or parts: the body (outer court), the soul (inner court or Holy Place), and the spirit (Most Holy Place).

Refer to the following charts at the end of this chapter:

T-1 The Tabernacle Plan - Old Testament / New Testament

T-2, T-3 The Body / Soul / Spirit Model

2 Cor. 6:16-17
16 ***For ye are the temple of the living God****; as God hath said, I will dwell in them, and walk in them; and I will be their God, and they shall be my people.*
17 Wherefore come out from among them, and be ye separate, saith the Lord, and touch not the unclean thing; and I will receive you,

1 Cor. 6:19-20
19 What? know ye not that ***your body is the temple of the Holy Ghost*** *which is in you, which ye have of God, and ye are not your own?*
20 For ye are bought with a price: therefore ***glorify God in your body, and in your spirit****, which are God's.*

- **The complete man is comprised of three parts: spirit, soul and body.**

1 Thess. 5:23
And the very God of peace sanctify you wholly (completely)*; and I pray God your whole* ***spirit*** *and* ***soul*** *and* ***body*** *be preserved blameless unto the coming of our Lord Jesus Christ.*

The Body (Outer Court)

The body, with its five senses of sight, hearing, taste, smell and touch, connects us with the earth, making us **world conscious**. This physical structure is comprised of bone, fiber of flesh and sinew, and vital organs: brain, heart, lungs, etc. It is that which begins to deteriorate as we grow older. Apostle Paul gives us this hope that, *"Though the outer man perishes the inner man is renewed day by day."*

The body is the outer shell, the tabernacle of the soul. It is compared to the outer court of the Old Testament tabernacle.

Although this lesson deals with dominion over sins of the body (flesh) and sins of the soul (self), the primary emphasis is on **self**. Early in our Christian walk we should gain dominion over the sins of the flesh (Gal. 5:19-21). Apostle Paul in his letter to the Christians in Rome states that sin should no longer have dominion over them.

Rom. 6:14
For sin shall not [any longer] exert dominion over you, *since now you are not under Law [as slaves], but under grace [as subjects of God's favor and mercy]. AMP*

The greater lifetime struggle will be with **self -- the soul (the will, mind and emotions)**:
- Self-will vs. God's will.
  - Self-ways (mind) vs. God's ways (mind).
    - Self-love vs. God's love.
      - Self-righteousness vs. God's righteousness.

The Soul (Holy Place)

The soul, the organ of our personality, is made up of the **will**, **mind** and **emotions;** it makes us **self-conscious**:
- The emotions are what we feel.
  - The intellect is what we think.
    - The will is what we desire and will do.

Your soul is the real you. It is who you are -- your individuality, personality, influence, intellect, natural talents, abilities and giftings.

The soul gives the physical body its use. The word "soul" in the Greek language is rendered "life". In Latin, it is rendered "anima" -- that which animates the body. The soul then, is that which gives life to this physical body:
- The brain is useless without intellect.
- The heart is cold and a mere muscular pump of blood, if there is no affection and love.
  Love makes the heart beat faster in the presence of a loved one.

Gen. 2:7
And the Lord God formed man of the dust of the ground (body), *And breathed into his nostrils the breath of life* (spirit); *And man became **a living soul*** (soul).

As soon as the breath of life (that created man's spirit) came into contact with man's body, **the soul was produced**. Therefore, the soul is the combination of man's body and spirit. Scripture calls man a living soul. Jesus said it is the Spirit that gives life. The breath of life comes from the Lord of creation. The inbreathing of God produced a two-part natural man (body and soul), and the spiritual man (spirit).

With the **second birth,** the breath of God causes a spiritual birth. Man becomes a new creature in Christ with God's Spirit dwelling in his spirit. With the born-again experience man receives a new Spirit. But he will not receive his new glorified body, until the resurrection.

The soul is the outer sheath of the spirit. It is compared to the inner court or Holy Place of the tabernacle. The soul is still part of the carnal man. Placed between two worlds; the natural and the spiritual, the soul is a part of both. Connected to the natural through the body; it is connected to the spiritual through the spirit of man.

Man was created with a soul that possesses a **free will**. If man's soul wills to obey God, it will allow the Spirit to rule; if not, it will suppress the Spirit and allow the fleshly desires to rule. The soul binds the body and spirit together. If one allows the Spirit of God to rule, it can influence the soul to subdue the body into obedience to God.

- **The soul with its will, intellect and emotions is the pilot of our entire being. For the Spirit of God to lead our life, the soul must give its consent.**

Man, with his own willpower, can conquer some sins of the flesh -- giving up drugs, alcohol and other bad habits. But on his own, he cannot make significant changes to his soul -- his will, mind and emotions. The composition of the soul is like software burned in a computer chip -- impossible to change.

- **The will of man is so strong that satan can't override it and God won't overrule it!**

- **The same transforming power of God that delivered us from the sins of the flesh is needed to deliver us from self - sins of the soul.**

God gives us His Spirit to provide the power to change our soul: *"He must increase but I must decrease":*
   - More of His will and less of mine.
    - More of His ways and less of mine.
     - More of His mind and less of mine.
      - More of His agape love and less of my limited human love.

Any improvement in this area will be determined by our hunger, desire and discipline to allow the Spirit to change us to be like Him.

Sins of the Soul
It is not sin, as we often define sin (violation of the Ten Commandments) or works of the flesh (defined in Galatians 5:19-21), that causes the greatest hindrance to a Christian's progress in the Kingdom of God. After we have dealt death to the flesh, there remains another step. There must be a death to self (our will, mind, and emotions) in order to fulfill the purpose of God.

There must be a rending of the veil of self. Refer to Chart T-9 at the end of this chapter.

- **Selfishness, self-righteousness and other self-centered traits are the greatest sins of the soul.**

-- From Webster's New World College Dictionary

Selfish - Obsessed with self, too much concerned with one's own welfare or interest and having little or no concern for others.

Self-righteous - Filled with or showing a conviction of being morally superior, or more righteous than others; smugly virtuous.[2]

The Greatest Challenge to Spiritual Growth is Dominion Over Self:

Self-advancement	Promoting one's own interest
Self-aggrandizement	Making one's self more powerful
Self-assertion	Demanding recognition for one's self, or insisting upon one's rights
Self-assurance	Confidence in one's ability, talent (vs. confidence in God)
Self-centered	Occupied or concerned with only one's affairs, egocentric
Self-complacent	Self-satisfied especially in a smug way
Self-conceit	Too high opinion of one's self, vanity
Self-deception	Deceiving of one's self as to one's true feelings and motives
Self-defense	Defense of one's rights and actions
Self-importance	Having or showing an exaggerated opinion of one's own importance
Self-indulgence	Indulgence in one's desires, impulses, etc.
Self-interest	Exaggerated regard for self at the expense of others
Self-opinionated	Stubbornly holding to one's own opinions, conceited
Self-proclaimed	Proclaimed or announced by one's self
Self-reliant	Reliant on one's own judgment and abilities

Self-satisfied	Feeling or showing an often smug satisfaction with one's self or one's accomplishments
Self-serving	Serving one's own selfish interest, especially at the expense of others
Self-sufficient	Independent, able to get along without help
Self-will	Persistent in carrying out of one's own will or wishes especially when in conflict with others, stubbornness, abstinent
Self	. . . . . .

The Holy Ghost gives us power for dominion over self:
- God gives us His Spirit on the basis of giving up sins of the flesh.
- The Holy Ghost is given for power to subdue and die to self.
- The Holy Ghost is not just a ticket to heaven, but a powerful change agent to change us from:
    - Selfish (us) to service (others).
        - Self-centered to Christ-centered.
            - Self-righteous to Christ's righteousness.

Acts 1:8
*But ye shall receive **power, after that the Holy Ghost** is come upon you:*

Rom. 8:14
*For as many as are **led by the Spirit of God**, they are the sons of God.*

God's Spirit Will Lead Us to:

Self-abasement	Humility
Self-denial	Sacrifice our desires
Self-discipline	Discipline to control our desires, actions, and habits
Selflessness	Devoted to the welfare or interest of others
Self-renunciation	Renouncing our own interests, especially for the benefit of others
Self-respect	Proper respect for ourselves and our worth as a person
Self-restraint	Self-control
Self-surrender	Surrender of self, our will

The Spirit (The Most Holy Place)

The spirit is the part of man that is immortal and undying. The spirit lies beyond man's self-consciousness and above the senses of the human mind. Here man unites and communes with God. It is our spirit that links us to God's Spirit, allowing us to commune with Him. It is by God's Spirit dwelling in our spirit that we discern and receive revelation of the truth.

The **spirit of man** is comprised of **conscience**, **communion** and **intuition**. The spirit of man makes us **God-conscious**.

-- From "The Spiritual Man"

Conscience is the discerning organ which distinguishes right and wrong; not through the influence of knowledge stored in the mind but rather by a spontaneous direct judgment. Often reasoning will justify things which our conscience judges to be wrong. The work of the conscience is independent and direct; it does not bend to outside opinions. If man should do wrong it will raise its voice of accusation.

Intuition is the sensing organ of the human spirit. It is so diametrically different from physical sense and soulical sense that it is called intuition. Intuition involves a direct sensing independent of any outside influence. That knowledge which comes to us without any help from the mind, emotion or volition comes intuitively. We really "know" through our intuition; our mind merely, helps us to "understand."

Communion is worshiping God. The organs of the soul are incompetent to worship God. God is not apprehended by our thoughts, feelings or intentions, for He can only be known directly in our spirits. Our worship of God and God's communications with us are directly in the spirit. They take place in "the inner man," not in the soul or outward man.

Before the believer is born again his spirit becomes so sunken and surrounded by his soul that it is impossible for him to distinguish whether something is emanating from the soul or from the spirit. The functions of the latter have become mixed up with those of the former. Furthermore, the spirit has lost its primary function towards God; for it is dead to God. All that this life possesses and all that it may become are in the realm of the soul. If we distinctly recognize what is soulical it will then be easier for us later on to recognize what is spiritual. It will be possible to divide the spiritual from the soulish.[3]

It is the Spirit that is always warring against the flesh and the flesh against the Spirit -- both striving for full mastery and control.

Gal. 5:16-18
16 But I say, walk and live [habitually] in the [Holy] Spirit [responsive to and controlled and guided by the Spirit]; then you will certainly not gratify the cravings and desires of the flesh (of human nature without God).

*17 For the **desires of the flesh are opposed to the [Holy] Spirit, and the [desires of the] Spirit are opposed to the flesh (godless human nature); for these are antagonistic to each other [continually withstanding and in conflict with each other]**, so that you are not free but are prevented from doing what you desire to do.   AMP*
18 Why don't you choose to be led by the Spirit and so escape the erratic compulsions of a law-dominated existence?   MSG

Three Levels of Living: The Body, Soul or Spirit Ruling
(Refer to Chart T-4)

1. The flesh ruling as the dominant member.

At this level there is minimal permanent victory in the Christian's life. Often the renewal of God's Spirit in one's life is soon lost due to carnal living. Like the five foolish virgins whom Jesus described in Matthew Chapter 25, the oil (Spirit of God) that once resided in their lives had leaked out. Like the children of Israel, they were out of Egypt (the world) but not all of Egypt (the world) was out of them.

1 Cor. 3:1-3
*1 However, brethren, I could not talk to you as to spiritual [men], but as to non-spiritual [**men of the flesh, in whom the carnal nature predominates**], as to mere infants [in the new life] in Christ [unable to talk yet!]*
2 I fed you with milk, not solid food, for you were not yet strong enough [to be ready for it]; but even yet you are not strong enough [to be ready for it],
*3 For you are still [unspiritual, having the nature] of the flesh [under the control of ordinary impulses]. For as long as [there are] envying and jealousy and wrangling and factions among you, **are you not unspiritual and of the flesh, behaving yourselves after a human standard and like mere (unchanged) men**?   AMP*

2. The soul (will, mind, or emotions) ruling as the dominant member.

At this level people love to go to God's house, and often donate their time and energy to the church. But in working for Him, they are still struggling with God's perfect will. While doing good and needed things in the church, they are often limiting themselves to only their natural abilities or talents.

Living at this level:
- With the **will** ruling they are pursuing their will vs. God's will.
- With the **emotions** ruling they exercise their limited human love toward others vs. the love of God flowing through their lives (God's unconditional agape love).
- With the **mind** ruling, working for God is motivated with their thoughts and ways rather than God's thoughts and ways.

-- From "The Spiritual Man"

Soulish believers are not behind others in the matter of works. They are very active, zealous, and willing. However, this is not to say that they labor this way because of God's command. Rather, they do so as they like and according to their own enthusiasm. They think that it is always good to do God's work, but they do not know that it is really good only when they do the work which God gives them. They work according to their own ideas, schemes and abilities. They have not sincerely sought the will of God.

Most soulish believers have a great deal of spiritual knowledge, but their experiences can never match what they know. Because they know much, they also condemn much. Thus, criticizing others becomes a common characteristic of soulish believers. They receive grace to have knowledge, but unlike spiritual believers, they do not receive grace to have humility.[4]

3. The Spirit ruling as the dominant member.

- **For the Spirit to rule in our life, it must be separated from, and then elevated to rule the soul (will, mind and emotions).**

The Word of God, that is sharper than a two-edged sword, will separate the soul (natural man) from the spirit (spiritual man). Refer to Chart T-2, "The Word Divides the Soul and Spirit", at the end of this chapter.

Heb. 4:12
*12 For the word of God is quick, and powerful, and sharper than any two-edged sword, piercing even to the **dividing asunder** of **soul** and **spirit**, and of the joints and marrow, and is a discerner of the thoughts and intents of the heart.*

*12 . . . It penetrates even **to dividing soul and spirit**. NIV*

*12 . . . It **cuts** all the way through, to **where soul and spirit meet** together. GNT*

He who allows the Spirit to be elevated above the soul will reach for the spiritual and will have an insatiable hunger for the things of God. Our hunger drives our pursuit. What we pursue, we will become addicted to. One may wish for wealth and remain poor; one may wish for health and remain sick; but the one who hungers and thirsts for righteousness shall be filled.

The final test of spiritual life is neither what we think (our mind) or feel (our emotions), but what we do (our will) to pursue God's will. When we are in the center of His will, He is in us and we are in Him. We have His Spirit and His Spirit has us.

Apostle Paul's prayer in 1 Thess. 5:23 should be our prayer today: *"May the very God of peace sanctify us wholly; and I pray God that our whole **spirit** and **soul** and **body** be preserved **blameless** unto the coming of our Lord Jesus Christ."*

Blameless in Body:
  - No desire or leaning toward carnal pleasures.
  - Eyes that see no evil, ears that hear no evil, lips that speak no evil and hands that touch no evil.

Blameless in Soul:
  - **Emotions** that can love our enemies and a lost world. A love (agape) driving us to sacrifice for the Kingdom of God.
  - A **mind** desiring to emulate our heavenly Father, desiring to know His ways. Hungering not just for more knowledge, but for more revelation of Him.
  - A submissive **will**, obedient to His will.
  - A pure appetite of the soul, reaching for eternal things.
  - A desire for anointing (divine ability) vs. our ability to do God's will and work.

Blameless in Spirit:
  - Awe and reverence for the sacred things of God -- careful not to grieve the Holy Spirit. *"And grieve not the Holy Spirit of God, whereby ye are sealed unto the day of redemption" (Eph. 4:30).*
  - Craving a higher level of spiritual life, with access to the Gifts of the Spirit, to fulfill the burden of the Lord -- seeking and saving the lost.
  - By faith, looking beyond the temporal, seeing the invisible, hearing the inaudible and believing for the impossible.
  - Having a conscience void of offense toward God and man. *"To have always a conscience void of offence toward God, and toward men" (Acts 24:16).*
  - Having a conscience refusing to be enticed by compromise of a carnal mind.
  - Praying for the deeper things of God -- for the infinite, the supernatural.
  - Having an ever increasing ability to hear the voice of the Spirit as we commune with God in fervent prayer.

- **As a Christian becomes more spiritual, he becomes less tolerant of worldly things. Conversely, as a Christian becomes more carnal, he becomes less tolerant of the things of the Spirit.**

Refer to Chart T-6, "Born Again Christian – Spiritual Vs. Carnal."

The Fading of the Outer Man

In autumn, green maple tree leaves turn to brilliant golden colors of bright gold, reds, pinks, and yellows. Actually, these colors have been present since spring. During the summer months, they are not visible because green chlorophyll in the leaves overpowers the colors. When the nights become cool and daylight hours are short, the tree stops manufacturing chlorophyll. Then the green fades and these beautiful colors emerge.

We are like those leaves. In our dual nature, we have an outer man and an inner man, a man of the flesh and a man of the Spirit. God's Spirit works through our inner spirit. Our problem is that we often try unsuccessfully to work for God through our outer person (with our natural talents and abilities). Like the green chlorophyll; our natural life is obscuring the power of the spiritual life within us. God wants that part to die. He wants the green to go. The veil of self must be removed to allow His spirit to be liberated to accomplish His will and work.

If we are to move into genuine apostolic ministry and the supernatural power of the Holy Ghost, there must be a death to the flesh. This voluntary death involves being crucified with Christ: *"And they that are Christ's have crucified the flesh with the affections and lusts" (Gal. 5:24).*

As the outer man fades, the glory of God, resident in the inner man, can come shining through as light to a dark and hopeless world. There will be a beautiful radiance; and a release of the supernatural that we have never experienced.

- **So the message is clear -- the green must go. If we are to move deeper into the power of the supernatural, it cannot be church and religion as usual. It cannot be routine, formatted religious behavior. The outer man must fade to reveal the radiance of God's beauty and supernatural power through the inner man.**

Who is on the Throne in Your Life?

King Saul is a type of the **flesh**. He was handsome and tall, and appealing to the people. But he could never completely obey the Word of God. As King Saul continued his downward spiral away from God, an evil spirit came upon him and he sought to kill David. King Saul told his son Jonathan that as long as David was alive, he would prevent him from ascending the throne and becoming king.

Jonathan is a type of the **soul**. He was born of Saul (flesh), but knit to David as the soul is attached to the spirit. He and David became best of friends. When Jonathan appealed to King Saul for David, Saul tried to kill him.

David is a type of the **spirit**. He was a great worshipper of God as shown in his many Psalms. He was a man after God's own heart because he did all the will of God.

Why did Jonathan have to die? As long as he lived, he was the rightful heir to the throne. However, David would never assume the throne as long as Jonathan was alive. Refer to Chart T-7, "Death of Self for the Spirit to Reign."

Key Message of This Story:

- **The flesh will ever be in conflict with the Spirit, fighting to subdue it and gain control.**

- **When the flesh becomes depraved, it will destroy the soul (will, mind, emotions):**
    - **Bringing mental and emotional damage.**
    - **Destroying the will to pursue the right paths of life.**

- **In the natural kingdom, the soul is the rightful ruler in our life -- with its will, intellect and natural talents.**

- **For God's Spirit to be elevated to the throne of our life, self must be crucified -- there must be a death to self.**

Let this song be our prayer: "Change Me, Lord":

"Change me Lord, change me Lord; don't let me stay the same,
For I want to be more like you.
Take my life; make my life, just what you want it to be,
Lord, please change me, change me, dear Lord."[5]

Refer to the following pages for the **"Transformation"** overview charts.

Chart T-1

THE TABERNACLE PLAN

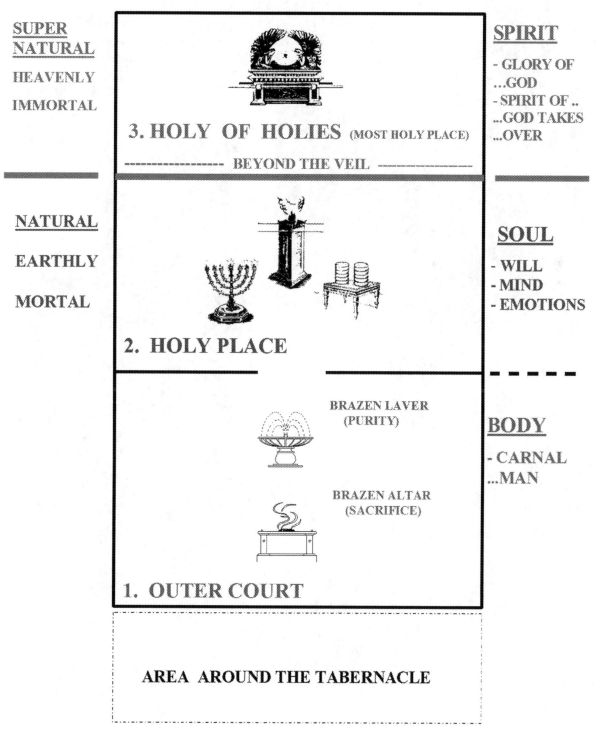

SUPER
NATURAL

HEAVENLY

IMMORTAL

SPIRIT

- GLORY OF
...GOD
- SPIRIT OF ..
...GOD TAKES
...OVER

3. HOLY OF HOLIES (MOST HOLY PLACE)

········ BEYOND THE VEIL ········

NATURAL

EARTHLY

MORTAL

SOUL

- WILL
- MIND
- EMOTIONS

2. HOLY PLACE

BRAZEN LAVER
(PURITY)

BODY

- CARNAL
...MAN

BRAZEN ALTAR
(SACRIFICE)

1. OUTER COURT

AREA AROUND THE TABERNACLE

Chart T-2

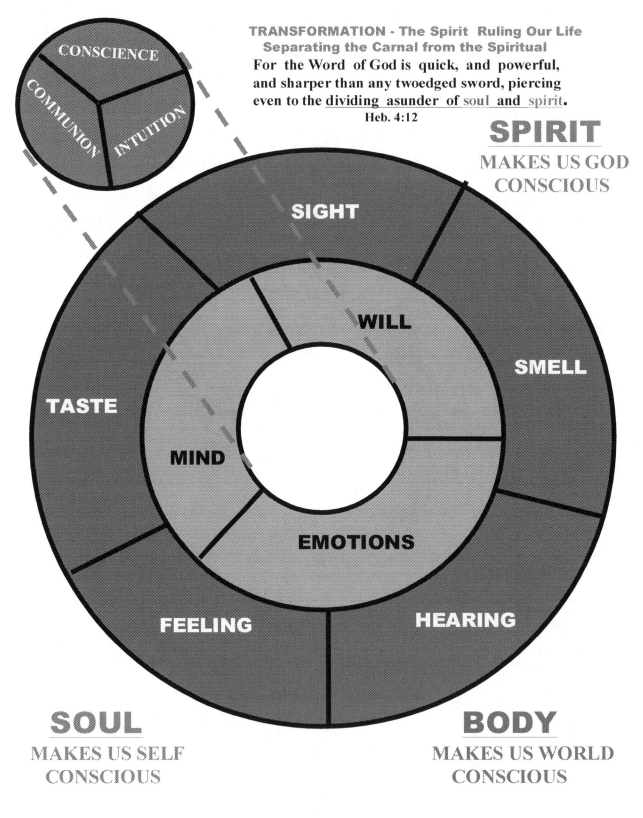

TRANSFORMATION - The Spirit Ruling Our Life
Separating the Carnal from the Spiritual
For the Word of God is quick, and powerful, and sharper than any twoedged sword, piercing even to the dividing asunder of soul and spirit.
Heb. 4:12

CONSCIENCE
COMMUNION
INTUITION

SPIRIT
MAKES US GOD
CONSCIOUS

SIGHT

WILL

SMELL

TASTE

MIND

EMOTIONS

FEELING

HEARING

SOUL
MAKES US SELF
CONSCIOUS

BODY
MAKES US WORLD
CONSCIOUS

Chart T-3

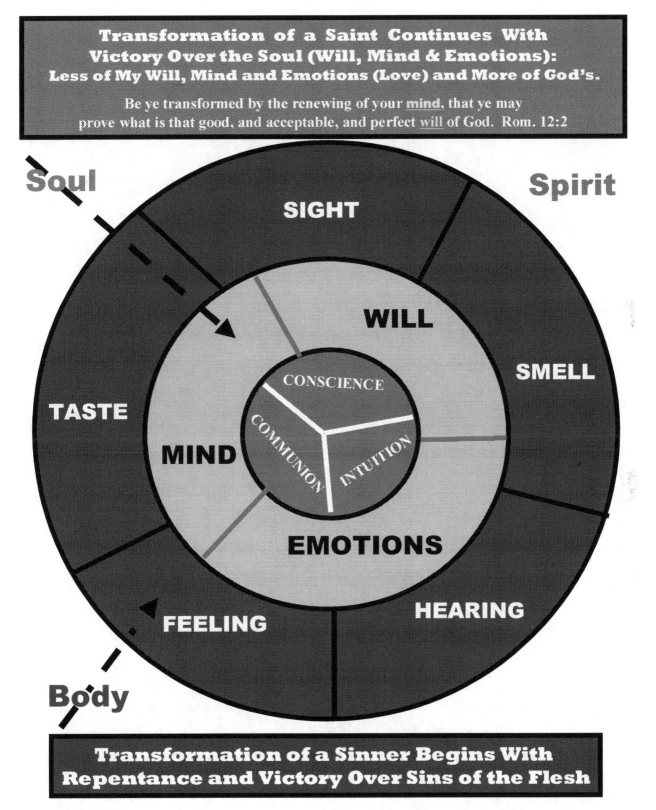

Chart T-4

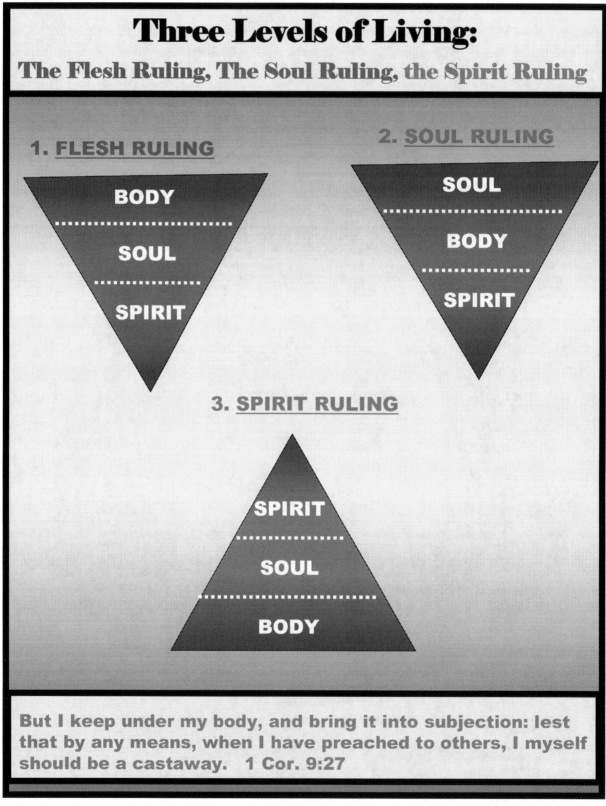

Three Levels of Living:
The Flesh Ruling, The Soul Ruling, the Spirit Ruling

1. FLESH RULING

BODY
SOUL
SPIRIT

2. SOUL RULING

SOUL
BODY
SPIRIT

3. SPIRIT RULING

SPIRIT
SOUL
BODY

But I keep under my body, and bring it into subjection: lest that by any means, when I have preached to others, I myself should be a castaway.   1 Cor. 9:27

Chart T-5

As a born-again Christian:

- Where are you?
- Which way are you going?

?? SPIRITUAL DEATH

SPIRITUAL LIFE
GROWTH & MATURITY

THE CARNAL MAN

THE FLESH RULING

SATAN'S WILL FOR YOUR LIFE
1. Little or no personal devotion of prayer and the Word.
2. Unfaithful to the house of God in attendance and service.
3. Other things have replaced God as the first priority in your life — job, entertainment, hobbies, etc.

BACKSLIDDEN

MAINTENANCE LEVEL
1. Consistent personal devotion of prayer and the Word.
2. Faithful to the house of God in attendance and offerings.
3. Struggling to do God's perfect will and put Him first in every area of your life.

THE SOUL (SELF) RULING

- Our Will Vs God's Will
- Our Mind Vs God's Mind
- Our Emotions Vs God's Emotions (love & compassion)

THE SPIRITUAL MAN

GOD'S WILL FOR YOUR LIFE
1. Consumed with the purpose, will and work of God.
2. Praying in the Spirit. Living in the Spirit.
3. Anointed to operate as a son of God in the supernatural realm — significantly affecting your personal harvest field.

THE SPIRIT RULING

Moving from a maintenance driven Christian to a harvest driven Christian

Chart T-6

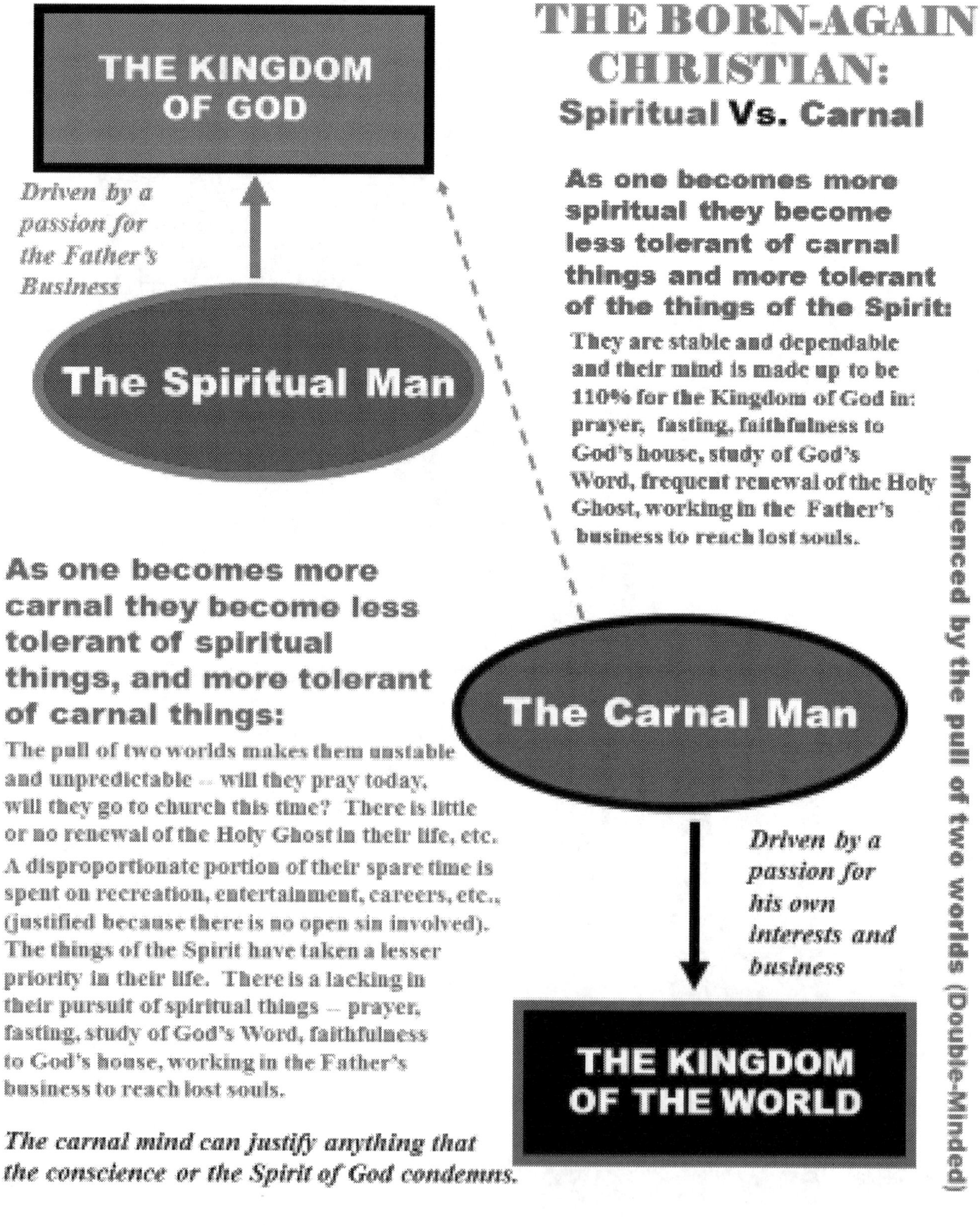

THE KINGDOM OF GOD

Driven by a passion for the Father's Business

The Spiritual Man

THE BORN-AGAIN CHRISTIAN:
Spiritual Vs. Carnal

As one becomes more spiritual they become less tolerant of carnal things and more tolerant of the things of the Spirit:

They are stable and dependable and their mind is made up to be 110% for the Kingdom of God in: prayer, fasting, faithfulness to God's house, study of God's Word, frequent renewal of the Holy Ghost, working in the Father's business to reach lost souls.

The Carnal Man

Driven by a passion for his own interests and business

THE KINGDOM OF THE WORLD

As one becomes more carnal they become less tolerant of spiritual things, and more tolerant of carnal things:

The pull of two worlds makes them unstable and unpredictable -- will they pray today, will they go to church this time? There is little or no renewal of the Holy Ghost in their life, etc. A disproportionate portion of their spare time is spent on recreation, entertainment, careers, etc., (justified because there is no open sin involved). The things of the Spirit have taken a lesser priority in their life. There is a lacking in their pursuit of spiritual things -- prayer, fasting, study of God's Word, faithfulness to God's house, working in the Father's business to reach lost souls.

The carnal mind can justify anything that the conscience or the Spirit of God condemns.

Influenced by the pull of two worlds (Double-Minded)

Chart T-7
Death of Self for the Spirit to Reign

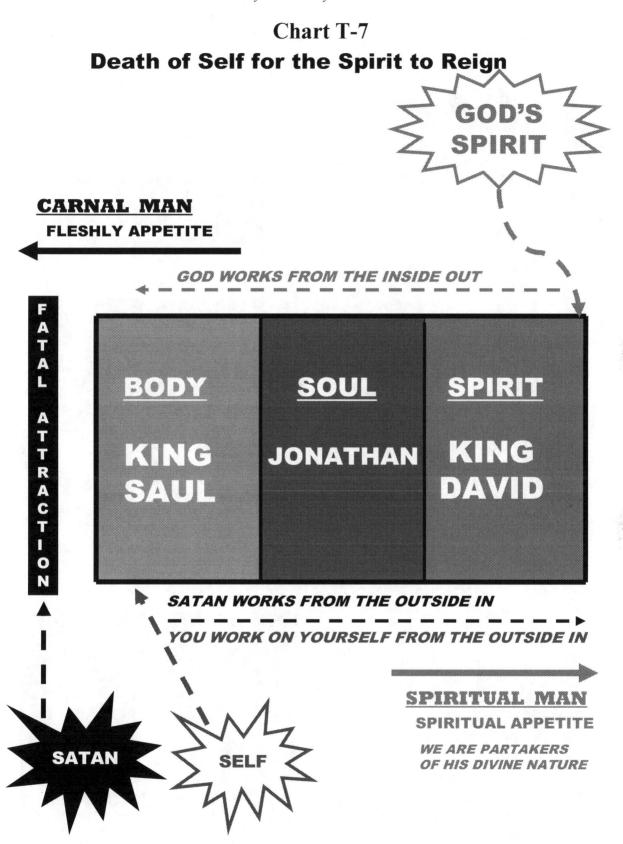

Chart T-8

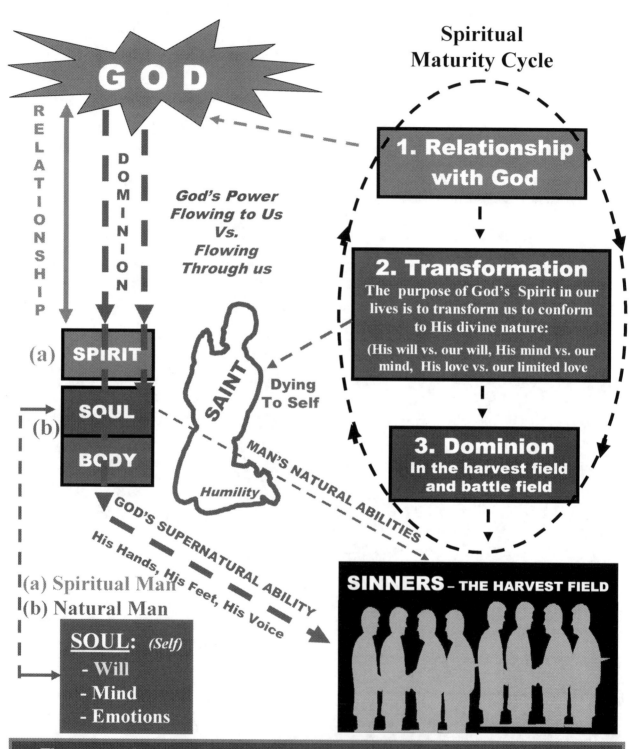

Spiritual Maturity Cycle

GOD

RELATIONSHIP

DOMINION

God's Power Flowing to Us Vs. Flowing Through us

(a) SPIRIT

SOUL

(b)

BODY

SAINT

Dying To Self

Humility

MAN'S NATURAL ABILITIES

GOD'S SUPERNATURAL ABILITY

His Hands, His Feet, His Voice

1. Relationship with God

2. Transformation
The purpose of God's Spirit in our lives is to transform us to conform to His divine nature:
(His will vs. our will, His mind vs. our mind, His love vs. our limited love

3. Dominion
In the harvest field and battle field

(a) Spiritual Man
(b) Natural Man

SOUL: *(Self)*
- Will
- Mind
- Emotions

SINNERS – THE HARVEST FIELD

There must be a continuous transformation. dying to self (our will, mind and emotions), to exercise dominion in the harvest field and battle field -- depending on God's supernatural ability vs. our limited natural abilities.

Chart T-9

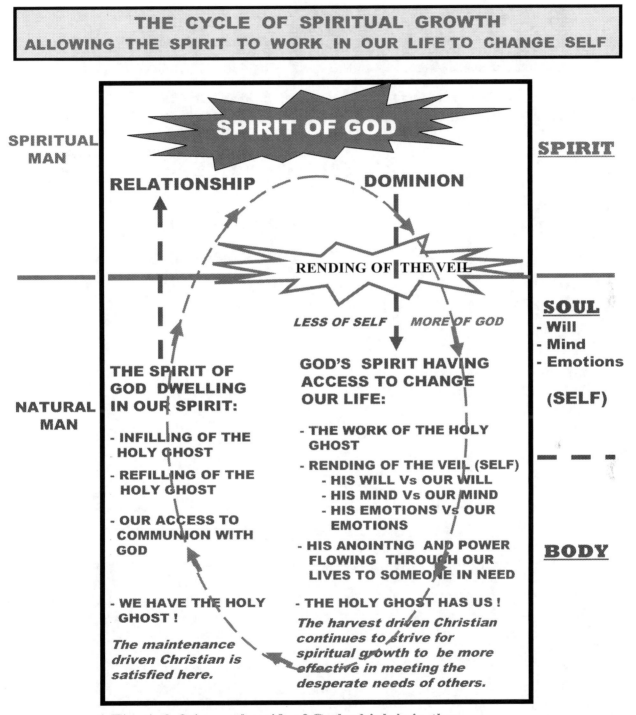

THE CYCLE OF SPIRITUAL GROWTH
ALLOWING THE SPIRIT TO WORK IN OUR LIFE TO CHANGE SELF

SPIRITUAL MAN

SPIRIT OF GOD

SPIRIT

RELATIONSHIP   DOMINION

RENDING OF THE VEIL

SOUL
- Will
- Mind
- Emotions

LESS OF SELF   MORE OF GOD

THE SPIRIT OF GOD DWELLING IN OUR SPIRIT:

- INFILLING OF THE HOLY GHOST

- REFILLING OF THE HOLY GHOST

- OUR ACCESS TO COMMUNION WITH GOD

- WE HAVE THE HOLY GHOST !

The maintenance driven Christian is satisfied here.

GOD'S SPIRIT HAVING ACCESS TO CHANGE OUR LIFE:

- THE WORK OF THE HOLY GHOST

- RENDING OF THE VEIL (SELF)
  - HIS WILL Vs OUR WILL
  - HIS MIND Vs OUR MIND
  - HIS EMOTIONS Vs OUR EMOTIONS

- HIS ANOINTNG AND POWER FLOWING THROUGH OUR LIVES TO SOMEONE IN NEED

- THE HOLY GHOST HAS US !

The harvest driven Christian continues to strive for spiritual growth to be more effective in meeting the desperate needs of others.

(SELF)

BODY

1 Tim 1:6 Stir up the gift of God which is in thee.

Fan into flame the gift of God, which is in you. ESV

Chart T-10

THE PATH TO THE SUPERNATURAL
FOR THE BORN-AGAIN BELIEVER

THE MIRACLE MINISTRY OF JESUS WILL FLOW THROUGH US UNRESTRICTED - WHEN SELF HAS COMPLETELY DIED

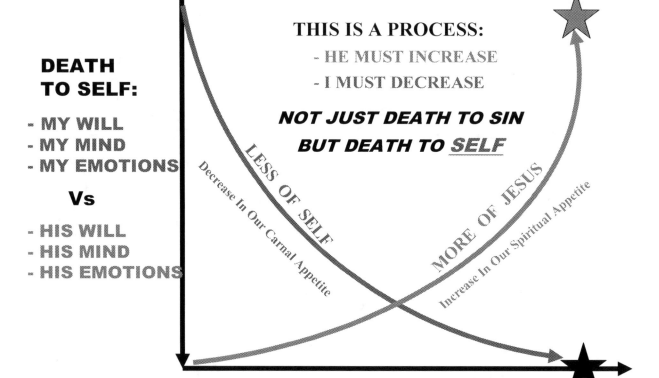

DEATH TO SELF:

- MY WILL
- MY MIND
- MY EMOTIONS

Vs

- HIS WILL
- HIS MIND
- HIS EMOTIONS

THIS IS A PROCESS:
- HE MUST INCREASE
- I MUST DECREASE

NOT JUST DEATH TO SIN
BUT DEATH TO SELF

LESS OF SELF
Decrease In Our Carnal Appetite

MORE OF JESUS
Increase In Our Spiritual Appetite

SPIRITUAL GROWTH - CHANGE OVER TIME

IN THE NEW TESTAMENT: (Why did John the Baptist have to die?)
John the Baptist was the forerunner of Jesus' miracle ministry. His message of "He must increase, but I must decrease", was a self-fulfilled prophecy when he was imprisoned, and put to death as the miracle ministry of Jesus began.

IN THE OLD TESTAMENT: (Why did Jonathan have to die?)
Saul is a type of the flesh, Jonathan is a type of the soul (self - the will, the mind, and the emotions), David is a type of the Spirit. Both Saul and Jonathan had to die before David could come to the throne.

Chart T-11

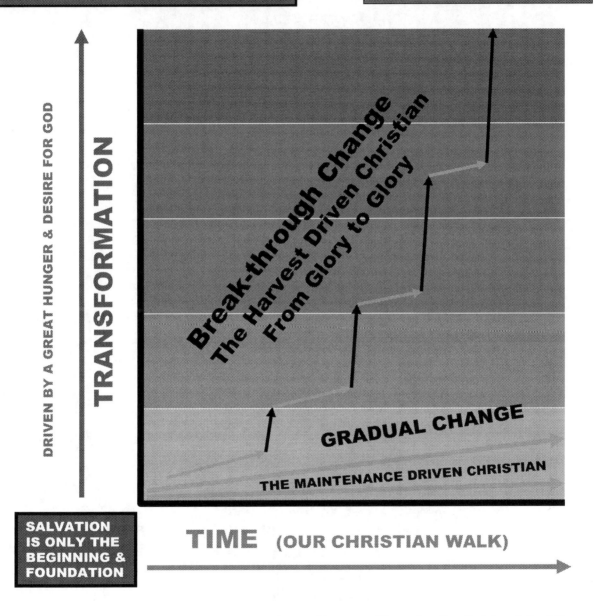

BREAK-THROUGH TO NEW LEVELS OF:
- **RELATIONSHIP** with God
- **DOMINION** - Partnering with God to fulfill His mission and His will and work on earth

GOD'S ETERNAL PURPOSE & WILL FOR OUR LIFE

DRIVEN BY A GREAT HUNGER & DESIRE FOR GOD

TRANSFORMATION

Break-through Change
The Harvest Driven Christian
From Glory to Glory

GRADUAL CHANGE

THE MAINTENANCE DRIVEN CHRISTIAN

SALVATION IS ONLY THE BEGINNING & FOUNDATION

TIME (OUR CHRISTIAN WALK)

" Changed into His image from Glory to Glory by the Spirit of God "

" Partakers of His Divine Nature "

Chart T-12

Spiritual Maturity
Life Cycle & Balance
(Driven by Love for God and Others)

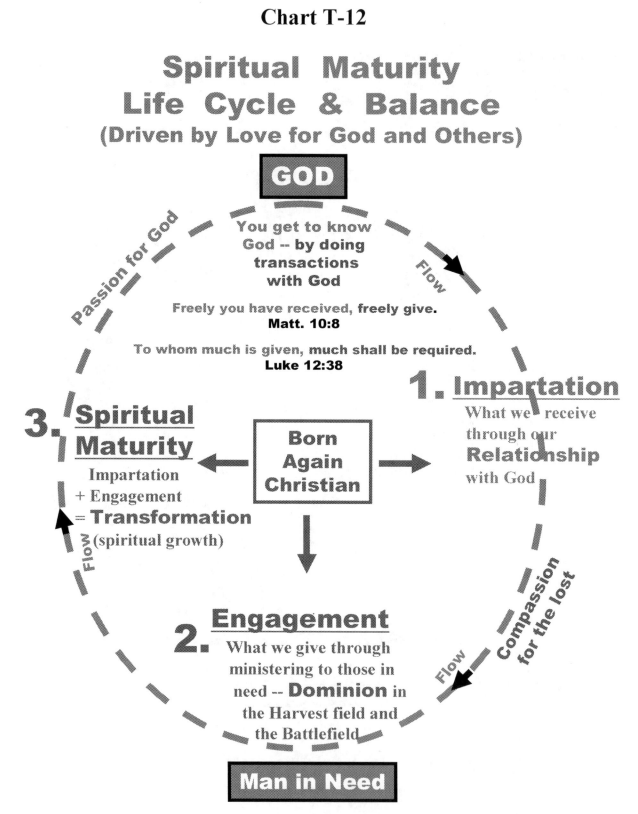

GOD

You get to know God -- **by doing transactions with God**

Freely you have received, **freely give.**
Matt. 10:8

To whom much is given, **much shall be required.**
Luke 12:38

Passion for God

Flow

1. Impartation
What we receive through our **Relationship** with God

3. Spiritual Maturity
Impartation + Engagement = **Transformation** (spiritual growth)

Born Again Christian

Flow

Compassion for the lost

2. Engagement
What we give through ministering to those in need -- **Dominion** in the Harvest field and the Battlefield

Flow

Man in Need

Ministering to someone in need benefits them - and in turn benefits you.

4. Dominion - Doing God's Will and Work

Theme Summary and Key Scripture Text

Dominion
God depending on man

Dominion: To dominate with authority and power, to rule in a territory or domain. This involves God sharing His authority and power with man in a partnership to fulfill His purpose, doing His will and work on earth.

- **Old Testament**
  - Physical Dominion

Let us make man in our image: and let them have dominion over all the earth. (Genesis 1:26)

You have put man in charge of everything you made; everything is put under his authority. (Psalms 8:6) TLB

- **New Testament**
  - Spiritual Dominion

The five-fold ministry and the laity have been given the same power and authority over sickness and satan.

Engagement in the Father's Business
As a physician, priest (intercessor), king, soldier, harvester

- Curse ye Meroz, said the angel of the LORD, curse ye bitterly the inhabitants thereof; because they came not to the help of the Lord, to the help of the Lord against the mighty. (Judges 5:23)

- Ye shall receive power after the Holy Ghost is come upon you, and ye shall be witnesses unto me in Jerusalem, and in all Judaea, and in Samaria, and unto the uttermost part of the earth. (Acts 1:8)

- Behold I give unto you power to tread on serpents and scorpions, and over all the power of the enemy: and nothing shall by any means hurt you. (Luke 10:10)

- **The 12 disciples represent the five-fold ministry:**
  He called His twelve disciples together, and gave them power and authority over all devils and diseases. (Luke 9:1)

- **The 70 given the same power, represent the laity:**
  The Lord appointed seventy also . . . heal the sick . . . I give you power over all the power of the enemy. (Luke 10:9, 19)

- The Great Commission of Jesus Christ -- Go: (Matthew 28:19, Mark 15:16, Luke 24:47, John 20:21, Acts 1:8).

Study References

Vol.	Book Name	Primary Study Section / Chapter	Elective Study
II	Dominion - Doing God's Will and Work	Sec. II, III	Sec. I, IV
IV	Unlimited Partnership With a Supernatural God	Sec. I / Ch. 2, 3	
V	Revival & Evangelism - Passion for God - Passion for Souls	Sec. II / Ch. 3-6	Sec. III / Ch. 2-4
VIII	Addendum Volume (PowerPoint Charts)	Charts at the end of this chapter	B2 - B7, G-1 - G-25, J-1 - J-35

From the beginning of time God's purpose for creating man included **relationship,** however, it was much more than that. It was to establish a partnership with Himself and give man **dominion** to carry out His mission, will and work on earth. Dominion means: to prevail against; to dominate with authority and power; to rule in a kingdom or domain.

There is the kingdom of this world and there is the Kingdom of God. It is God's plan for us, His children, to prevail against His enemies -- the kingdom of this world, the god of this world (satan). God wants us to rule and participate with Him in His domain, His Kingdom business: *"And they went forth, and preached everywhere, **the Lord working with them, and confirming the word** with signs following" (Mark 16:20).*

If we are going to rule and reign with Him on this earth in the by and by, then we must rule and reign with Him in the here and now: *"Blessed and holy is he that hath part in the first resurrection: on such the second death hath no power, but they shall be priests of God and of Christ, and shall reign with Him a thousand years" (Rev. 20:6).*

God's plan has never changed. Man was made to rule the earth for God -- to have dominion, authority and power. He was to reflect the glory of God, revealing God to those who did not know Him. In the Old Testament God gave man dominion over the earth: *"Be fruitful, and multiply, and replenish the earth, and subdue it: and have dominion over the fish of the sea, and over the fowl of the air, and over every living thing that moveth upon the earth" (Gen. 1:28).*

In the New Testament, God gave every born-again Christian (five-fold ministry and laity) the same dominion over satan and sickness: *"He called His twelve disciples together, and gave them power and authority over all devils and diseases" (Luke 9:1). "The Lord appointed seventy also . . . heal the sick . . . I give you power over all the power of the enemy" (Luke 10:1, 9, 19).*

God's decision to do nothing on earth except through man is a wonderful truth. In making this choice, God placed Himself in a relationship that He would need man to carry out His work and will. God needs man; man needs God. Those who say God doesn't need you or me, do not understand the key principle of relationship. And that is, both parties must have a mutual need and a dependence on one another. Otherwise, it is one-sided and not a valid relationship or contract.

We can rejoice in the fact that God needs us and depends on us to carry on His work. And, Oh God, we need You. We need Your help and wisdom to work out impossible situations and problems in our lives that we could not solve in a lifetime.

- **God created this earth and He owns it, but He has assigned it to man to govern and rule. He has chosen man to be the intercessor here, to carry on His work, His will and His purpose.**

Psalms 115:16
*16 The heaven, even the heavens, are the LORD's: **but the earth hath He given to the children of men.***

*16 The heavens belong to the Lord, **but He has given the earth to all mankind.** TLB*

*16 . . . **the earth He has assigned to men.** MOF*

God has put man in charge on earth, for God, with God and under God. God created man in His image because He wanted a son who would:
- Look like Him.
- Think like Him.
- Love what He loves.
- Hate what He hates.
- Do His will in carrying on His business here on earth.

He assigned man to govern the earth. Man is God's representative or intercessor in the battle against the forces of evil and the mission of the harvest -- to seek and save the lost.

God made Adam in His image, He put His breath in Him, He put His glory on him, and then He told him: "I am giving you dominion. You are in charge. You are My agent to carry out My mission and work on earth. You are My hands, My feet, My eyes, My ears, and My mouthpiece on the earth." King David declared this awesome concept in his writings:

Psalms 8:3-6
3 When I consider thy heavens, the work of thy fingers, the moon and the stars, which thou hast ordained;
4 What is man, that thou art mindful of him? and the son of man, that thou visitest him?
*5 For thou hast made him **a little lower than the angels,** and hast crowned him with glory and honor.*
*6 Thou madest him to have **dominion** over the works of thy hands; thou hast **put all things under his feet:***

Psalms 8:5 **(Man made a little lower than deity)**
5 For thou hast made him but little lower than God, and crownest him with glory and honor. ASV

5 Yet you made him inferior only to yourself; you crowned him with glory and honor. TEV

- **Man is much more valuable to God than angels. When the angels committed one sin, God did not lift a finger to recover or save them, but instead He cast them out of heaven to be doomed forever. But one man sinned and God promised that He would come and die for him.**

Jude 6
And the angels which kept not their first estate, but left their own habitation, He hath reserved in everlasting chains under darkness unto the judgment of the great day.

Man is a beloved son of God. In the New Testament we are His bride, His love. He loved us so much that He suffered, shed His blood and died for us. We are important to God. God needs us and we surely need Him. This is a great partnership and relationship.

- **God's purpose for creating man in the beginning and His purpose for the New Testament church are the same -- relationship and dominion.**

Dominion -- Old Testament

This chapter is a reminder of familiar Old Testament examples of the children of Israel going beyond their role of relationship with God and stepping into their dominion role of fulfilling God's purpose.

Israel's Relationship with God

The children of Israel were in relationship with God in the Old Testament because they inherited the covenant relationship that God had made with Abraham, their father. When they were fulfilling their part of the covenant, they were involved in the dominion role of doing God's will. When they were faithful to God, they enjoyed His favor.

Israel's Dominion Role

God's plan was to partner with man and empower him to carry out His mission and work on earth. Throughout the Old Testament history it was God's will for Israel to:

- Wage war and join in the battle with God against His enemies.
- Be involved in conquest to claim the territory promised to their forefathers.
- Be a channel for the rest of the earth to be blessed.
- Allow God to work through them to display His mighty power as a witness to the heathen nations.

Gen. 13:14-17 (God gave Abram the land, but he had to walk through it and possess it)
14 And the LORD said unto Abram, after that Lot was separated from him, Lift up now thine eyes, and look from the place where thou art northward, and southward, and eastward, and westward:
15 For all the land which thou seest, to thee will I give it, and to thy seed forever.
16 And I will make thy seed as the dust of the earth: so that if a man can number the dust of the earth, then shall thy seed also be numbered.
*17 Arise, **walk through the land in the length of it and in the breadth of it; for I will give it unto thee.***

Ex. 23:30-33 (Defeating the enemy was a partnership of man and God)
*30 By little and little **I will drive them out** from before thee, until thou be increased, and inherit the land.*
*31 And I will set thy bounds from the Red sea even unto the sea of the Philistines, and from the desert unto the river: for I will deliver the inhabitants of the land into your hand; and **thou shalt drive them out before thee.***
32 Thou shalt make no covenant with them, or with their Gods.
33 They shall not dwell in thy land, lest they make thee sin against me: for if thou serve their Gods, it will surely be a snare unto thee.

Deut. 11:22-25
22 For if ye shall diligently keep all these commandments which I command you, to do them, to love the LORD your God, to walk in all his ways, and to cleave unto him;
23 Then will the LORD drive out all these nations from before you, and ye shall possess greater nations and mightier than yourselves.
*24 **Every place where on the soles of your feet shall tread shall be yours**: from the wilderness and Lebanon, from the river, the river Euphrates, even unto the uttermost sea shall your coast be.*
25 There shall no man be able to stand before you: for the LORD your God shall lay the fear of you and the dread of you upon all the land that ye shall tread upon, as he hath said unto you.

Projecting the Old Testament into the New Testament

The entire Israelite history is a type of the redemption of mankind by Jesus Christ. The deliverance of the Jews from their enemies is a symbol of the great deliverance of people in the world from the powers of satan. Israel's history tracks the New Testament church (born on the Day of Pentecost) through its decline after the first century, the Dark Ages, and its restoration that began in the early 1900s. Refer to Chart D-7, "Restoration -- The History of the Nation of Israel and the Church", at the end of this chapter.

It is God's will for us to be a part of the restoration of the church today, involving ourselves in a dominion role in the last day harvest. To do this, we must be willing to go beyond where we have been before into new places in the Spirit.

To be led by the Spirit:
- Allow the Spirit to be more dominant in our lives through a closer relationship with God.
- Allow the Spirit to **lead us into the dominion role** by taking dominion over satan and sickness.

God only claims us as a son if we allow His Spirit to lead us: *"For as many as are led by the Spirit of God, they are the sons of God" (Rom. 8:14).* The Spirit will always lead us further into His mission, purpose and work.

To better understand this, let us examine the Old Testament experiences and how God worked through His chosen people to accomplish His purpose.

Gal. 3:24
Wherefore the law was our schoolmaster to bring us unto Christ, that we might be justified by faith.

The Old Testament is the New Testament concealed (types and shadows). The New Testament is the Old Testament revealed. Many things that happened in the physical in the Old Testament are revealed as spiritual concepts in the New Testament church today. These things were written for us to better understand how God deals with man and what He requires of man.

Heb. 8:5
*Who serve unto the **example and shadow of heavenly things**, as Moses was admonished of God when he was about to make the tabernacle: for, see, saith he, that thou make all things according to the pattern shewed to thee in the mount.*

1 Cor. 10:1, 6
1 Moreover, brethren, I would not that ye should be ignorant, how that all our fathers were under the cloud, and all passed through the sea; 6 Now these things were our examples.

1 Cor. 10:11
Now all these things happened unto them for ensamples: and they are written for our admonition, upon whom the ends of the world are come.

Old Testament and New Testament Comparison

The focus of the Old Testament was:	The focus of the New Testament is:
• Physical nation (God's chosen people)	• Spiritual nation (church - God's chosen people)
• Physical kingdom with physical kings	• Spiritual kingdom with spiritual kings
• Physical priesthood with physical priests	• Spiritual priesthood with spiritual priests
• Physical anointing	• Spiritual anointing
• Physical battles with physical dominion	• Spiritual battles with spiritual dominion
• Conquest for physical territory	• Conquest for spiritual territory
• Physical enemies to fight	• Spiritual enemies to fight
• Physical warfare with physical weapons	• Spiritual warfare with spiritual weapons
• Blood covenant with physical circumcision	• Blood covenant with a spiritual circumcision (baptism)
• Laws of God physically written on stone	• Laws of God written on men's hearts
• Physical tabernacle with three parts: (outer court, Holy Place, Holy of Holies)	• Spiritual tabernacle with three parts: body, soul and spirit
• Physical veil between the Holy Place and the Holy of Holies	• The veil of self (our will, mind and emotions) between the soul and the spirit. Refer to Charts T-1, 8, 9 at the end of Chapter 3.
• Physical sacrifices of animals (bulls, lambs, goats)	• Spiritual sacrifice of our lives (worship, praise, service)
• Coming out of Egypt (baptized in the cloud and the sea) 1 Cor. 10:2. Crossing the Red Sea (leaving the old life of the past)	• Coming out of the world: (baptized in water, Spirit) Deliverance from sin and separation from the world (leaving the old life of the past)
• Going into the Promised Land: Crossing the Jordan River to Canaan and restoration to the physical inheritance of their forefathers (future)	• Going into God's will and purpose: Restoration of God's people to the spiritual place of their forefathers -- the apostolic ministry of the first church in the book of Acts (our future)
• Physical death for an entire generation unwilling to get involved in God's purpose and will to drive out the enemy and possess Canaan land • The angel of the Lord placed a curse on those that did not get involved in the battle against Sisera (Judg. 5:23)	• Spiritual death for those who do not get involved in God's purpose and will for their lives in His Kingdom Refer to Chart D-8, "Egypt to Canaan Journey", at the end of this chapter.

God Empowers Available and Willing People for Supernatural Feats

God miraculously used women and men in the Old Testament who had no natural abilities to overcome the impossible challenges that they faced. The principle of dominion is that God uses those who are willing to step into His will and purpose to perform His miraculous work -- availability vs. ability. Some of these are recorded by Apostle Paul in the hall of faith:

Heb. 11:7-8, 17, 22-24, 30-34, 36-39
*By faith Noah . . . By faith Abraham . . . By faith Moses . . . By faith the walls of Jericho fell down . . . By faith the harlot Rahab. And what shall I more say? for the time would fail me to tell of Gideon, and of Barak, and of Samson, and of Jephthae; of David also, and Samuel, and of the prophets: Who through faith **subdued kingdoms, wrought righteousness, obtained promises, stopped the mouths of lions,** Quenched **the violence of fire, escaped the edge of the sword, out of weakness were made strong, waxed valiant in fight, turned to flight the armies of the aliens**. And others had trial of cruel mockings and scourgings, yea, moreover of bonds and imprisonment: They were stoned, they were sawn asunder, were tempted, were slain with the sword: they wandered about in sheepskins and goatskins; being destitute, afflicted, tormented; (Of whom the world was not worthy:) they wandered in deserts, and in mountains, and in dens and caves of the earth. And these all, having obtained a good report through faith, received not the promise:*

Refer to the following pages for a summary of some of the Old Testament heroes of faith.

Old Testament Character	Miraculous Accomplishments
Deborah (a prophetess and a judge)	Deborah's prophecy inspired Barak, the leader of Israel's army to battle against the army of Sisera: *"And Barak said unto her, If thou wilt go with me, then I will go: but if thou wilt not go with me, then I will not go".* *(Judg. 4:8)*
Jael (a housewife)	Jael, with just a hammer and nail, like David with a sling and stone, killed Sisera and secured the victory. God used two women in a dominion role for this great victory. Normally this role in Old Testament battles would be reserved for men. Thank God for women who will exercise dominion and step into the battle to be used by God. **To all the godly women in the New Testament church, we salute and commend you -- you are very valuable. There is no limitation to your taking dominion in the Kingdom of God. We need you and God needs you.**
David (a young shepherd boy)	A young shepherd boy with just a rock and a sling defeated the giant Goliath when all the warriors in Israel's army were afraid.
Samson (the strongest man)	When the Spirit of God moved on Samson he performed feats of supernatural strength in defeating the enemy that had dominion over Israel: *"For at that time the Philistines had dominion over Israel".* *(Judg. 14:4)*
Four sick lepers (the weakest men)	The Assyrians had besieged Samaria and created a great famine in the city. Four starving lepers outside the gates of Samaria, in partnership, with God defeated the entire army of the Assyrians.
Esther (a young orphan girl in Babylonian captivity)	A young orphan girl, with the favor of God, was chosen to be queen. She risk her life by identifying with her people and saved the Jews from annihilation: *"And in every province, and in every city, whithersoever the king's commandment and his decree came, the Jews had joy and gladness, a feast and a good day. And many of the people of the land became Jews; for the fear of the Jews fell upon them."* *(Est. 8:17)*
Shadrach, Meshach, and Abednego (young men in Babylonian captivity)	These three young men risk their life by refusing to bow to the king's idol. They were protected from the flames of the fiery furnace by the fourth Man in the fire. Then Nebuchadnezzar, the ruler of the world, made a proclamation: *"Therefore I make a decree, That every people, nation, and language, which speak anything amiss against the God of Shadrach, Meshach, and Abed-nego, shall be cut in pieces, and their houses shall be made a dunghill: because there is no other God that can deliver after this sort."* *(Dan. 3:29)*

Old Testament Character	Miraculous Accomplishments
Daniel (in Babylonian captivity)	God gave Daniel the king's dream and the interpretation saving many from death. He was protected from death in the lion's den. Became of God's favor he became a prince in the Babylonian captivity. Then the king made this decree: *"That in every dominion of my kingdom men tremble and fear before the God of Daniel: for he is the living God, and steadfast forever, and his kingdom that which shall not be destroyed, and his dominion shall be even unto the end. He delivereth and rescueth, and he worketh signs and wonders in heaven and in earth."* (Dan. 6:26-27)
Gideon (the least qualified)	This fearful and unqualified man was chosen by God to lead 300 men in defeating the large Assyrian army that had oppressed Israel for seven years.
Moses (the meekest man)	After leaving Egypt in defeat and being a lowly shepherd in the wilderness for 40 years, he was chosen by God to defy the dynasty of Egypt and deliver Israel from the oppression of the most powerful nation in the world.
Caleb (85 year old man)	At the age of 85 God had miraculously preserved his strength as it was when he was 40. After crossing Jordan for conquest of Canaan, he requested the most difficult territory (strong fortified cities) to conquer for a possession.
Joshua (leader of Israel)	When needing more daylight to secure the victory against the enemy Joshua commanded the sun to stand still: *"And he said in the sight of Israel, Sun, stand thou still upon Gibeon; and thou, Moon, in the valley of Ajalon. And the sun stood still, and the moon stayed, until the people had avenged themselves upon their enemies. So the sun stood still in the midst of heaven, and hasted not to go down about a whole day. And there was no day like that before it or after it, that the Lord hearkened unto the voice of a man: for the Lord fought for Israel"* (Josh. 10:12-14).
Rahab (a harlot)	Rahab, the harlot, risk her life to hide and save the two spies sent by Joshua to spy out the city Jericho. Because of this heroic deed she and her family were spared in the battle of Jericho. She turned to the God of Israel and became a part of the lineage of Jesus Christ -- the great, great, great, grandmother of Jesus Christ.

Dominion -- New Testament

Apostle Paul's writings in Ephesians 4:11-12 identify the two purposes for which God created the New Testament church:

1. **Perfect the saints** (Relationship)

2. **Equip the saints for the work of the ministry** (Dominion)

Eph. 4:11-12
11 And He gave some, apostles; and some, prophets; and some, evangelists; and some, pastors and teachers;
12 For the: (1) **Perfecting of the saints**, *(2) For the* **work of the ministry**, *for the edifying of the body of Christ:*

12 **For the equipping of the saints for the work of ministry** *. . . NKJV*

12 **To prepare God's people for works of service**, *so that the body of Christ may be built up. NIV*

We have well accepted **relationship** as the first purpose for which God created man. Relationship with God brings the blessings of God in our lives. But we have understood less about the second purpose, **dominion** -- to carry out His purpose and work on earth.

While relationship brings God's blessings; fulfilling the role of dominion brings His favor. Everyone wants to be in relationship with God to receive His blessings, but fulfilling the dominion role as a son of God is also a part of His eternal purpose and will for our lives.

In the Christian culture we often lead people to a relationship with God, but fail to help them understand and take the next important step -- exercising dominion in the Kingdom of God. This lesson emphasizes the foundational concept that God works only through man to accomplish His will and work on earth. The three concepts of relationship, transformation and dominion working together in a believer's life will bring balance, spiritual growth and fulfillment.

God and man dominion roles include: **Great Physician** / physician; **Great High Priest** / priest; **Great Commander** / soldier; **King of Kings** / king; **Lord of the Harvest** / harvester.

Our Heavenly Father is:	It is His will for us as sons of God to be:
The **Great Physician,** the great healer of the complete man: body, soul and spirit.	A **physician** healing the hurting of our generation. The world is full of people dying from physical and spiritual (sin) diseases, crying out in their despair and hopelessness, desperately in need of caregivers that have been commissioned by the Great Physician.
The **Commander-in-Chief** in the war against satan and sin.	A **soldier** engaging in spiritual warfare against the kingdom of satan. The forces of evil that are set in array against the purpose and mission of the church. The kingdom of satan has issued its challenge to the church. What will be our response?
The **King of Kings,** the omnipotent, omniscient, omnipresent ruler of the universe.	A **king** serving in His Kingdom with dominion over satan, the prince of this world.
The **Great High Priest,** the great intercessor that once and for all offered the atoning sacrifice for our sins.	A **priest**, a holy and anointed man to serve as an intercessor to His lost world. It is His will for us to be a go-between reconciling the world unto Christ: *"Jesus Christ hath given to us the ministry of reconciliation" (2 Cor. 5:18).*
The **Lord of the Harvest.**	A **laborer** in His harvest field. The Lord of the Harvest is calling every born-again Christian to work in His business, as the sun sets on the harvest field. **Jesus' only prayer request** still rings out today: *"Pray ye therefore the Lord of the harvest, that he will send forth labourers into his harvest."*

The first message in Acts is for the unconverted to begin their **relationship** with God. But there is a second message of **dominion** that is often overlooked. This is a challenging message for the believer, that tells what the early church did, how they did it, and the miraculous results that they received. There was prayer, fasting, apostolic authority and dominion, resulting in intense evangelism with deliverance, salvation and miracles.

We have cracked open the door of evangelism and miracles from time to time, and we rejoice and thank God when this happens. But we must press with prayer and fasting, and move further into the **dominion** role until the doors of evangelism and miracles burst open; and the power of God, as recorded in the book of Acts, flows from our lives and churches to those bound in prisons of sin, sickness and abuse. We should be praying for and expecting this to happen in our individual lives and in our churches.

If Jesus Christ (God in the flesh) used authority and dominion over disease and the power of satan to launch and advance His ministry, how can the church operate without the same today? If the New Testament church in the book of Acts needed a miracle ministry, with signs, miracles and wonders, to confirm the Word and reach their world, how much more the church needs the same today. This will only happen as we fervently seek Him and fulfill our dominion role.

God had an eternal purpose and will for our lives before we were born. The more we move into the center of God's eternal purpose and will, the more complete and fulfilled our lives will be.

The Challenge

There are insurmountable problems and issues of a generation that has been affected by sickness, sin and abuse. There has been an absence of godly influence and guidance passed down from the prior generation. There is very little time to reach our world, because we are living in the endtime, just before the second coming of Jesus Christ. As of 2015 the population of the world has reached 7.3 billion. That is approximately 24 times more people in the world today than at the time of Christ and the first century church in the book of Acts. The church is not keeping up with this incredible and overwhelming increase in the population.

The Solution

The only solution is the supernatural power of God, working in the born-again believer, with authority over satan and sickness: *"The Lord working with them, and confirming the word with signs following" (Mark 16:20).*

Impartation + Encounter and Engagement (Dominion)
= Release of Power for Miracles

Impartation is what we receive through our relationship with God. Encounter and engagement is our active involvement in the Father's business (harvest field and battlefield) exercising our dominion role. Refer to Chart D-6 at the end of this chapter. May we embrace the miraculous work of the Spirit and hunger for the operation of the supernatural in our lives and our churches -- allowing Him to: *"Do exceeding abundantly above all that we ask or think, according to the power that worketh in us" (Eph. 3:30).*

Key Foundational Requirements for Dominion in the Supernatural

Some of the key foundational requirements for dominion in the supernatural include the following:
- Growing in Love for God.
- Growing in Obedience (not only saying to "no" to satan but "yes" to God's will).
- Growing in Burden (passion for God, compassion for lost souls).
- Growing in Sacrifice: *"Present your bodies a living sacrifice holy and acceptable unto God which is your reasonable service" (Rom. 12:1).*
- Growing in Anointing (God's divine ability working in our lives).
- Growing in Charity (love in action to those in need).
- Growing in Spiritual Gifts (spiritual gifts flow through the charity channel) 1 Cor. 1:1-3.

The three key overarching elements in this process upon which the others rest and operate are: **love** for God, **obedience** to the will of God, and the **burden** of the Lord that is reflected in our passion to do His will and work:

- None of the above principles will work in our life without a true love for God.

- God will not recognize nor bless our efforts working in His Kingdom if we are not living in obedience to His Word and will. It is not enough to just say "no" to satan, we must say "yes" to God's will for our lives.

- Our working in the Kingdom will only be effective unless it is driven by a burden -- a passion for God and compassion for souls.

Refer to the following pages for the **"Dominion"** overview charts.

Chart D-1

Dominion

**Kingdom comes from two words:
King and domain – The King's Domain**

Domain is a land or territory that a ruler or government rules or controls

Dominion means to dominate with authority and power – to rule in a territory or domain

God and Man Dominion Roles:

Our Heavenly Father is:	As a son of God I Am:
- The Great Physician	- A physician healing hurts and sickness in our world
- The Great High Priest	- A priest interceding for the needs of our world
- The Great Commander	- A soldier fighting the battle against evil of sin and Satan
- The King of Kings	- A king with dominion over the kingdom of Satan
- Lord of the Harvest	- Harvester working in the harvest field of lost souls

Chart D-2

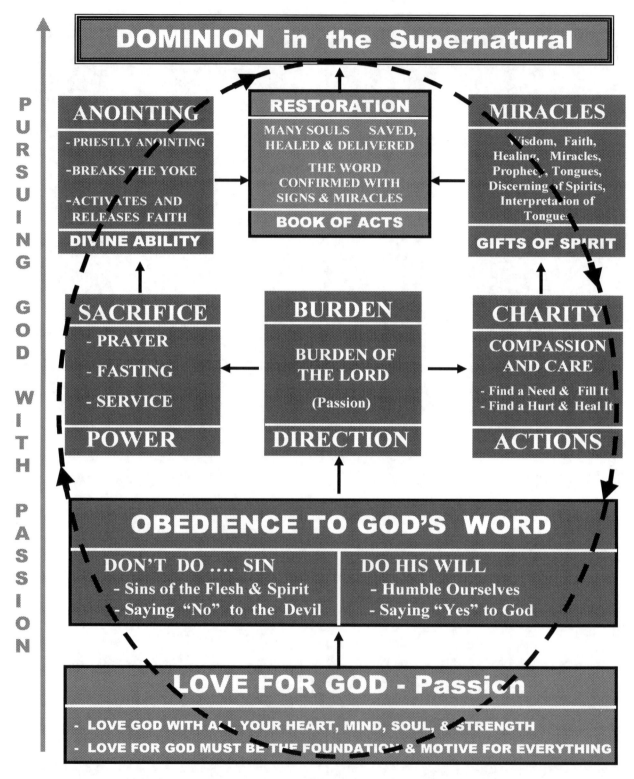

Fundamental truths comprise the foundation upon which others operate and are supported.

Chart D-3

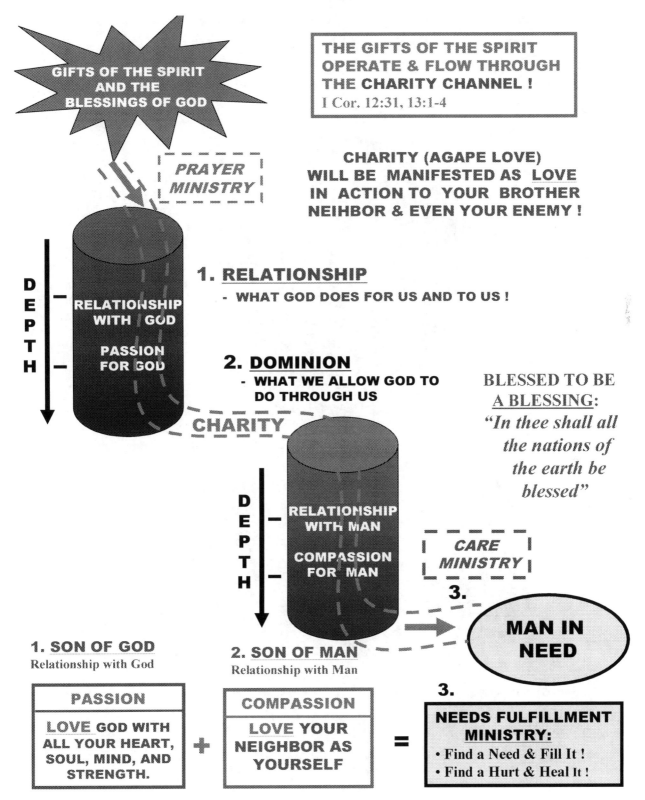

THE GIFTS OF THE SPIRIT OPERATE & FLOW THROUGH THE **CHARITY CHANNEL !**
I Cor. 12:31, 13:1-4

CHARITY (AGAPE LOVE) WILL BE MANIFESTED AS LOVE IN ACTION TO YOUR BROTHER NEIHBOR & EVEN YOUR ENEMY !

GIFTS OF THE SPIRIT AND THE BLESSINGS OF GOD

PRAYER MINISTRY

DEPTH

RELATIONSHIP WITH GOD

PASSION FOR GOD

1. RELATIONSHIP
- WHAT GOD DOES FOR US AND TO US !

2. DOMINION
- WHAT WE ALLOW GOD TO DO THROUGH US

CHARITY

BLESSED TO BE A BLESSING: *"In thee shall all the nations of the earth be blessed"*

DEPTH

RELATIONSHIP WITH MAN

COMPASSION FOR MAN

CARE MINISTRY

3.

MAN IN NEED

1. SON OF GOD
Relationship with God

2. SON OF MAN
Relationship with Man

3.

PASSION		COMPASSION		NEEDS FULFILLMENT MINISTRY:
LOVE GOD WITH ALL YOUR HEART, SOUL, MIND, AND STRENGTH.	+	LOVE YOUR NEIGHBOR AS YOURSELF	=	• Find a Need & Fill It ! • Find a Hurt & Heal It !

Chart D-4

JESUS LEADS HIS INNER CIRCLE FIRST FURTHER INTO THE SUPERNATURAL

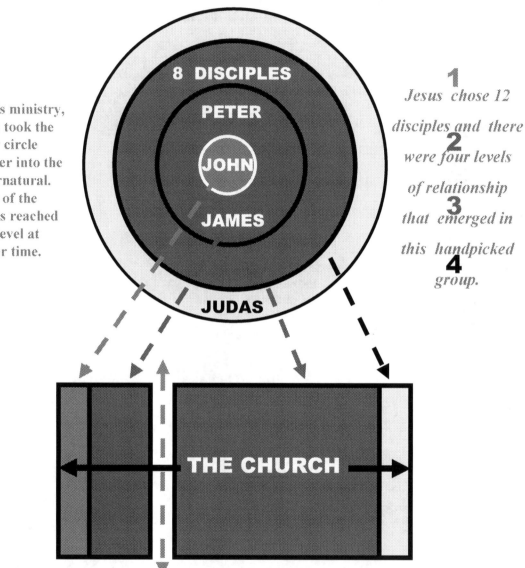

In His ministry, Jesus took the inner circle further into the supernatural. Most of the others reached that level at a later time.

8 DISCIPLES

PETER

JOHN

JAMES

JUDAS

1 *Jesus chose 12*
disciples and there
2 *were four levels*
of relationship
3 *that emerged in*
this handpicked
4 *group.*

THE CHURCH

FOLLOWING JESUS' EXAMPLE OF LEADERSHIP INTO THE SUPERNATURAL:

There is an inner circle (20-30%) within the church that is ready to make the changes required for:
- A greater REVELATION of Jesus (e.g. Matt 17:1, Mark 9:2 Mt. Transfiguration experience)
- A deeper move into SUPERNATURAL ACTIONS (e.g. Mark 5:37, Luke 8:51 - Raising the dead)
- A greater depth in PRAYER - POWER (e.g. Luke 9:28, Mark 14:33 Gethsemane prayer - NOT MY WILL)
- More challenging TEACHING (e.g. Mark 13:3)

These are the those in the church that are a part of the inner circle and are ready NOW to make the radical change (paradigm change) necessary to move into the supernatural. As this group is led further into the supernatural, others will follow over time.

Chart D-5

Chart D-6

Impartation + Encounter and Engagement with the Forces of Satan and Sickness Releases Supernatural Power!

GOD

Passion for God

You become more Christlike **with more Christlike actions!**

- Partakers of His divine nature.
- Power to become a son of God.
- Freely you have received, **freely give.**

Flow

3. Releases Supernatural Power

Signs and Miracles Following the Believer.
Mark 16:17-18

Flow

Operating as a son of God

1. Impartation
(Revival)
Being Full of the Spirit

Compassion for the lost

2. Encounter & Engagement
With the Opposing Forces of Satan and Sickness
(Evangelism)

Flow

Jesus came out of the wilderness in the power of the Spirit and His miracle ministry began.
Luke 4:14

Jesus went into the wilderness full of the Spirit.
Luke 4:1

Man in Need

Ministering to someone in need blesses them - and in turn blesses you.

Chart D-7

RESTORATION - THE HISTORY OF THE CHURCH

It is God's will for history to repeat itself – for us to go back (full circle) to the original pattern of the first church in the Book of Acts!

"The glory of this latter house shall be greater than the former"

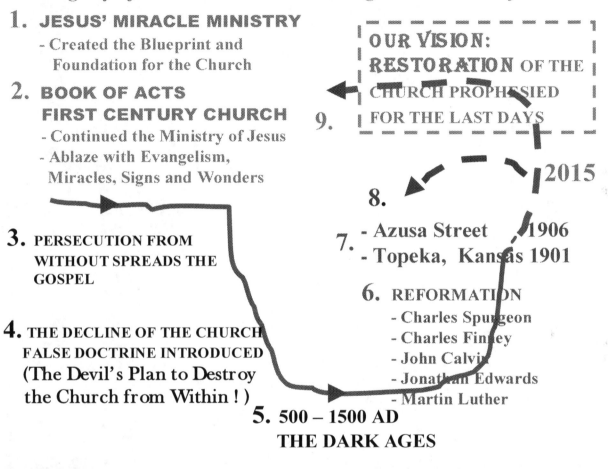

1. JESUS' MIRACLE MINISTRY
- Created the Blueprint and
  Foundation for the Church

**2. BOOK OF ACTS
FIRST CENTURY CHURCH**
- Continued the Ministry of Jesus
- Ablaze with Evangelism,
  Miracles, Signs and Wonders

**OUR VISION:
RESTORATION OF THE
CHURCH PROPHESIED
FOR THE LAST DAYS**

9.

8.

2015

7. - Azusa Street   1906
- Topeka, Kansas 1901

**3. PERSECUTION FROM
WITHOUT SPREADS THE
GOSPEL**

6. REFORMATION
- Charles Spurgeon
- Charles Finney
- John Calvin
- Jonathan Edwards
- Martin Luther

**4. THE DECLINE OF THE CHURCH
FALSE DOCTRINE INTRODUCED
(The Devil's Plan to Destroy
the Church from Within !)**

**5. 500 – 1500 AD
THE DARK AGES**

OUR CHOICE – Today in 2015, the beginning of the 3rd Millennia:

8. TAKE A SHORT CUT? – Be part of the falling away (II Thess. 2:3)
   (Deception - The devil's plan to destroy the Church from within)

9. PAY THE PRICE FOR RESTORATION? (A Deeper Relationship with Him)
   We must not look at Restoration as a heaven or hell issue for us:
   It is a heaven or hell issue for our Harvest Field! If we fall short of
   Restoration, there will be many SOULS that will be LOST!

Chart D-8

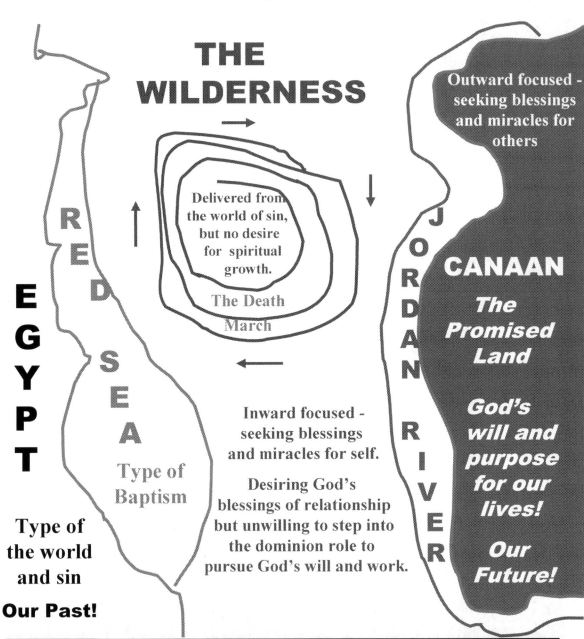

THE WILDERNESS

→

Delivered from the world of sin, but no desire for spiritual growth.

The Death March

←

Outward focused - seeking blessings and miracles for others

R E D   S E A

Type of Baptism

E G Y P T

Type of the world and sin

Our Past!

Inward focused - seeking blessings and miracles for self.

Desiring God's blessings of relationship but unwilling to step into the dominion role to pursue God's will and work.

J O R D A N   R I V E R

CANAAN

The Promised Land

God's will and purpose for our lives!

Our Future!

The Children of Israel had God's miraculous blessings of provision because of their <u>relationship</u> privileges. But since they were not willing to step into the <u>dominion</u> role of His will and purpose, they did not have His favor:

Ps 95:10 Forty years long was I grieved with this generation, and said, It is a people that do err in their heart, and they have not known my ways:

Heb 3:17 But with whom was he grieved forty years? was it not with them that had sinned, whose carcases fell in the wilderness?

5. Dominion -- Soul Winning Like Jesus

Summary and Key Scripture Text

Basic Soul Winning Concepts

Using our dual nature like Jesus as a:

- **son of man** (natural)
  Building relationships, breaking bread, doing kind deeds, being a friend.
- **son of God** (supernatural)
  Ministering to needs of healing and salvation.

Ministering to man's complete needs: physical, mental, emotional, spiritual.

The Father's business (soul winning) is a partnership between God and man.

Jesus Ministering as Son of Man

Jesus sitting down with sinners; breaking bread; ministering to their relationship needs first:

- When the Pharisees saw it, they said unto his disciples, Why **eateth** your Master with **publicans and sinners**? (Matt. 9:11-12)
- The Son of man . . . a **friend of publicans and sinners**. (Matt. 11:19)
- And when they saw it, they all murmured, saying, That he was gone to be **guest with a man that is a sinner**. (Luke 19:7)
- How is it that he **eateth and drinketh with publicans and sinners**? (Mark 2:16)

Jesus Ministering as Son of God

Jesus (God in human form) came to earth to see and feel (as Son of man), touch and heal (as Son of God):

- And Jesus **saw** a great multitude, and was **moved with compassion** toward them, and he **healed** their sick. (Matt. 14:14)
- And he **healed** many that were sick of divers diseases, and **cast out many devils**; and suffered not the devils to speak, because they knew him. (Mark 1:34)
- And Jesus, **moved with compassion**, put forth his hand, and **touched** him, and saith unto him, I will; **be thou clean**. (Mark 1:41)
- When the Lord **saw** her, he had **compassion** on her, and said unto her, Weep not. And he came and **touched** the bier: And he said, Young man, I say unto thee, **Arise**. (Luke 7:13-14)
- And he said unto Jesus, Lord, remember me when thou comest into thy kingdom. And Jesus said unto him, Verily I say unto thee, To day shalt thou be with me in paradise. (Luke 23:42-43)

Study References

Vol.	Book Name	Primary Study Section / Chapter	Elective Study
IV	Unlimited Partnership With a Supernatural God	Sec. I / Ch. 2, 3	Sec. III / Ch. 6
V	Revival & Evangelism - Passion for God - Passion for Souls	Sec. I / Ch. 3, Sec. II / Ch. 3, 4	Sec. III / Ch. 4
VIII	Addendum Volume (PowerPoint Charts)	Charts at the end of this chapter	G1 - G27, J-1 - J-35, K-1 - K-17

The greatest challenge for the five-fold ministry is to recruit, teach and train people to be soul winners. This need is emphasized by Jesus' only prayer request: *"Then saith he unto his disciples, The harvest truly is plenteous, but the labourers are few; Pray ye therefore the Lord of the harvest, that he will send forth labourers into his harvest"* (Matt. 9:37-38).

To learn from Jesus Christ, the greatest soul winner of all times, we must return to the Bible, the original soul winning manual. Recorded in Matthew, Mark, Luke and John are His life, His deeds and how He ministered to the needs of people. May we study the actions of Jesus Christ and follow in His footsteps in ministering to the needs of our generation. "What would Jesus do?" (WWJD) is a provoking question -- a good model for living our lives and working in His Kingdom. An equally important question is: "How would Jesus do it?" (HWJD).

Jesus' Example as Son of Man and Son of God

A unique thing about Jesus was His dual nature -- He was both Son of God and Son of man. When we are born again of the water and the Spirit, we become the tabernacle of God's Spirit with a dual nature as a son of man and a son of God.

In the role of "Son of man", Jesus was a friend to sinners. At least eight times in the New Testament it is recorded that Jesus sat down to eat with sinners. When the religious leaders condemned Jesus for this association, He responded: *"They that are whole have no need of the physician, but they that are sick: I came not to call the righteous, but sinners to repentance"* (Mark 2:17). In the role of "Son of God", He performed miracles of healing and deliverance from satan's power.

To be great soul winners, in the role of "son of man", we must make friends with sinners. The church has isolated itself too much from the world. We must separate ourselves from sin --

but not from the sinner. We must separate ourselves from the world system but not from the people in the world.

We can't reap a harvest in the farm house; we must go into the field. We can't catch fish in the camp house; we must go to where they are. We sure can't catch them if our initial approach is to explain to them the fillet plan -- "You can't do this and you can't do that." Like Jesus, we must first build a bridge to them through a relationship of love.

In most cases, we should not confront the unconverted with the plan of salvation until we have a confirmation that God has opened the door of their soul. The unsaved must first see and feel God in us before they hear about changes required in their life. Often their unspoken message is, "Do you care about me and my needs; is there any hope?"

Jesus, the greatest soul winner, did not come to this world to bring condemnation. Sometimes Christians try to persuade sinners that they are sinners: *"For all have sinned, and come short of the glory of God" (Rom. 3:23)*. Although this is a truth from God's Word, this is not the starting point in soul winning. Jesus addressed this when He stated that sinners are condemned already:

John 3:17-18
*17 For God **sent not** his son into the world to **condemn the world**; but that the world through him might be saved.*
18 He that believeth on him is not condemned: but he that believeth not is condemned already, because he hath not believed in the name of the only begotten Son of God.

Jesus Extends Mercy and Forgiveness to the Adulterous Woman

When the religious leaders brought to Jesus a woman caught in adultery, He did not join in their condemnation. The greatest day of her life was when God, in flesh, became her defense attorney. Jesus turned the condemning finger to her religious accusers harboring their hidden sins; they dropped their stones and silently walked away.

John 8:4-11
4 They say unto him, master, this woman was taken in adultery, in the very act.
5 Now Moses in the law commanded us, that such should be stoned: but what sayest thou?
6 This they said, tempting him, that they might have to accuse him. But Jesus stooped down, and with his finger wrote on the ground, as though he heard them not.
*7 So when they continued asking him, he lifted up himself, and said unto them, **he that is without sin among you, let him first cast a stone at her.***
8 And again he stooped down, and wrote on the ground.
9 And they which heard it, being convicted by their own conscience, went out one by one, beginning at the eldest, even unto the last: and Jesus was left alone, and the woman standing in the midst.
10 When Jesus had lifted up himself, and saw none but the woman, he said unto her, woman,

where are those thine accusers? Hath no man condemned thee?
*11 She said, no man, Lord. And Jesus said unto her, **neither do I condemn thee: go, and sin no more.***

Jesus did not say, "Don't stone her." He said, "Go ahead and stone her, but let the one without sin cast the first stone." He was the only sinless One, the only One qualified to have stoned her. He did not condemn her for past sins, but forgave her and encouraged her to live a life free from sin.

Jesus Invites Himself to the Home of the Hated Tax Collector
(Possibly the most notable conversion in the New Testament)

Many great conversions are recorded in the New Testament. The conversion of Apostle Paul is often suggested as the most notable one. In one day, he was changed from a killer of Christians to a follower of Jesus. However, Apostle Paul was a devout, religious leader who had fervently studied the Law and zealously followed its statutes. His atrocities against the Christians were committed out of ignorance, convinced he was doing his religious duty. He merely needed a course correction -- the revelation that Jesus was the mighty God of the Old Testament manifested in the flesh.

Zacchaeus was probably the most hated man in his city, and possibly in all of Israel. He was a tax collector, who cheated and overcharged people on their taxes. His wealth was obtained at the expense of the poor and rich alike. They could do nothing about this injustice, possibly because the Romans were a part of the scheme. This unfair treatment made Zacchaeus the target of hatred and disgust.

Zacchaeus wanted to see Jesus having heard of His great miracles of healing. So when Jesus was passing through Jericho he climbed a tree to see Him, possibly to hide from the insults of the people. Jesus, knowing all things and seeing his heart, approached the tree – reaching out to a hated outcast.

Many would have condemned Zacchaeus, calling him a criminal and thief who was disobeying all of the Ten Commandments. But Jesus invited Himself to dine in Zacchaeus' home, angering the self-righteous religious leaders.

Jesus built a bridge to him without condemning him -- treating him as a friend, breaking bread with him. Zacchaeus experienced this unlikely encounter with Jesus (as **Son of man**) taking time to visit on his turf -- building a bridge to him over the dinner table. As he began to feel the presence of the **Son of God**, he confessed, repented and promised to make restitution to all he had wronged.

Luke 19:1-10
1 And Jesus entered and passed through Jericho.
*2 And, behold, there was a man named Zacchaeus, which was the **chief among the publicans**, and he was rich.*

3 And he sought to see Jesus who he was; and could not for the press, because he was little of stature.
4 And he ran before, and climbed up into a sycamore tree to see him: for he was to pass that way.
*5 And when **Jesus** came to the place, he looked up, and saw him, and **said unto him,** Zacchaeus, make haste, and come down; for today **I must abide at thy house.***
6 And he made haste, and came down, and received him joyfully.
7 And when they saw it, they all murmured, saying, that he was gone to be guest with a man that is a sinner.
*8 And Zacchaeus stood, and said unto the Lord; behold, Lord, **the half of my goods I give to the poor; and if I have taken anything from any man by false accusation, I restore him fourfold.***
9 And Jesus said unto him, this day is salvation come to this house, forsomuch as he also is a son of Abraham.
*10 For the **son of man is come to seek and to save that which was lost**.*

This miraculous conversion, a 180 degree turnaround in the life of a terrible, hated sinner, must have been big news in Jericho, when the refund checks began arriving. In our day it would have been everyone buying new cars with the refund of years of overpaid taxes -- the poor buying economy cars, the more wealthy buying luxury cars. What a story, what a miraculous conversion and tremendous example for us, with Jesus using His dual nature to restore a seemingly unreachable sinner:

- Jesus functioned as a **Son of man**, by simply inviting himself to the home of Zacchaeus for food and fellowship.

- Without verbal condemnation by Jesus, the awesome presence of the **Son of God** caused a sinner to repent and invite Jesus into his life -- becoming free from bondage to satan and sin.

The salvation of sinners occur as:
- The Spirit of God draws them: *"No man can come to me, except the father draw him"* *(John 6:44).*
- The Spirit draws them as we sons of God, lift Him up: *"And I, if I be lifted up from the earth, will draw all men unto me" (John 12:32).*

As a son of man, we lift Him up with our **good works**, then the Spirit of God in us, as a son of God, will **draw them**.

Matt. 5:16
*Let **your light so shine** before men, that they may **see your good works**, and glorify your Father which is in heaven.*

Let your light shine -- not preaching, not condemnation. The first step is good works -- what we can do with our natural abilities building a bridge to them through relationships. This involves doing kind deeds by ministering to their physical needs first and taking time to find common ground (breaking bread with them).

Our Faith Perfected With Good Works

Our good works not only benefit the sinner, but gives us God's favor as we love and reach for His lost children. We should light up the world with our smile, sweet spirit and kind deeds.

James 2:14-22
14 What doth it profit, my brethren, though a man say he hath faith, and have not works? Can faith save him?
15 If a brother or sister be naked, and destitute of daily food,
16 And one of you say unto them, depart in peace, be ye warmed and filled; notwithstanding ye give them not those things which are needful to the body; what doth it profit?
*17 Even so **faith, if it hath not works, is dead, being alone.***
*18 Yea, a man may say, thou hast faith, and I have works: **shew me thy faith without thy works, and I will shew thee my faith by my works.***
19 Thou believest that there is one God; thou doest well: the devils also believe, and tremble.
*20 **But wilt thou know, o vain man, that faith without works is dead?***
21 Was not Abraham our father justified by works, when he had offered Isaac his son upon the altar?
*22 Seest thou how faith wrought with his works, and **by works was faith made perfect***?

We do not receive salvation by our works, but by the grace of Jesus Christ and the infilling of His Spirit. *"Not by works of righteousness which we have done, but according to his mercy he saved us, by the washing of regeneration, and renewing of the Holy Ghost" (Titus 3:5).*

But salvation through faith in Jesus Christ will bring about some changes in our lives -- changes that allow Him to work through us in reaching His lost world. Jesus clearly described the **final test at the Judgment** to be works -- actions of ministering to others. This encompasses the needs of the complete man -- physical, emotional and spiritual needs.

Matt. 25:31-36, 40-41, 45-46
31 When the son of man shall come in his glory, and all the holy angels with him, then shall he sit upon the throne of his glory:
32 And before him shall be gathered all nations: and he shall separate them one from another, as a shepherd divideth his sheep from the goats:
33 And he shall set the sheep on his right hand, but the goats on the left.
34 Then shall the King say unto them on his right hand, come, ye blessed of my Father, inherit the kingdom prepared for you from the foundation of the world:

*35 For I was an hungred, and **ye gave me meat**: I was thirsty, and **ye gave me drink**: I was a stranger, and ye took me in:*

*36 Naked, and **ye clothed me**: I was sick, and **ye visited me**: I was in prison, and **ye came unto me**.*

*40 And the king shall answer and say unto them, verily I say unto you, **inasmuch as ye have done it unto one of the least of these my brethren, ye have done it unto me**.*

41 Then shall he say also unto them on the left hand, depart from me, ye cursed, into everlasting fire, prepared for the devil and his angels:

45 Then shall he answer them, saying, Verily I say unto you, Inasmuch as ye did it not to one of the least of these, ye did it not to me.

46 And these shall go away into everlasting punishment: but the righteous into life eternal.

Ministering to the Complete Man (Body, Soul, Spirit)

As discussed in Chapter 3, man, like the tabernacle of Moses, has three divisions -- body, soul and spirit. Refer back to Charts T-1 and T-2 in that chapter.

1 Thess. 5:23
*And the very God of peace sanctify you **wholly** (completely); and I pray God your whole **spirit** and **soul** and **body** be preserved blameless unto the coming of our Lord Jesus Christ.*

The **body** is compared to the outer court of the Old Testament tabernacle. With its five senses of sight, hearing, taste, smell and touch, it connects us with the earth, making us **world conscious**. The body is the outer shell, the tabernacle of the soul.

The **soul** is compared to the inner court or Holy Place of the tabernacle. It is made up of the will, mind and emotions, and makes us **self-conscious**. Your soul is the real you. It is who you are -- your individuality, personality, influence, intellect, natural talents and abilities.

The **Spirit** is compared to the Most Holy Place of the tabernacle. It is, "the secret place of the Most High", the dwelling place of God. The spirit of man is comprised of conscience, communion and intuition. It is man's spirit that makes him **God conscious**. Man's spirit lies beyond man's self-consciousness and above the senses of the human mind. It is our spirit that links us to God's Spirit, allowing us to commune with Him. The spirit is the part of man that is immortal and undying.

Our heavenly Father, the Great Physician, desires that we minister to the sick, the hurting and the lost, as He did. We are the physicians whom He has commissioned to tend to human needs. When a doctor receives his certificate, he announces it to the world. When we are born again of the water and the Spirit, we receive our commission as a physician, and are given authority over sickness and disease (Luke 9:1, 10:19).

The Great Physician's mission statement was recorded by Luke: *"The Spirit of the Lord is upon me, because He hath anointed me to preach the gospel to the poor; He hath sent me to heal the brokenhearted, to preach deliverance to the captives, and recovering of sight to the blind, to set at liberty them that are bruised" (Luke 4:18).*

- **Just as a natural doctor must study the anatomy of the body to effectively administer wellness and healing remedies, we as sons of the Great Physician should understand the anatomy of the complete man (body, soul and spirit). With this understanding we should be better prepared to minister to the needs of people.**

In ministering to the needs of man, there are three roles that relate to the tri-part man:

1. That which God leaves to man -- doing kind deeds (ministering in the outer court, the **body** -- physical needs; e.g. taking a sick neighbor a cup of soup, running an errand for them, etc. -- befriending and building relationships).
2. The part God shares with man (ministering in the inner court of the **soul** -- teaching biblical concepts -- particularly the plan of salvation).
3. The area where only God can work (ministering in the Most Holy Place, the **spirit of man** -- speaking to man and filling him with His Spirit).

The key to successful soul winning is to understand the division of roles. We must do our part and let God do His part. Refer to Chart S-2, "Soul Winning -- a Partnership With God", at the end of this chapter.

As we minister to lost souls, we must understand when to operate as son of man (with our natural abilities) and when to operate as son of God (with God's supernatural abilities). We must follow the example of Jesus to effectively reach His lost world:

- As a son of God, building a relationship with God -- our spirit connecting to His Spirit.
- As a son of man, breaking bread and building relationships with sinners. The love of God flows through relationships.
- As a son of God, reaching to fallen man and reaching to our great God -- using the ministry of reconciliation to bring the lost to Him: *"And all things are of God, who hath reconciled us to himself by Jesus Christ, and hath given to us the ministry of reconciliation" (2 Cor. 5:18).*

Refer to the following charts at the end of this chapter:
Chart S-1 Ministering as Son of Man and Son of God
Chart S-4 The Soul Winning Cycle

Ministering in the Outer Court First as a Son of Man

Listening is one of the greatest personal soul winning tools. Too often the Christian is inclined to do all the talking -- telling the sinner what he needs to do. One of the greatest tools for soul winning is to listen -- discovering their fears, hurts and needs. Hurting sinners don't care how much we know, until they know how much we care.

In conversations with friends and relatives, we are talking too much if we speak more than 50% of the time if two of us are talking, or more than 33% of the time when three are involved in the conversation. Communication with those we are trying to win to Jesus Christ is most effective and successful when we listen more and talk less (e.g. 80% / 20%. They must feel like they have been heard, accepted and appreciated:

- Be totally attentive when they are speaking.

- Encourage them to talk by asking leading questions about themselves (location of home, career, children, needs, etc.).

- Don't try to sell the church to them. Don't tell them what they need. Determine their needs because that is the open door for continued follow-up and the beginning of a relationship.

We would not choose a doctor who did all the talking without listening, telling us of his great practice with technology advancements, etc.; nor would we return to a doctor who made a diagnosis before he knew our problem. If he ordered an MRI on our head when we had a broken foot, we would seek help from another physician.

Yet, sometimes that is the way Christians deal with sinners, bypassing the outer court of their pressing physical needs and offering solutions to their spiritual ones. If we care, we will spend time to build a relationship with them -- discovering and ministering to their concerns and needs.

-- From Effective Evangelism

Evangelism needs to be less about telling and more about listening: think conversation not proclamation. **Listen to soul cravings.** I believe everyone has cravings for purpose, meaning and significance in life. By listening to and speaking into a person's cravings, you can delicately awaken them to recognize the fulfillment of all their cravings that can only be found in God Himself. **Develop relationships.** Jesus was the complete expression of the Father's love to the world; the love of God flowed like a spring of living water from the life of Jesus. I believe that in many cases, God's love can be more compelling than scientific evidence of God or a theological argument. Is God's love flowing through you? Are people in your life compelled by how passionately and personally you care about them? [1]

Jesus, our example of the greatest soul winner, always **ministered in the outer court (physical needs) first.** His objective was ultimately to minister to their soul and spirit. He came to earth as a Son of man to build a bridge of love and relationship with man.

When the Gospels record that Jesus sat down to eat with sinners, their conversations were not disclosed in Holy Writ because they were personal -- outer court conversations, with Jesus listening to their interests and needs. Associating with and befriending sinners was not compromise, although religious leaders accused Jesus of such. This first step was reaching them by ministering in the outer court and building a bridge on common ground.

- **Love is the bridge over which truth is transported.**

The beginning of soul winning is building a bridge on common ground in the outer court. Common ground issues involve their interests (careers, children, hobbies, food, etc.), not ours. The greatest opportunity for common ground is breaking bread together. This initial relationship with them is based on what we have in common, not our differences. Differences divide; commonality brings people together.

Vincent Donovan states: "Evangelization is a process of bringing the Gospel to people where they are, not where you would like them to be." Refer to Chart S-3, "Ministering at the Point of Need", at the end of this chapter.

Apostle Paul, the great missionary and soul winner, was a bridge builder. He built relationships in the outer court with people on common ground to win them to Christ.

1 Cor. 9:20-23
20 When I was with the Jews, I lived like a Jew to bring the Jews to Christ. When I was with those who follow the Jewish law, I too lived under that law. Even though I am not subject to the law, I did this so I could bring to Christ those who are under the law.
21 When I am with the Gentiles who do not follow the Jewish law, I too live apart from that law so I can bring them to Christ. But I do not ignore the law of God; I obey the law of Christ.
*22 When I am with those who are weak, I share their weakness, for I want to bring the weak to Christ. Yes, **I try to find common ground with everyone, doing everything I can to save some.***
23 I do everything to spread the Good News and share in its blessings. NLT

Second is Superior to the First
The second Adam (Jesus Christ) is superior to the first Adam. The second birth (spiritual birth) is better than the first birth (natural birth). But there is a progression -- the first must precede the second.

The inner court is better than the outer court; the Most Holy Place is better than the Holy Place. But the progression must be in sequence. To move into the inner court, one must first come through the outer court.

The Bread of Life (Word of God) is better than natural bread; it feeds man's spiritual needs. Natural bread can only satisfy man's natural needs. But there is a progression. The ministry that Jesus exampled for us was:

- First, ministering to physical needs (breaking bread and building relationships with sinners).
- Second, breaking the bread of life as He taught the multitudes the principles of His Kingdom.

We must win the unsaved to us before we can win them to Christ. We must be patient like fishermen -- fishers of men. If we omit the outer court ministry and go directly to the next level prematurely, they may become argumentative and reject the Gospel message. We must allow God to open the door of their soul before we address their deeper spiritual needs.

Refer to Appendix 1, "Soul Winning and Breaking Bread Experiences", for examples of ministering in the outer court first.

Ministering in the Inner Court as a Son of God

This ministry is shared by man (son of God) and God. After we have built a relationship and ministered to someone's physical needs, God will open the door of their soul for ministry to their spiritual needs. Here we share the story of Jesus Christ -- His miraculous birth and miracle ministry, and His great love displayed in His death, burial and resurrection. As we continue this journey, we can impart the plan of salvation -- repentance, burial through baptism in Jesus name, and resurrection by the infilling of God's Spirit.

Soul winning is a partnership with God. When we do our part as a son of man with our natural abilities, God will partner with us as a son of God to minister to man's spiritual needs.

Ministering in the Most Holy Place by God

Once each year the high priest alone was permitted to minister in the innermost sanctum of the tabernacle. Likewise, only our Great High Priest (Jesus Christ) can work in this innermost court of man's spirit. This ministry is beyond the realm of man and the natural because it involves a supernatural experience – the infilling of God's Spirit.

God's Spirit (capital letter "S") filling man's spirit (small letter "s") is a supernatural experience that only Jesus Christ, our Great High Priest can perform. It completes the new birth experience described by Jesus -- born of the water (baptism in Jesus name); and born of the Spirit (receiving the gift of the Holy Ghost): *"Jesus answered and said unto him, Verily, verily, I say unto thee, Except a man be born again, he cannot see the kingdom of God. Nicodemus saith unto him, How can a man be born when he is old? can he enter the second time into his mother's womb, and be born? Jesus answered, Verily, verily, I say unto thee, Except a man be born of water and of the Spirit, he cannot enter into the kingdom of God. That which is born of the flesh is flesh; and that which is born of the Spirit is spirit. Marvel not that I said unto thee, Ye must be born again" (John 3:3-7).*

This "born again" new birth experience was referenced again by Jesus at the Feast of the Passover: *"In the last day, that great day of the feast, Jesus stood and cried, saying, If any man thirst, let him come unto me, and drink: He that believeth on me, as the scripture hath said, out of his belly shall flow rivers of living water. (But this spake he of the Spirit, which they that believe on him should receive: for the Holy Ghost was not yet given; because that Jesus was not yet glorified)" John 7:37-39.*

Examples of those receiving this "new birth" experience are recorded in: Acts 2 (Jews), Acts 8 (Samaritans), Acts 9 (Apostle Paul's conversion), Acts 10 (Gentiles) and Acts 19 (John the Baptist's followers).

Christ's Sufferings Provided Healing for the Complete Man: Body, Soul and Spirit

At Calvary, Jesus' natural life ended with tremendous physical, mental and spiritual suffering -- more than any human would ever be called on to endure. Thus, we can never question God's understanding of our trials, because He empathizes with every heartache and pain.

It was within Jesus' power to escape these sufferings, yet He willingly offered His body to endure immeasurable torture and pain for healing of the body, soul and spirit. Never did He resist until, *"All was finished" (John 19:28). AMP*

That was the ultimate price that Jesus Christ (God tabernacled in flesh) paid to provide physical, mental, emotional and spiritual healing.

The greatest message of hope that we as believers can give to the hopeless and lost of our world is that the sufferings of Christ provided complete healing for their entire being:
- The body (physical wounds and sickness).
- The soul (mental and emotional wounds).
- The spirit (deep wounds inflicted by sin, sickness and separation from God).

All that man would ever suffer was executed upon the physical body of Jesus Christ:

1. Healing for the Body
Who can fathom the physical sufferings of the Lord Jesus from His inhumane beating and crucifixion on the cross? Man sins with his body through the five senses; he suffers physical ailments and pain. Therefore, Christ's body accordingly had to be the recipient of punishment. Christ's sufferings in the body are clearly foretold in the Messianic writings of the prophets: *"They have pierced my hands and feet" (Psalms 22:16); "Him whom they have pierced" (Zech. 12: 10).*

Isa. 53:5

He was wounded for our transgressions, He was bruised for our guilt and iniquities; the chastisement [needful to obtain] peace and well-being for us was upon Him, and with the stripes [that wounded] Him we are healed and made whole. AMP

- **The back of Jesus was terribly beaten. His hands and feet were torturously nailed to the cross. The precious blood that flowed from these wounds provided healing for the body.**

2. Healing for the Soul (mental and emotional wounds)

The punishment of the cross meant shame, also. It was used to execute runaway slaves who had neither property nor rights. His body belonged to his master; he could be executed in this most shameful way. Jesus took the place of a slave and was crucified in shame as the soldiers stripped Him of His garments (John 19:23).

Isaiah 53 cites the suffering of His soul: *"His soul was made an offering for sin"*; *"His soul travailed"*; and *"He poured out His soul to death."* A week before the Passover Jesus said: *"Now is my soul troubled" (John 12:27)*. While in the Garden of Gethsemane Jesus was again heard to say: *"My soul is very sorrowful, even to death" (Matt. 26:38)*. These passages underscore the suffering of His soul.

- **The long razor-sharp thorns pierced deep into the head of Jesus. From those wounds, the blood that flowed down His tear-stained face provided mental and emotional healing for the soul.**

3. Healing for the Spirit (sickness from sin and separation from God)

The spirit of Christ suffered immensely, also. The spirit is the segment of man that communes with God. The Son of God was holy, blameless, unstained and separated from sin. His spirit was united with the Holy Spirit in perfect oneness. Upon announcing that He would be betrayed and die on the cross, He was, *"Troubled in spirit" (John 13:21)*.

Apostle Paul said Jesus took the form of a slave. As such, He came to rescue us who are subject to bondage of sin. We were slaves in bondage to sin and satan. Yet Jesus died to liberate us from this bondage.

As the life of Jesus ebbed away on the cross, He cried, *"My God, my God, why hast thou forsaken me?" (Matt. 27:46)*. His spirit was split asunder from God. How intensely He felt the loneliness, the desertion, the separation. Yet He obeyed and yielded to the will of the Father as He became the *"lamb slain from the foundation of the world"* to atone for the sins of lost mankind.

The last act of torture by the Roman soldiers came after His death when they plunged a spear into His side, releasing blood and water.

- **The Roman spear pierced deep into Jesus' side and heart. The blood and water that flowed from His side became a cleansing fountain for healing of the spirit -- a healing from the awful sickness of sin and separation from God.**

Over 500 years before Christ, Zechariah described Calvary in his prophetic writings: *"On that day a fountain will be opened for the dynasty of David and for the people of Jerusalem, **a fountain to cleanse them from all their sins and impurity**. And on that day, says the Lord of Heaven's Armies, I will erase idol worship throughout the land, so that even the names of the idols will be forgotten" (Zech. 13:1-2).*

Whatever judgment could come upon the **body, soul** and **spirit** of sinners was poured upon Jesus. He took our place and paid the price for our healing and the penalty for our sins. His death is reckoned as our death, and His judgment as our judgment: *"There is therefore now no condemnation for those who are in Christ Jesus" (Rom. 8:1).*

- **The suffering and death of Jesus provided healing for the complete man -- body, soul and spirit.**

Refer to the following pages for the **"Soul Winning"** overview charts.

Chart S - 1

Ministering as son of man and son of God

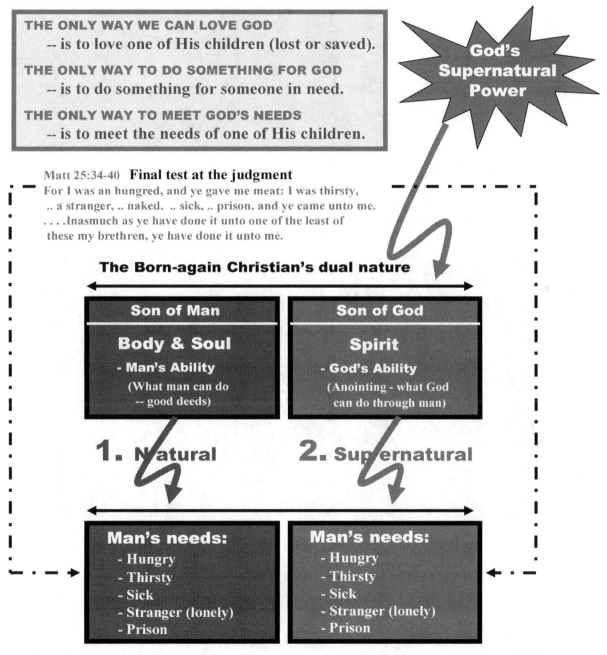

THE ONLY WAY WE CAN LOVE GOD
-- is to love one of His children (lost or saved).

THE ONLY WAY TO DO SOMETHING FOR GOD
-- is to do something for someone in need.

THE ONLY WAY TO MEET GOD'S NEEDS
-- is to meet the needs of one of His children.

God's Supernatural Power

Matt 25:34-40 **Final test at the judgment**
For I was an hungred, and ye gave me meat: I was thirsty,
.. a stranger, .. naked, .. sick, .. prison, and ye came unto me.
....Inasmuch as ye have done it unto one of the least of
these my brethren, ye have done it unto me.

The Born-again Christian's dual nature

Son of Man	Son of God
Body & Soul	**Spirit**
- Man's Ability	- God's Ability
(What man can do -- good deeds)	(Anointing - what God can do through man)

1. Natural   **2. Supernatural**

Man's needs:	Man's needs:
- Hungry	- Hungry
- Thirsty	- Thirsty
- Sick	- Sick
- Stranger (lonely)	- Stranger (lonely)
- Prison	- Prison

(1) Building a relationship with someone in need by doing kind deeds, as a **son of man**. These good deeds (what we can do) begin to open up the channel of God's love and compassion in our lives for the second step.

(2) God's supernatural power -- what God can do through us, as a **son of God**, to minister to their needs.

Chart S - 2

Soul Winning - a Partnership With God

The FATHER'S Business (Soul Winning) is a Partnership between God and man :

1. Son of man (you and I) begin to work in the outer court.

2. *GOD* alone begins to work in man's spirit, the most holy place.

3. *GOD* and a son of God (you and I) work together in the inner court.

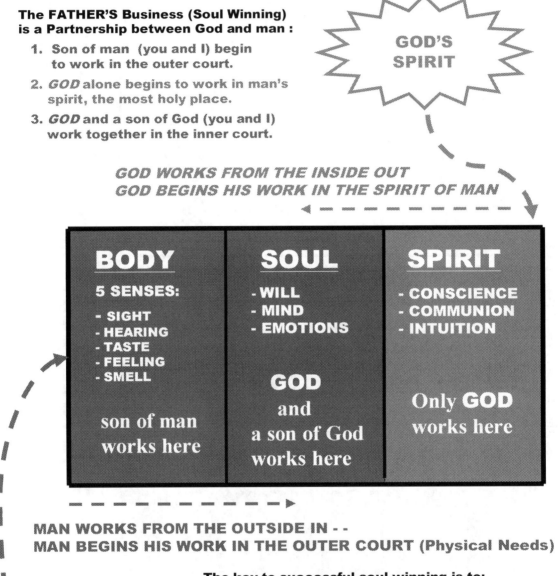

GOD WORKS FROM THE INSIDE OUT
GOD BEGINS HIS WORK IN THE SPIRIT OF MAN

BODY	SOUL	SPIRIT
5 SENSES: - SIGHT - HEARING - TASTE - FEELING - SMELL son of man works here	- WILL - MIND - EMOTIONS GOD and a son of God works here	- CONSCIENCE - COMMUNION - INTUITION Only GOD works here

MAN WORKS FROM THE OUTSIDE IN - -
MAN BEGINS HIS WORK IN THE OUTER COURT (Physical Needs)

The key to successful soul winning is to:

1. Understand GOD's part and your part.

2. Do your part and let GOD do His part. Don't get ahead of GOD or play GOD.

3. Understand that you have a dual nature, and when to operate as a son of man, and when to operate as a son of GOD. JESUS, the greatest soul winner, exampled this for us in His earthly ministry, when He sat down to eat with sinners and ministered to their physical needs first.

Chart S - 3

MINISTERING AT THE POINT OF NEED STARTING WHERE THEY ARE

- 1. **SINNER**
  - Unchurched

- 2. **CONVERTED**
  - Believer Seeking
  - Backslider

- 3. **NEW CONVERT**
  - Born Again

- 4. **SAINT**

- 5. **DISCIPLE**
  - Soul Winner

MAN
MINISTERING IN THE OUTER COURT - (BODY)

- PHYSICAL NEEDS (Sick, Lonely, Discouraged, etc.)
- FOOD & FELLOWSHIP
- CAREERS
- FAMILY
- HOBBIES
- INTERESTS
- PRAYER

MAN & GOD
MINISTERING IN THE INNER COURT - (SOUL)

- SPIRITUAL NEEDS
- HBS (Old Testament)
- HBS (New Testament)
- PRAYER

GOD
MINISTERING IN THE HOLY OF HOLIES -- (SPIRIT)

Chart S – 4

THE SOUL WINNING AND SPIRITUAL MATURITY CYCLE
(Fulfilling God's Will and Purpose)

1. Building a Relationship with God
(Faithfulness in Prayer, the Word, the House
of God, Fasting, Tithes and Offerings, etc.)
If it stops here, we become religious (self righteous) vs.
becoming spiritual -- and spiritual growth will stagnate.

2. Operating as Son of Man (See and Feel)

Building a relationship and bridge on common ground by
breaking bread and doing good deeds with compassion.

If it stops here, we have done some good deeds, but the
deeper needs of the person will not be met and permanent
change will most likely not occur.

3. Operating as Son of God (Touch and Heal)

Dominon in the Supernatural - Using our dual nature
like Jesus with the ministry of reconciliation (touching
God and touching man). God's miraculous power flowing
through our lives with the gifts of the Spirit operating to
meet the needs of man.

Soul winning is a spiritual process and will only be successful and have lasting
results as we operate in the Spirit. To operate at this level the first two processes
are foundational and cannot be bypassed. You cannot have compassion on
someone that you cannot see and touch. As we complete this cycle over and
over again, true and lasting spiritual growth of the born-again Christian occurs.

Chart S – 5

SPIRITUAL GROWTH OF THE SAINT AND WORKING IN GOD'S KINGDOM TO REACH THE LOST - GO HAND IN HAND

Going to God for man (Prayer)   before going to man for God (Care) !

> **GOD WORKING THROUGH MAN TO DO HIS WORK**
> **GOD HAS NO OTHER PLAN THAN TO USE MAN**

- Our heavenly Father will give us more of His power and authority when we use what He has already given to us.
- When there is growth and expansion in our relationship with our heavenly Father, there will be **growth and expansion** in our role as His son to carry on His mission to reach the lost.
- As we reach out to the needs of others, a greater hunger and desire for more of God in our lives is created to meet the need.

6. Perfect Love

The Highest Law and Strongest Force in the Kingdom

Summary and Key Scripture Text

Perfect Love

Love is the only motive accepted by God for working in His Kingdom: *"Though I have all spiritual gifts . . . give all my goods to the poor . . . give my body to be burned, and have not love, it is nothing"* (1 Cor. 13:1-3).

Perfect love is still required to create the atmosphere of humility demanded for the "one mind and one accord" unity evident at the miraculous birth of the first century church.

"First love" is flowing the perfect love of God, that we receive from the perfect Head of the body, first to the brotherhood, the body of Christ, of which every believer is a part. And in the measure we flow God's perfect love to the brotherhood we flow it back to the source -- our heavenly Father. Refer to Chart L-4 at the end of this chapter.

Three things will last forever -- faith, hope and love -- and the greatest of these is love. *(1 Cor. 13:13) NLT*

Love is the Life Flow in the Body of Christ

- Master, which is the great commandment in the law? Jesus said unto him, Thou shalt love the Lord thy God with all thy heart, and with all thy soul, and with all thy mind. This is the first and great commandment. And the second is like unto it, Thou shalt love thy neighbour as thyself. On these two commandments hang all the law and the prophets. (Matt. 22:36-40)
- For in Jesus Christ neither circumcision availeth anything, nor uncircumcision; but faith which worketh by love. (Gal. 5:6)
- And above all these things put on charity, which is the bond of perfection. (Col. 3:14)
- I demand that you love each other as much as I love you. (John 15: 12) TLB
- If we love one another, God dwelleth in us, and His love is perfected in us. (1 John 4:12)
- By this shall all men know that ye are my disciples, if ye have love one to another. (John 13:35)
- We must love one another, just as he commanded us. Those who obey God's commandments remain in fellowship with Him, and he with them. (1 John 3:23-24) NLT
- We will speak the truth in love, growing in every way more and more like Christ, who is the head of his body, the church. (Eph. 4:15-16) NLT
- There is no fear in love; but perfect love casteth out fear. He that feareth is not made perfect in love. (John 3:18) NLT
- And this commandment have we from Him, that he who loveth God love his brother also. (1 John 4:21)
- Most of all, let love guide your life, for then the whole church will stay together in perfect harmony. (Col. 3:14) TLB
- Finally, all [of you] should be of one and the same mind (united in spirit), sympathizing [with one another], loving [each other] as brethren [of one household], compassionate and courteous (tenderhearted and humble). (1 Peter 3:8-12) AMP

Study References

Vol.	Book Name	Primary Study Section / Chapter	Elective Study
IV	Unlimited Partnership With a Supernatural God		Sec. III / Ch. 1, 6
VI	Perfect Love - The Highest Law and Strongest Force	Sec. I / Ch. 2-7	Sec. I / Ch. 8-13
VIII	Addendum Volume (PowerPoint Charts)	Charts at the end of this chapter	N-6 - N-15

The primary purpose and scope of this lesson are directed and driven by two of the greatest foundational principles and challenges for spiritual growth of the Christian:

(1) The greatest commandment is to love God and others: *"Love the Lord your God with all your heart, soul, and mind. This is the first and greatest commandment. The second most important is similar: Love your neighbor as much as you love yourself. All the other commandments and all the demands of the prophets stem from these two laws and are fulfilled if you obey them. Keep only these and you will find that you are obeying all the others"* (Matt. 22:37-40). TLB

(2) The command to grow and increase in the love of God: *"That ye, being **rooted and grounded in love**, may be able to comprehend with all saints what is the breadth, and length, and depth, and height; And to know the love of Christ, which passeth knowledge, that ye might be filled with all the fulness of God"* (Eph. 3:17-19).

*"And may the Lord make you to **increase and excel and overflow in love** for one another and for all people"* (1 Thess. 3:12). AMP

*"But concerning the pure brotherly love that there should be among God's people . . . Indeed, your love is already strong toward all the Christian brothers. Even so, dear friends, we beg you to **love them more and more**"* (1 Thess. 4:9-10).

*"My prayer for you is that you **will overflow more and more with love for others**, and at the same time keep on growing in spiritual knowledge and insight"* (Phil. 1:9). TLB

To address these two foundational principles and challenges, we will review some of the attributes and effects of God's divine love and affirm that:

(1) Love is the only motive accepted by God for working in His Kingdom: *"Though I have all spiritual gifts . . . give all my goods to the poor . . . give my body to be burned, and have not love, it is nothing"* (1 Cor. 13:1-3).

(2) The source of God's perfect love is the Spirit. It is produced by the Spirit: *"The fruit of the Spirit is **love**, joy, peace, longsuffering, gentleness, goodness, faith, meekness, temperance."* Therefore the only way to have more of God's divine agape love is to be emptied of self and filled with His Spirit, allowing it to change and control us: *"Be filled with the Holy Spirit and controlled by Him" (Eph. 5:18). TLB*

(3) Love is the key element required to produce the humility and unity essential for evangelism and miracles, like the first century church in the book of Acts that shook their known world.

Also a significant emphasis is placed on love for the brotherhood (the body of Christ) since:

- Loving God and loving our brother in Christ are completely and indivisibly linked, because we are members of one body.

- Our love for God is manifested and measured by our love for our brother.

- Our heavenly Father elevates His Church, His Bride, above all others: *"Now you are no longer strangers to God and foreigners to heaven, but you are members of God's very own family, citizens of God's country, and you belong in God's household with every other Christian" (Eph. 2:19). TLB*

- The Word of God demands a special love and treatment for those in the household of faith: *"As we have therefore opportunity, let us do good unto all men, **especially unto them who are of the household of faith**" (Gal. 6:10). "Respect everyone, and **love your Christian brothers and sisters**. Fear God, and respect the king" (1 Peter 2:17). NLT*

Perfect Love is the Highest Law and Strongest Force

John 3:16	**Love is greater than doctrine**. It is the bridge over which truth is transported.
Gal. 5:6	**Love is greater than faith**, for faith worketh by love.
1 Cor. 13:2	**Love is greater than miracles**, because all of the spiritual gifts flow through the love channel.
1 Cor. 13:3	**Love is greater than sacrifice or service**: *"Though I give all my goods to the poor give my body to be burned, and have not love, it is nothing."*
John 4:18	**Perfect love removes all fear**, creating an atmosphere for faith to work.
1 Cor. 13:13	Three things will last forever: faith, hope and love -- and **the greatest of these is love.**

If we had only one word to describe God, it would be "l-o-v-e." If we had only one word to describe the entire Bible, it would be **"l-o-v-e"** -- a love story of God's love for mankind, a love letter to mankind.

The scarlet cord of love is woven through every book of the Bible from Genesis to Revelation. God's love is so beautiful and strong that it encompasses every person and every circumstance for man and God relationships:

- God's love for everyone on earth.
  - Our love for God.
    - Our love for the brotherhood (household of faith).
      - Our love for our neighbor - every person on earth.
        - Our love for our enemies.

We cannot fully understand God's **perfect love** and words fail us in trying to describe it. But, everything that we need to know we learned at an early age in Sunday school; and that is -- **"Jesus loves me this I know, for the Bible tells me so."**

"Jesus loves me" is the central affirmation of the Christian faith and the cornerstone of His church. When God says, "I love you", He is expressing that you matter to Him; you are a person of worth; you are valuable to Him. Regardless of what others think, in the eyes of your heavenly Father, you have great value and He loves you completely. The most vivid characteristic of God is not simply that God "loves," but that God is love itself. Love is not merely one of His attributes, but His very nature. Two times in the same chapter the Apostle John repeats the truth that: **"God is love"**.

1 John 4:8
*He that loveth not knoweth not God; for **God is love**.*

1 John 4:16
***God is love**; and he that dwelleth in love dwelleth in God, and God in him.*

Man's Love Vs. God's Love

Man's love is natural and finite. God's love is supernatural and infinite. God's love is perfect: unfathomable, in-explainable, unspeakable, unending, unselfish, unmerited, redeeming, compassionate, and so much more. His love is perfect because God is perfect in all His ways. His love supersedes human love because it is impartial, unconditional and eternal. God's agape love is freely given by the Lover and it expects nothing in return. He loved us while we were still in sin and did not love Him: *"God commendeth his love toward us, in that, while we were yet sinners, Christ died for us" (Rom. 5:8).*

The English language limits the description of love because there is only one word (love) with many meanings, emotions and degrees of intensity. For example, if we said, "I love my son, I love my car, or I love candy", obviously we are not using "love" in the same degree or meaning.

-- From "Four Types of Love"

In the New Testament period there were four major Greek words that were used for love:

Eros Love - A word that was not actually used in the New Testament but was alluded to. It meant physical passion; its gratification and fulfillment. The Greek word is probably not used in the New Testament because the origin of the word came from the mythical God Eros, the God of love. It is inferred in many Scriptures and is the only kind of love that God restricts to a one-man, one-woman relationship within the bounds of marriage (Heb. 13:4; Song 1:13; 4:5-6; 7:7-9; 8:10; 1 Cor. 7:25; Eph. 5:31).

Storge Love - Storge is the natural bond between mother and infant, father, children, and kin. William Barclay states, "We cannot help loving our kith and kin; blood is thicker than water" (N.T. Words, 1974).

Phileo Love - Phileo love is a love of the affections. It is delighting to be in the presence of another, a warm feeling that comes and goes with intensity. The Bible encourages it but it is never a direct command. God never commands phileo since this type of love is based on the feelings. God Himself did not phileo the world but rather operated in agape love towards us. I cannot have a warm tender feeling toward an enemy but I can agape love them.

Agape Love - Agape love is God's kind of love. It is seeking the welfare and betterment of another regardless of how we feel. Agape does not have the primary meaning of feelings or affection. Jesus displayed it when he went to the cross and died for you and me regardless of how He felt. In the gospels Jesus prayed, "Father, if it be possible, let this cup pass from me: nevertheless, not as I will, but as thou wilt" (Mt. 26:39; Mk. 14:36; Lk. 22:41-43; Jn. 18:11). Jesus sought the betterment of you and me, regardless of His feelings. Matthew 7:12 states it this way, *"So whatever you wish that men would do to you, do so to them; for this is the law and the prophets."*[1]

Apostle Paul in 1 Corinthians 13 declares that if we do many good things that includes human love (Phileo, Storge, and Eros), but have not God's love (Agape), we are nothing. Agape is a love that is freely given by the Lover, expecting nothing in return.

Definition of God's Perfect Agape Love

The Word of God describes the most beautiful and complete definition of **perfect love** -- agape love. This description in 1 Corinthians 13 cannot be surpassed by any human description, because it is defined by God. Man's love is natural and finite. God's love is infinite and supernatural -- agape love.

1 Cor. 12:31, 13:1-8, 13

*31 But covet earnestly the best gifts: and yet shew I unto you a **more excellent way**.*

13:1 Though I speak with the tongues of men and of angels, and have not charity, I am become as sounding brass, or a tinkling cymbal.

2 And though I have the gift of prophecy, and understand all mysteries, and all knowledge; and though I have all faith, so that I could remove mountains, and have not charity, I am nothing.

3 And though I bestow all my goods to feed the poor, and though I give my body to be burned, and have not charity, it profiteth me nothing.

4 Charity suffereth long, and is kind; charity envieth not; charity vaunteth not itself, is not puffed up,

5 Doth not behave itself unseemly, seeketh not her own, is not easily provoked, thinketh no evil;

6 Rejoiceth not in iniquity, but rejoiceth in the truth;

7 Beareth all things, believeth all things, hopeth all things, endureth all things.

8 Charity never faileth: but whether there be prophecies, they shall fail; whether there be tongues, they shall cease; whether there be knowledge, it shall vanish away.

13 And now abideth faith, hope, charity, these three; but the greatest of these is charity.

This is called the "love chapter" because it gives a very detailed definition of the boundaries and attributes of God's agape love. Verses 4-8 gives sixteen defining aspects of agape love:

*1. **Suffereth Long*** - This word means patient endurance in trying circumstances. This characteristic of love never retaliates.

*2. **Is Kind*** - This word refers to words and actions of goodness toward others. Genuine love always respects and blesses others.

*3. **Envieth No**t* - Is not jealous over the abilities or possessions of others, but is pleased when they do well.

*4. **Vaunteth Not Itself*** - Is not boastful and never draws attention to itself or to what it is doing.

*5. **Is Not Puffed Up*** - Is not arrogant or proud. Recognizes that any talents we possess are from God.

*6. **Does Not Behave Itself Unseemly*** - Is never rude, but it always treats others with compassion and respect! Keeps emotions in control under conditions of stress.

*7. **Seeketh Not Her Own*** - Never self-centered, but seeks what is best for others. Puts the interest of others ahead of their own.

*8. **Is Not Easily Provoked*** - Does not react in an unloving way to the unkind words or acts of others. Stops the cycle of violence by returning good for evil.

*9. **Thinketh No Evil*** - Attaches the best possible meaning to the motives, words and conduct of others. Does not keep a record of evils done to it.

10. Rejoiceth Not In Iniquity - Does not gossip or find pleasure in hearing when another person falls, but grieves over the fallen brother.

11. Rejoiceth In The Truth - Rejoices when truth is proclaimed and wins the victory over falsehood and evil. Celebrates the goodness and virtues of others and is pleased when they do well.

12. Beareth All Things - Endures hurts and evils, and covers the wrongs of others (1 Peter 4:8). Conceal, or allow to pass unnoticed the offences of others (as far as can be lawfully done).

13. Believeth All Things - Is trusting and gives others the benefit of the doubt. Places the most favorable interpretation on everything that happens.

14. Hopeth All things - Always holds out hope that things will work out right in the end. Always expects the best possible outcome.

15. Endureth All Things - Continues in spite of persecution and ill treatment. Does not complain and bears up under wrong treatment at the hands of a fellow man.

16. Charity Never Faileth - When everything else in this world has passed away, when everything held in such high esteem is gone, it is the great constant that will last throughout.

- **You will grasp more clearly the meaning of perfect love at the personal level by substituting your name in place of charity or love in the following verses:**

1 Cor. 12:4-7
*[I am] very **patient** and [I am] **kind,** [I am] **never jealous or envious**, [I am] **never boastful or proud,** [I am] **never haughty or selfish or rude**. [I do] **not demand [my] own way.** [I am] **not irritable or touchy**. [I do] **not hold grudges** and will **hardly even notice when others do it wrong**. [I am] **never glad about injustice**, but **rejoice whenever truth wins out**. If [I] love someone, [I] will be **loyal to him** no matter what the cost. [I] will **always believe in him, always expect the best of him**, and **always stand my ground in defending him**. TLB*

How does this sound with your name in this passage? To the extent that this is not true, we see how much we must change to exhibit the agape love of Christ. If we live our lives in the context of this definition of love, we will offend fewer people. And in turn, this will eliminate much of the difficulty and pain in broken relationships and the humility required for restoration and reconciliation.

Those striving for the Kingdom and desperate for the unity that ignited revival and evangelism in the first century church will be the only ones progressing toward the goal of perfect love. God will test every born-again believer with opportunities to improve in forgiveness and reconciliation of relationships. The process of perfect love (agape love) to grow in our lives is to pass it on to the brotherhood and all mankind in the measure that we receive it from God.

- **The most wonderful privilege in the world is to experience the perfect love of God. May we understand, that the pure joy of this wonderful love, is to impart it in the same measure that we receive it to everyone -- whether they be friend or foe.**

The importance of loving one another is emphasized by every New Testament writer:

Matthew	*For if ye love them which love you, what reward have ye? Do not even the publicans the same?*
Mark	*Thou shalt love thy neighbor as thyself. There is none other commandment greater than these.*
Luke	*If you love those who love you, what credit is that to you? Even sinners love those who love them. NIV*
John	*By this shall all men know that ye are my disciples, if ye have love one to another.* *We know that we have passed from death to life, because we love our brothers. Anyone who does not love remains in death.* *If we love one another, God dwelleth in us, and his love is perfected in us.*
Peter	*Above all things have intense and unfailing love for one another, for love covers a multitude of sins [forgives and disregards the offenses of others]. AMP*
James	*If ye fulfil the royal law according to the scripture, Thou shalt love thy neighbour as thyself, ye do well: But if ye have respect to persons, ye commit sin, and are convinced of the law as transgressors.*
Paul	*For the whole Law can be summed up in this one command: "Love others as you love yourself." TLB*

Rick Warren said, "Learning to love God and others is to be our highest goal, our greatest aim, our first priority, our deepest aspiration, our strongest ambition, our constant focus, our passionate intention, and the dominant life value of our lives. The more we learn how to love authentically, the more like Jesus we become."

God's Warning to the Church of Ephesus -- "You Have Left Your First Love"

Recorded in bold, clear and sobering detail is:

1. God's commendation of the wonderful traits of the Ephesian believers.
2. God's condemnation of the single failure of the heart that seemingly negated the wonderful works of the church.
3. God's warning of judgment for having left their first love and the commandment to repent.

4. God's gracious offer of forgiveness if true repentance is made.

5. God's wonderful promise of eternal life to the overcomer.

Rev. 2:1-7

1 Unto the angel of the church of Ephesus write; These things saith he that holdeth the seven stars in his right hand, who walketh in the midst of the seven golden candlesticks;
2 I know thy works, and thy labor, and thy patience, and how thou cannot bear them which are evil: and thou hast tried them which say they are apostles, and are not, and hast found them liars:
3 And hast borne, and hast patience, and for my name's sake hast labored, and hast not fainted.
*4 Nevertheless I have somewhat against thee, **because thou hast left thy first love.***
*5 Remember therefore from whence thou art fallen, and repent, and do the first works; or else I will come unto thee quickly, **and will remove thy candlestick out of his place, except thou repent.***
6 But this thou hast, that thou hatest the deeds of the Nicolaitans, which I also hate.
7 He that hath an ear, let him hear what the Spirit saith unto the churches; To him that overcometh will I give to eat of the tree of life, which is in the midst of the paradise of God.

*4 But I have this complaint against you. **You don't love me or each other as you did at first!** NLT*

There were so many good things about the Ephesus church that it seems they were almost perfect. But the Lord said, *"I have somewhat against you"* -- only one thing against you -- ***"Thou hast left thy first love."***

The Ephesian church had done many things well:

1. They were commended for their labor. *"I know thy works, and thy labour."* The church at Ephesus was hard working.

2. They were commended for their patience. God noted both the external works and their heart of longsuffering.

3. They stood for the truth of God's Word and actively exposed false doctrine. For a church to mix a little error with truth is an unforgivable sin that causes people to be deceived and lost.

4. They were commended for removing false teachers from their congregation.

Their one fault began in their heart. The Lord can do without our achievements, but not without our love. The saints at Ephesus were not reprimanded with having changed their doctrinal views. But Jesus placed His finger on their heart and said: "There has been a change here."

The greatest challenge as Christians is to guard our heart: *"Keep thy heart with all diligence; for out of it are the issues of life"* (Prov. 4:23).

"First Love" is Love for the Body of Christ

The last voice of the Bible was penned by the Apostle John, now an elderly man on the isle of Patmos. In this last book, the book of Revelation, he identified the potentially fatal flaw in the church of Ephesus -- *"You have left your **first love**." "You don't love me or each other as you did at first" (Rev. 2:4) NLT.* His writings warned them to repent and do their first works or their light would be turned to darkness by God.

The Apostle John recorded only a few verses related to our love for God. However, his extensive writings regarding love pertain to loving the brotherhood.

-- From "The Apostle John"

There is a church tradition, which says, that when John was evidently an old man in Ephesus, he had to be carried to the church in the arms of his disciples. At these meetings, he was accustomed to say no more than, **"Little children, love one another!"** After a time, the disciples wearied at always hearing the same words, asked, "Master, why do you always say this?" **"It is the Lord's command,"** was his reply. **"And if this alone be done, it is enough!"**[2]

It would be very easy to accept the principle that **"first love"** refers only to our love for God, because loving Him is easy. He is magnificent, loving, kind, gracious, merciful, and beautiful. He is longsuffering, forgiving and everything wonderful. He is omnipotent, omniscient, omnipresent, infinite, indescribable, immeasurable and so much more. He holds our very breath and life in His hand and will be our Judge at the end of our sojourn.

Serving, worshipping and loving God must be our first priority. But the pre-condition to truly loving God is to first love our brother. Jesus demands such and accepts us as His disciples only as we love one another -- the body of Christ. **"First love"** includes love for God and love for the brotherhood because both are a part of one body and the body of Christ cannot be divided or separated.

Love for the brotherhood is emphasized here because our love for God is measured by our love for our brother:

(1) Loving God with all our heart includes loving our brother.

The term, "I love the Lord with all my heart" is probably the most misused and untrue statement in all of Christianity. Because the only way for this to be true, is to love our brother with all our heart: *"Esteeming him better than yourself" (Phil. 2:3).* Our love for God is manifested and measured by our love for the brotherhood: *"I demand that you love each other as much as I love you" (John 15:12) TLB. "If we love one another, His love is perfected in us" (1 John 4:12).*

(2) **Loving God and loving our brother are completely and indivisibly linked**, because our love for God is manifested by our love for our brother. Our love for God *(the invisible)* is manifested by our love for our brother *(the visible)*, as shown by many Scriptures penned by the Apostle John.

1 John 4:20-21
*20 If anyone says, I love God, and detests his brother [in Christ], he is a liar; **for he who does not love his brother, whom he has seen, cannot love God, Whom he has not seen.***
21 And this command (charge, order, injunction) we have from Him: that he who loves God shall love his brother [believer] also. AMP

(3) The Apostle John states that we cannot be in true fellowship with God if we do not love our brother: *"And this is his commandment: We must love one another, just as he commanded us. Those who obey God's commandments remain in fellowship with Him, and he with them"* (1 John 3:23-24). NLT

(4) Believers proclaim their love for God, but often struggle with reconciliation of relationships within the brotherhood.

(5) It is sometimes believed in Christian circles that one can love God separately from loving his brother.

(6) It is the visible evidence of our love for an invisible God:
"Your strong love for each other will prove to the world that you are my disciple" *(John 13:35). TLB*

"By this shall all [men] know that you are My disciples, if you love one another [if you keep on showing love among yourselves]" *(John 13:35). AMP*

(7) A deficiency of brotherly love is possibly satan's greatest tool to disrupt unity and hinder apostolic revival.

(8) Pursuing **perfect love** will produce **humility** in the brotherhood required to create the *"one mind and one accord"* **unity** evident at the birth of the church.

(9) Only the **perfect love** of God, growing and flowing in our lives, will allow us to reach our full potential for God's purpose and will for our lives.

(10) Any good or evil done to your brother, your heavenly Father considers it as having been done to Him. *"When you did it unto the least of these, **ye did it to me**"* (Matt. 25:40).
*"He who oppresses the poor, reproaches, mocks, and **insults his Maker**, but he who is kind and merciful to the needy honors Him"* (Prov. 14:31). AMP

*"Mocking the poor is **mocking the God** who made them" (Prov. 17:5). TLB*

(11) If your relationship with your brother is not right, your relationship with the Father is not right. *"Forgive us our sins, just as **we have forgiven those who have sinned against us**" (Matt. 6:12). TLB*

(12) Biblical **forgiveness involves reconciliation** of the relationship. Getting right with God includes getting right with your brother:

*"So if you are presenting a sacrifice at the altar in the Temple and you suddenly remember that someone has something against you, leave your sacrifice there at the altar. Go and be **reconciled** to that person. Then come and offer your sacrifice to God" (Matt. 5:23-24). NLT*

*". . . Abandon your offering, leave immediately, go to this friend and **make things right**. Then and only then, come back and work things out with God." MSG*

(13) When we act in an unloving way toward a brother (critical, judgmental, isolation, etc.) we are negatively affecting the body of Christ. And this causes a blockage in the flow of our love back to the head of the body -- Jesus Christ:

*"So that there should be no division or discord or lack of adaptation [of the parts of the body to each other], but the members all alike should have a mutual interest and care for one another. **Now you [collectively] are Christ's body and [individually] you are members of it**, each part severally and distinct [each with his own place and function]" (1 Cor. 12:25, 27). AMP*

*"Instead, we will **speak the truth in love**, growing in every way more and more like Christ, who is the head of his body, the church. He makes the **whole body fit together perfectly**. As each part does its own special work, it helps the other parts grow, so that the **whole body is healthy and growing and full of love**" (Eph. 4:15-16). NLT*

- Andrew Murray, a dynamic preacher from the 1800s declares that: **"Our greatest gift to God is our personal holiness, which is attached to our love and unity within the body of Christ."**

- **When we love the brotherhood with the perfect love of God, we are actually loving God because He accepts it as having been done to Him. Our love to members of the body flows love back to the Head of the body -- Jesus Christ.**

- **The message of perfect love is being continuously transmitted from the Head to the members of the body. And may there be no blockage by individual members that create a restriction of that flow to other members in the body of Christ and back to the Head.**

- **Perfect love** creates **humility** and in turn produces **unity** required for another Pentecost with the operation of apostolic power and authority, accompanied by the supernatural.

Refer to Chart L-4, "Our Love to God is Measured by Our Love to Our Brother."

Jesus Warns of Love Growing Cold

In the Olivet discourse recorded in Matthew 24, Jesus answered His disciples' question: "*What shall be the sign of thy coming, and of the end of the world?* The last sign listed was the sign of "love growing cold": "*Because iniquity shall abound, **the love of many shall wax cold**.*" This is speaking of Christians, because for love to grow cold, it must have been hot at a prior time.

May we prayerfully and seriously search our hearts and make the appropriate changes in our life to ensure that we are not included with the *many* Christians (the majority vs. the minority) whose love will grow cold in the perilous last days of the Church Age.

Matt. 24:12
*Because of the increase of wickedness, **the love of most will grow cold**. NIV*

Many: NT: 4118 4183 pleistos; the largest number. KJV - very great, most.[3]

God's **perfect love** is something that should grow and increase in our lives. Our love for God is like a fire that, if intentionally tended will burn brighter, affecting people in need of a Savior. But like an unattended fire, its intensity will decrease and begin to grow lukewarm and cold.

When our ardent, agape love for Christ subsides:
- The Bible is neglected.
- Witnessing and soul winning cease.
- Selfishness replaces sacrifice and self-denial.
- Church attendance is neglected or becomes mechanical.
- Prayer becomes a form of survival (for self) instead of revival prayers (for the lost).
- Unreconciled relationships within the brotherhood result in ill feelings, critical comments and isolation.
- Other priorities replace God as number one.

We should pray every day and ask God to search our hearts and forgive us of any defects He sees in our love for Him and others:
- When our work for God becomes routine and motivated out of duty, there is cause for repentance.
- When we seek recognition or promotion of self, there is cause for repentance.
- When we have not restored fractured relationships, especially those in the household of faith, there is cause for repentance.

- When we are judgmental and criticize others, especially those in the household of faith, there is cause for repentance.
- When we are not submissive to godly leaders, there is cause for repentance.

• **God cares more about our character and conduct than about our position and work in the church.**

• **Like the saints of the Ephesus church, we may feel very secure in our doctrine and work for God. But we must make sure that we have a true love for God and others,** *"Especially those in the household of faith -- the body of Christ."*

To be pleasing to God and most effective, we must excel in love -- God's **perfect love.** Love has the greatest value to God.

Loving God With All Our Heart

To return the great love that God has for us, we should completely fall in love with Him. May we be so in love with Him that our purpose is lost in His; our kingdom is lost in His. God's first and greatest commandment is to love Him with all of our heart, soul, mind and strength.

• **"All" puts Him in the very center of our lives -- our relationships, our plans and our daily activities.**

Love for God is the oil that greases the wheels of obedience. Obedience is not only saying "no" to satan and the world, but it is also saying "yes" to God and His will. True love for God directs and energizes us to pursue His will. Without love, we will struggle with obedience to His will.

When We Love Jesus Christ with All Our Heart, Soul and Mind – Perfect Love:
- We love to talk about Him.
- We love to talk to Him in prayer (Relationship, Transformation, and Dominion prayers).
- We love to go to His house.
- We love to think about Him. He is always on our mind.
- We love to study about Him.
- We return His great love by ministering to His needs (those of His saved and lost children).
- We put Him first in the resources He has given us -- time, health (strength), wealth.
- We extend His love, mercy and forgiveness to reconcile fractured relationships.

God is a Jealous Lover
This intimate love relationship between God and man is depicted as a bride and groom relationship. The heavenly Bridegroom is wooing His bride, desiring to destroy all the other lovers in her life. He demands to be first in our lives. Everything in our lives must pale in comparison to our love for Him.

What do we love?   What are the loves in our life?   What are the priorities in our life? How do we manage the resources (time, health and wealth) that God has given to us?   God is a jealous Groom -- a jealous lover of our soul. He demands to be first, because He will not tolerate idolatry and fornication, the two sins for which He destroyed Israel in the Old Testament. When He is not first in our life -- we have an idol in our life. And when He is not first, we have another lover in our life. The late Bishop Kilgore stated: "If He is not Lord of all, He is not Lord at all."

Ex. 20:5, Deut. 5:9
*Thou shalt not bow down thyself to them, nor serve them: for I the Lord thy God am a **jealous** God, visiting the iniquity of the fathers upon the children unto the third and fourth generation of them that hate me;*

Ex. 34:14
*For thou shalt worship no other God: for the Lord, whose name is **Jealous**, is a **jealous** God:*

Deut. 4:24
*For the Lord thy God is a consuming fire, even a **jealous** God.*

Zech. 8:2
Thus saith the lord of hosts; I was jealous for Zion with great jealousy, and I was jealous for her with great fury.

Eternal Life is Promised to Those Who Love God

Malachi, the last voice of the Old Testament, pronounced a blessing of eternal life on those who truly fear and love God and a curse of eternal death on those who do not.

Mal. 3:16-17
*16 Then those who feared and loved the Lord spoke often of him to each other. And he had a **Book of Remembrance** drawn up in which he recorded the names of **those who feared him and loved to think about him**.*
*17 **"They shall be mine,"** says the Lord Almighty, **"in that day when I make up my jewels**. And I will spare them as a man spares an obedient and dutiful son."*

Mal. 3:17-18, 4:1
*17 "They will be my people," says the Lord of Heaven's Armies. "On the day when I act in judgment, **they will be my own special treasure**. I will spare them as a father spares an obedient child.*
18 Then you will again see the difference between the righteous and the wicked, between those who serve God and those who do not."
4:1 The Lord of Heaven's Armies says, "The day of judgment is coming, burning like a furnace. On that day the arrogant and the wicked will be burned up like straw. They will be consumed -- roots, branches, and all." NLT

Loving Our Neighbor and Enemies

Jesus, in His answer to the question, *"Who is my neighbor"*, related the parable of the Good Samaritan. Its message discloses the truth that anyone in need is our neighbor, and we should display God's love to them with kind deeds -- **love in deed is love indeed.**

The commandment of God under both the Old and New Covenants demands that we love our neighbors and our enemies -- treating well those who despitefully use and persecute us.

Ex. 23:4-5
*4 If you come upon your enemy's ox or donkey that has strayed away, take it back to its owner. 5 If you see that the donkey of **someone who hates you** has collapsed under its load, do not walk by. Instead, stop and help. NLT*

Prov. 25:21, Rom. 12:20
If your enemy is hungry, give him food! If he is thirsty, give him something to drink!

Matt. 5:44, 46
44 But I say unto you, Love your enemies, bless them that curse you, do good to them that hate you, and pray for them which despitefully use you, and persecute you;
46 For if ye love them which love you, what reward have ye? do not even the publicans the same?

Rom. 12:14, 16-19, 21
Bless those who persecute you . . . Pray that God will bless them. Live in harmony with each other . . . Never pay back evil with more evil . . . Do all that you can to live in peace with everyone . . . Never take revenge. Leave that to the righteous anger of God. For the Scriptures say, "I will take revenge; I will pay them back," says the Lord. Don't let evil conquer you, but conquer evil by doing good. NLT

1 Thess. 5:15
See that none of you repays another with evil for evil, but always aim to show kindness and seek to do good to one another and to everybody. AMP

May we follow the example of Jesus, who in His dying moments prayed for the cruel men who were torturing and killing Him:

Luke 23:33-34
33 And when they were come to the place, which is called Calvary, there they crucified him, and the malefactors, one on the right hand, and the other on the left.
*34 Then said Jesus, **Father, forgive them; for they know not what they do**. And they parted his raiment, and cast lots.*

1 Peter 2:22-23
22 He was guilty of no sin, neither was deceit (guile) ever found on His lips [Isa. 53:9].

23 When He was reviled and insulted, He did not revile or offer insult in return; [when] He was abused and suffered, He made no threats [of vengeance]. AMP

- **Some people are too mean and evil to love with our natural human love. But when the perfect love of Christ is working in us, we can love those who hate and persecute us. This will bring the favor of the Father, because He is reaching for them (His lost children) with His perfect love flowing through us.**

- **Jesus Christ is the author and finisher of our faith. His greatest desire is to complete the work of perfect love that He has begun in our lives.**

Refer to the following pages for the **"Perfect Love"** overview charts.

Chart L-1

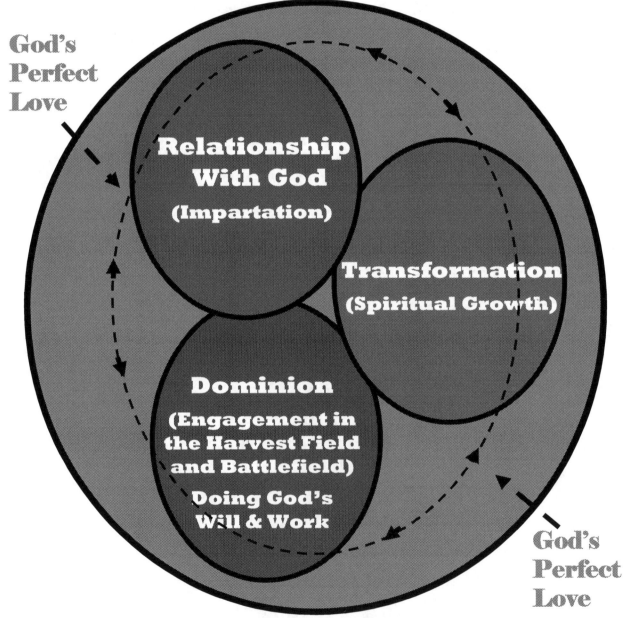

The Ecosystem of God's Kingdom

Just as oxygen is the key element in our natural ecosystem for us to live, PERFECT LOVE is the key element in God's ecosystem for the spiritual man to grow and be productive. It is the key element and driving force in a growing relationship with God, transformation of the inner man and dominion in the harvest field and battlefield.

God's Perfect Love

Relationship With God (Impartation)

Transformation (Spiritual Growth)

Dominion (Engagement in the Harvest Field and Battlefield) Doing God's Will & Work

God's Perfect Love

God is love -- in His perfect love we live and move and have our being!

Chart L-2

L O V E

Intense deep devotion for someone or something.

Love in its purest form would drive someone to give their life for a cause or a person.

Love is inconveniencing yourself for someone's benefit.

Love will drive you to sacrifice your time, energy and finances for someone in need.

LOVE WILL ALWAYS HAVE TWO COMPONENTS: "COMPASSION & CARE"

Compassion is the Emotion -

It is the deep sorrow and sympathy for the suffering or trouble of others accompanied by a strong urge to help.

Care is the Action -

It means to provide for or protect against trouble and want. It is feeling a great responsibility and concern for the welfare of someone to the extent that action will be taken to do something to affect their welfare and comfort.

Jesus came to earth to:
- **See and Feel   (Compassion)**
- **Touch and Heal   (Care)**

Chart L-3

HOW TO LOVE GOD MORE
Growing In Our Love For God

LOVING GOD
IS
LOVING PEOPLE

1 John 4:20
He that loveth not his brother whom he hath seen, how can he love God whom he hath not seen?

Gal 5:14
For all the law is fulfilled in one word, even in this; Thou shalt love thy neighbour as thyself.

Matt 25:37-40 <u>The final test at the judgment.</u>

37 Then shall the righteous answer him, saying, Lord, when saw we thee an hungred, . . . thirsty . . . stranger . . . naked . . . sick . . . in prison?

40 And the King shall answer and say unto them, Verily I say unto you, Inasmuch as ye have done it unto one of the least of these my brethren, ye have <u>done it unto me</u>.

THE ROYAL LAW

James 2:8-9
If ye fulfil the royal law according to the scripture, thou shalt love thy neighbour as thyself, ye do well: But if ye have respect to persons, ye commit sin.

Chart L-4

Our Love to God is Measured by Our Love to Our Brother

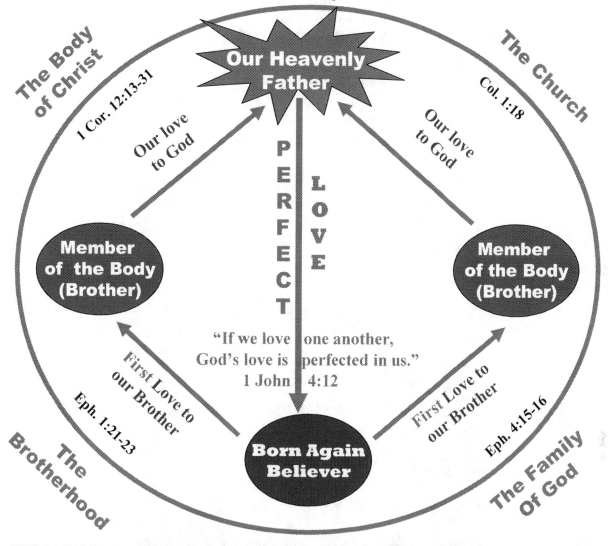

Our love to God is manifest and measured by our love to the brotherhood.
When love **FIRST** flows within the family of God, the brotherhood,
it is then most effective in ministering to the needs of our lost world !

*Christ puts us together in one piece, whose very breath and blood flow through us.
He is the Head and we are the body. (Col. 2:19) MSG*

There should be no division or discord or lack of adaptation [of the parts of the body to each other]. (1 Cor. 12:25) AMP

Do good unto all men, especially unto them who are of the household of faith. (Gal. 6:10)

I have somewhat against thee, because thou hast left thy first love. (Rev. 2:4)

Chart L-5
LOVE
Is the bridge over which truth is transported!

Eph. 4:15 We will speak the truth in love, growing in every way more and more like Christ, who is the head of his body, the church.

John 3:16 For God so loved the world, that he gave his only begotten Son, that whosoever believeth in him should not perish, but have everlasting life.

Luke 10:27 Thou shalt love the Lord thy God with all thy heart, with all thy soul, with all thy strength, and with all thy mind; and thy neighbour as thyself.

GOD'S SUPPLY:

- **Truth**
  > Doctrine

- **Spirit**
  > Gift of the Holy Ghost

  > Gifts of the Spirit
  - Wisdom
  - Knowledge
  - Faith
  - Healing
  - Miracles
  - Prophecy
  - Discerning of Spirits
  - Tongues
  - Interpretation of Tongues
  (1 Cor. 12:7-11)

MAN'S NEED:

- **Salvation**
- **Healing**
- **Deliverance**

GOD >>>>> God uses man to flow His love and truth to those in need >>>>> MAN

2 Cor. 5:18 God hath reconciled us to himself by Jesus Christ, hath given to us the ministry of reconciliation

---

Power is safe only in the hands of love!

The gifts of the Spirit flow through the charity (love) channel:

1 Cor. 13:2 And though I have the gift of prophecy, and understand all mysteries, and all knowledge; and though I have all faith, so that I could remove mountains, and have not charity, I am nothing. **3** And though I bestow all my goods to feed the poor, and though I give my body to be burned, and have not charity, it profiteth me nothing.

Chart L-6

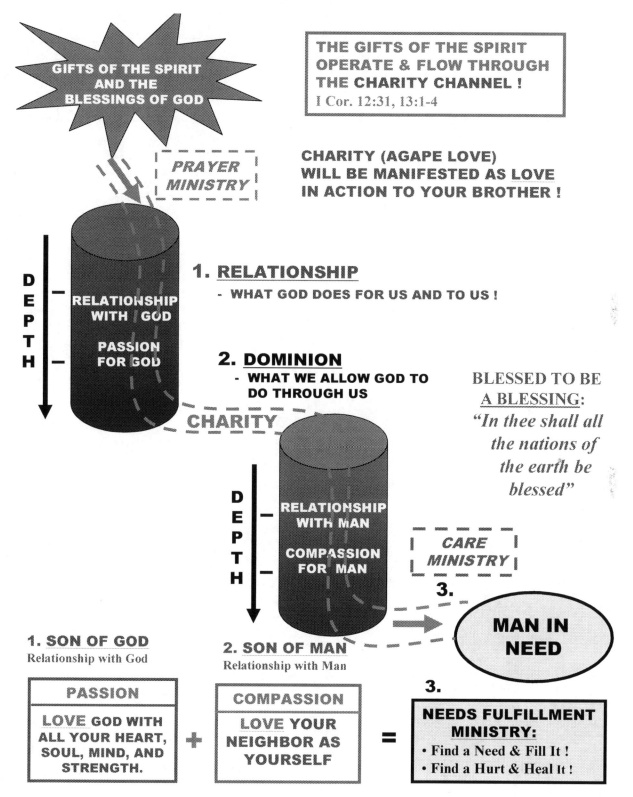

7. Humility and Unity

Theme Summary and Key Scripture Text

7.1 Humility

Humility is the foundation of all the other virtues hence, in the soul in which this virtue does not exist, there cannot be any other virtue except in mere appearance. (Saint Augustine)

"It is a great contradiction to speak of daily fellowship with a despised and rejected Christ, and of bearing His cross, if the meek and lowly, kind and gentle humility of the Lamb is scarcely evident in our daily lives."[4]

Paul explained to the church in Philippi the basic requirement for humility: *Esteeming and treating others better than ourselves.*

7.2 Unity

To be a book of Acts church, there must be unity in essentials, tolerance in non-essentials and love in all things.

In 1 Corinthians 12, Paul uses an extensive comparison between the human body and the body of Christ (the church) to describe how God wants His church to operate. This comparison emphasizes the horizontal connection and unity among the many different members as well as the dramatic diversity of many members working with complete unity in one body.

Like a natural healthy body where all actions within the members are unified and directed by the head, so should it be in the body of Christ. Any unkindness toward a member of the body of Christ indicates **a serious spiritual disorder because that action** is <u>not</u> directed by the Head of the body, Jesus Christ.

Humility Created by Perfect Love -- the Key to Unity

- If my people, who are called by my name, shall humble themselves and pray . . . then will I hear from heaven . . . and heal their land. (2 Chron. 7:14)
- For thus saith the high and lofty One . . . I dwell in the high and holy place, with him . . . who is of a contrite and humble spirit . . . (Isa. 57:15)
- Always be humble and gentle. Be patient with each other, making allowance for each other's faults because of your love. (Eph. 4:2) NLT
- Don't be selfish; don't live to make a good impression on others. Be humble, thinking of others as better than yourself. (Phil. 2:3) TLB
- Put on therefore, as the elect of God, holy and beloved, [tender mercies], kindness, humbleness of mind, meekness, longsuffering; (Col. 3:12)

Unity -- the Key to Another Pentecost

- And when the day of Pentecost was fully come, they were all with **one accord** in one place. (Acts 2:1)
- I urge and entreat you, brethren, by the name of our Lord Jesus Christ, that all of you be in perfect harmony and full agreement, and that there be no dissensions or factions or divisions among you, but that you be perfectly united in your common understanding and in your opinions and judgments. (1 Cor. 1:10) AMP
- There should be no division or discord or lack of adaptation [of the parts of the body to each other], but the members all alike should have a mutual interest and care for one another. (1 Cor. 12:25)
- So God has put the body together in such a way that extra honor and care are given to those parts that might otherwise seem less important. . . so that the parts have the same care for each other that they do for themselves. All of you together are the one body of Christ, and each one of you is a separate and necessary part of it. (1 Cor. 12:24-25, 27) TLB
- With all lowliness and meekness, with longsuffering, forbearing one another in love; Endeavouring to keep the unity of the Spirit in the bond of peace. (Eph. 4:2-3)

Study References

Vol.	Book Name	Primary Study Section / Chapter	Elective Study
V	Revival and Evangelism • Passion for God • Compassion for Souls		Sec. II / Ch. 5
VI	Perfect Love -- the Highest Law and Strongest Force	Sec. I / Ch. 6, 7	
VIII	Addendum Volume (PowerPoint Charts)	Charts at the end of this chapter	

Humility and Unity are discussed together with the subject of perfect love since:

- A *"one mind and one accord"* **unity** among the brotherhood is vital and mandatory for a revival that will reach our lost world in a significant way.

- Genuine **humility** is vital and mandatory for **unity** to operate among the brotherhood.

- **Perfect love** is vital and mandatory to create a spirit of **humility** in the brotherhood.

7.1 Humility Created by Perfect Love -- the Key to Unity

The dictionary defines humility as, "modesty, believing that we are not superior to others, the act or posture of lowering oneself in relation to others, meekness." True worship is humbling ourselves to the lowest state while exalting God to the highest; the difference between the two is the measure of our worship.

Saint Augustine stated: "It was **pride** that changed angels into devils; it is **humility** that makes men as angels."

J. Vaughan, M. A. states: "(1) If you are humble before God, you will be humble before men. (2) Exercise inward discipline to stop the first budding of pride. (3) Do acts of humility. (4) God always empties before He fills; He will humble before He will use a person."

To begin the discussion of "humility", let's tap into the insight and perspective of an author from the 1800s, to help establish the critical importance of this subject.

-- From "Humility" by Andrew Murray

In the daily interactions of the home and social life, in the more special fellowship with Christians, in the direction and performance of work for Christ -- alas! how much proof there is that humility is not esteemed the cardinal virtue. Humility is the only root from which the graces can grow, the one indispensable condition of true fellowship with Jesus. Meekness and lowliness of heart are the chief mark by which they who follow the meek and lowly Lamb of God are to be known.

What a solemn thought, that our love to God will be measured by our everyday interactions with men and the humility it displays; and that our love to God will be found to be a delusion, except that its truth is proved in standing the test of daily life with our fellowmen. It is easy to think we humble ourselves before God. **Humility towards men will be the only sufficient proof that our humility before God is real**; that humility has taken up its abode in us; and become our very nature; that we actually, like Christ, have made ourselves of no reputation.

And so **pride, or the loss of this humility, is the root of every sin and evil**. In heaven and earth, pride, self-exaltation, is the gate and the birth, and the curse, of hell. It was when the serpent breathed the poison of his pride, the desire to be as God, into the hearts of our first parents, that they from their high estate fell into all the wretchedness in which man is now sunk. Hence it follows that nothing can be our redemption, but the restoration of the lost humility, the original and only true relation of the creature to its God.[1]

Pride (the Opposite of Humility) is Listed with the Sins of the Flesh

Pride is the opposite of humility, modesty and meekness and is listed with the worst of sins: (sexual immorality, theft, murder, adultery, coveting, deceit, sensuality, envy, slander, ***pride*** . . .): *"For from within, out of a person's heart, come evil thoughts, sexual immorality,* *theft, murder, adultery, greed, wickedness, deceit, lustful desires, envy, slander, **pride**, and foolishness. All these vile things come from within; they are what defile you" (Mark 7:21-23). NLT*

God Hates Pride and Rewards Humility

King Solomon gives us a summary of what God hates -- and the first thing at the top of the list is "pride":

Prov. 6:16-19
16 These six things doth the Lord hate: yea, seven are an abomination unto him:
*17 A **proud look**, a lying tongue, and hands that shed innocent blood,*
18 An heart that deviseth wicked imaginations, feet that be swift in running to mischief,
19 A false witness that speaketh lies, and he that soweth discord among brethren.

Psalms 18:27
*You deliver the **humble** but condemn the **proud** and haughty ones. TLB*

Luke 14:11, Luke 18:14
*For whosoever exalteth himself shall be abased; and he that **humbleth** himself shall be exalted.*

1 Peter 5:5
*All of you serve each other with humble **spirits**, for God gives special blessings to those who are **humble**, but sets himself against those who are **proud**. TLB*

James 4:6
God resisteth the proud, but giveth grace unto the humble.

When we consider how much God hates pride, it should cause us to ask Him in prayer every day to search our hearts to reveal and remove any trace of pride.

Humility Brings Death to Self

Humility is the path of death to self. In death to self, humility is perfected. Jesus humbled Himself unto death, and patterned humility in which we too must walk: *"And after He had appeared in human form, He abased and humbled Himself [still further] and carried His obedience to the extreme of death, even the death of the cross"* (Phil. 2:8). AMP

- **It is a great contradiction to speak of daily fellowship with a despised and rejected Christ, and of bearing His cross, if the meek and lowly, kind and gentle humility of the Lamb is scarcely evident in our daily lives.**[1]

Humility will lead us to die to self as we follow in the footsteps of the master Teacher and become His true disciple. Self (our will, mind and emotions) encompasses all the evils of our fallen nature.

146

When Apostle Paul declared, ***"I die daily"***, he was not struggling with sin; he was battling self -- the process of self-decreasing and of Christ increasing. To have God's favor we too must submit ourselves to the brutal process of self-demotion and Christ's promotion:

 - Less of my will and more of His.

  - Less of my mind and more of His.

   - Less of my limited human love and more of His abundant **perfect love**.

Self-denial and its resulting humility is the downward path taught by Jesus for promotion: *"And whosoever shall exalt himself shall be abased; and he that shall **humble** himself shall be exalted" (Matt. 23:12).* Apostle James declares that going down in God's Kingdom actually leads up: *"**Humble** yourselves in the sight of the Lord, and he shall lift you up" (James 4:10).*

Pastor and revivalist, Andrew Murray, stated: "Self is the whole evil of fallen nature; self-denial is our capacity of being saved -- humility is our savior. Self is the root, the branches, and the tree, of all the evil of our fallen state. All the evils of fallen angels and men have their birth in the pride of self. On the other hand, all the virtues of the heavenly life are the virtues of humility. The great struggle for eternal life lies in the strife between pride and humility. **Pride and humility are the two master powers, the two kingdoms in strife for the eternal possession of man.**"[1]

Refer to Chart T-10, "The Path to the Supernatural -- He Must Increase, but I Must Decrease", at the end of Chapter 3.

The ambition to be great is a very common weakness in our human nature. The carnal nature of man craves greatness, to be first, to be the king (no matter how small the kingdom). It craves power, to execute its own agenda and plans, to control men and circumstances. This appeals and fascinates the natural man. But, it is so devastating and destructive to the spiritual man. The only cure for these selfish desires is genuine humility -- created by God's **perfect love** working in our lives.

Genuine humility requires a constant willingness to deny self and be critical of self. Apostle Paul explained to the church in Philippi the basic requirement for humility: ***"Esteeming and treating others better than ourselves."***

- **In our kingdom there are two sides to a conflict; in God's Kingdom, there is one side -- the "humble side". If we don't choose it, He will humble us.**

The Humility of Jesus Christ is Our Example

God coming to the earth in human form exemplified humility in its purest form. He descended from the highest of heaven's glory to the lowest of earth's estate.

The descent from His heavenly throne to His birth in extreme unfavorable conditions, in an animal stable, is an incalculable distance. The Bible makes it clear that He came "down" from the very highest to the very lowest.

He descended to a tiny speck in the universe called the Milky Way Galaxy, further down to the outer perimeter of the Milky Way Galaxy to a tiny speck in the universe -- our solar system. He came down further to a small speck in our solar system called earth -- then to the little town of Bethlehem: *"But thou, Bethlehem Ephratah, though thou be **little among the thousands of Judah**, yet out of thee shall he come forth unto me that is to be ruler in Israel; whose goings forth have been from of old, from everlasting" (Micah 5:2).*

The One worthy of all worship and the source of all power was born as a helpless baby in a dirty animal stable. Jesus never stopped descending and humbling Himself:
  - The King of kings became a servant to all.
  - The source of all Truth was falsely accused and judged guilty of blasphemy.
  - The Creator of all things was spit on by His creation.
  - The source and giver of life was crucified on a cross and died in agony, bleeding and gasping for air.
  - The One who possessed everything became poor so that we could be rich.

2 Cor. 8:9
Though he was so very rich, yet to help you he became so very poor, so that by being poor he could make you rich. TLB

In Christ's humility He exampled and modeled for us what it means to possess true humility. He showed us that to attain greatness, we must descend (not ascend).

Phil. 2:3-5, 7-8
*3 **In the true spirit of humility (lowliness of mind) let each regard the others as better than and superior to himself [thinking more highly of one another than you do of yourselves]**.*
4 Let each of you esteem and look upon and be concerned for not [merely] his own interests, but also each for the interests of others.
5 Let this same attitude and purpose and [humble] mind be in you which was in Christ Jesus: [Let Him be your example in humility:]
7 He stripped Himself [of all privileges and rightful dignity], so as to assume the guise of a servant (slave).
*8 And after He appeared in human form, He abased and humbled Himself **[still further] and carried His obedience to the extreme of death, even the death of the cross! AMP***

Humility Vs. Pride

From the world's perspective, the upward path of self-promotion is the preferred direction to go. In every human exist a proud ego reaching up for recognition, power and greatness. To the carnal man, humility is a brutal downward path of self-demotion. But the spiritual man understands that it leads to fulfillment, joy and promotion from the Father.

- **Pride, the loss of humility, is the root of every sin. This evil from hell is deeply innate in the heart of humanity.**

Without radical surgery by the Spirit to remove pride and replace it with humility, it will:
- Cause us to be critical and judgmental.
- Cause us to justify our unwillingness to initiate reconciliation of a relationship with a brother.
- Drain joy and fulfillment from our lives.
- Prevent spiritual growth.
- Greatly hinder the Great Commission of reaching souls.
- Possibly cause us to lose the precious gift of eternal life.

-- From The Spirit of Prayer

The truth is this: **Pride must die in you, or nothing of heaven can live in you.** Pride brings death, and humility brings life; the one is all evil, the other is all good. So much as you have of pride within you, you have of the fallen angels alive in you; so much as you have of true humility, so much you have of the Lamb of God within you.[2]

- **When we make critical remarks about a brother, a spirit of pride or self-righteousness is being asserted because it implies: "I am better than my brother."**

- **Apostle Paul declares it is unwise to measure ourselves among ourselves. But when we use the Word of God to measure ourselves, we are quickly humbled with the understanding that we have a long way to go to be like Him.**

- **Humility is the only soil where the fruit of the Spirit will grow and the supernatural Gifts of the Spirit will work.**

- **PERFECT LOVE creates HUMILITY and in turn produces UNITY, required for the complete restoration of apostolic ministry with the unrestrained operation of the supernatural.**

Refer to Chart H-1, "Perfect Love is the Foundation for Humility and Unity Required for Another Pentecost", at the end of this chapter.

7.2 Unity -- the Key to Another Pentecost

God's perfect love creates an atmosphere of humility among the brotherhood. Here the beautiful spirit of, *"one mind and one accord"*, unity can operate to create the explosion of revival and evangelism evident at the birth of the New Testament church.

Unity is defined as: "A condition of harmony or unification; the quality or state of being made one; a balanced pleasing or suitable arrangement of multiple parts. The opposite of unity is: confusion, disorganization, tension, disconnectedness, disjointedness, incompatibility, isolation." There is power in the natural world in unity and togetherness. For example one horse can pull six tons, while two horses can pull thirty-six tons. In the business world where there is unity (synergy) in a team, much more can be accomplished than individuals working alone.

Moses declared in Deuteronomy that with God's help against the enemy: *"One will chase a thousand and two [working together in unity] will put ten thousand to flight."* In the Kingdom of God there is unlimited power in unity, because it invites and allows the miraculous power of God to work with us.

Unity is simply having agreement, harmony and oneness in purpose and action. It is the glue in the body of Christ that allows us to be one. Even with all of our differences (perspectives, experiences, stages of spiritual growth, talents, ages, etc.) we can celebrate our great King, Jesus Christ, and work together in harmony for the greater cause. King David speaks of the beauty of unity in *Psalms 133:1, "Behold, how good and how pleasant it is for brethren to dwell together in unity."*

Jesus Christ declares that He will meet with His children when they come together in unity and harmony. Unified agreement in the body of Christ brings His very presence into our midst with answers to our prayers and fulfillment of our needs:

Matt. 18:19-20
*19 Again I tell you, if **two of you on earth agree (harmonize together)** about whatever [anything and everything] they may ask, it will come to pass and be done for them by My Father in heaven.*
*20 For wherever **two or three are gathered** (drawn together as My followers) in My name, there I am in the midst of them. AMP*

- **If unity brings the favor and power of God to His people, disunity brings God's disfavor and hinders His power working among us.**

- **To be a book of Acts church, there must be unity in essentials, tolerance in non-essential and love in all things.**

- **To enjoy unity, one must contribute to it. Every believer should be in unity with the Holy Spirit, to those in authority and with members of the body of Christ.**

Unity in the body of Christ is not uniformity. We all have a unique fingerprint, voice print, retina print, DNA, different personalities and talents. The church is composed of many individuals from a diversity of backgrounds, with different ideas and ways of doing things.

This diversity can cause an atmosphere unfavorable and sometimes hostile to the Spirit of unity in the church. The world culture establishes a mindset of maintaining the individual independence. It emphasizes the initiative, action, interests and conduct of the individual.

In the Kingdom of God, we as diverse members of one body, must contend for unity working together toward one common goal -- reaching a lost world. And as believers, we must fight and oppose the world's culture of individualistic principles and values.

Human Body Compared to Unity in the Body of Christ

The human body is the most amazing of all of God's creation. It is marvelously complex, yet it is unified with unparalleled harmony and interrelatedness. It is one unit and cannot be subdivided into several bodies. If the body is divided, the part that is cut off ceases to function and dies. The rest of the body loses some function and effectiveness. The complete human body is immeasurably more than the sum of its parts, likewise the body of Christ.

Paul uses an extensive comparison between the human body and the body of Christ (the church) to describe how God wants His church to operate. This comparison emphasizes the horizontal connection and unity among the many different members as well as the dramatic diversity of many members working with complete unity in one body.

1 Cor. 12:12-18, 20, 25-27
12 For as the body is one, and hath many members, and all the members of that one body, being many, are one body: so also is Christ.
*13 For by [means of the personal agency of] one [Holy] Spirit we were all, whether Jews or Greeks, slaves or free, baptized [and by baptism united together] into **one body**, and all made to drink of **one [Holy] Spirit**.*
14 For the body does not consist of one limb or organ but of many.
15 If the foot should say, Because I am not the hand, I do not belong to the body, would it be therefore not [a part] of the body?
16 If the ear should say, Because I am not the eye, I do not belong to the body, would it be therefore not [a part] of the body?
*17 If the whole **body were** an eye, where [would be the sense of] hearing? If the whole body were an ear, where [would be the sense of] smell?*
*18 But as it is, **God has placed and arranged the limbs and organs in the** body, each [particular one] of them, just as He wished and saw fit and with the best adaptation.*
20 And now there are [certainly] many limbs and organs, but a single body.

25 So that there should be no division or discord or lack of adaptation [of the parts of the body to each other], but the members all alike should have a mutual interest and care for one another.
26 And if one member suffers, all the parts [share] the suffering; if one member is honored, all the members [share in] the enjoyment of it.

27 Now you [collectively] are Christ's body and [individually] you are members of it, each part severally and distinct [each with his own place and function]. AMP

Apostle Paul, in his letters to the Ephesians and Colossians, emphasizes the **vertical connection** and unity of the various members of the body to the Head of the body, Jesus Christ:

Eph. 4:15-16
*15 But speaking the truth in love, may grow up into him in all things, which is **the head, even Christ**:*
16 From whom the whole body fitly joined together and compacted by that which every joint supplieth, according to the effectual working in the measure of every part, maketh increase of the body unto the edifying of itself in love.

Col. 1:18
***He is the Head of the body** made up of his people -- that is, his Church which he began; and he is the Leader of all those who arise from the dead, so that he is first in everything. TLB*

Col. 2:19
*Christ puts us together in one piece, whose very breath and blood flow through us. **He is the Head and we are the body.** We can grow up healthy in God only as he nourishes us. MSG*

Apostle Paul developed the analogy of the body to teach us about our relationship with one another. We are dependent on each other. It is through cooperation that we make our contribution and, in turn, are helped and aided to grow. Individualism in today's culture, with its emphasis on who is the "best" and "greatest", is unhealthy and destructive to the body of Christ.

-- From Teacher's Commentary

The whole spirit of the Corinthian church was individualistic. They were unable to see that each person needed the other and they were interdependent, not independent.

How much we need to rediscover the reality of the body of Christ today! For our age too is ruggedly individualistic -- exalting competitiveness and individual achievement. We find it hard to work with others in a team relationship. But we are a body. And it is as a body - honoring each part, ministering and being ministered to - that we must learn to live in God's family. The more excellent way to experience life in Christ's body, and to find fulfillment in ministry, is to live the life of love that binds us together in harmonious unity.

Paul's fullest treatment of the theme relational unity (1 Cor. 12:12-27) consists of an extended comparison between the human body and the church in order to emphasize horizontal union among the members of Christ's body and to demonstrate dramatically both diversity within unity (12:14-19) and unity out of diversity (12:20-27).

For Paul, the urgent need for humility, interdependence, and love within the Christian community is grounded in this dynamic horizontal unity between members of the body of Christ, a union that overcomes even the most imposing racial and social barriers (1 Cor. 12:13; cf. Gal. 3:28; Eph. 2:16). Horizontal, social relations between members are grounded in the vertical union each member enjoys with Christ (Rom. 12:5; 1 Cor. 10:16-17; 12:13).

The head is not merely one body part among many, but Christ's role as Head over the church entails authority and supremacy (Eph. 1:22; 5:24; Col. 1:18). Moreover, this head-body relationship between Christ and the church stands at the center of God's plan for the entire cosmos over which Christ has been established as sovereign (Eph.1:20-23).[3]

- **An important mark of human maturity and self-awareness is a growing respect and care for one's own body. There is a parallel in our spiritual life: as we mature in Jesus Christ, we will gain a deeper understanding of the need for care and protection for every member in the body of Christ.**

- **Like a natural healthy body where all actions within the members are unified and directed by the head, so should it be in the body of Christ. Any unkindness toward a member of the body of Christ indicates a serious spiritual disorder because that action is <u>not</u> directed by the Head of the body, Jesus Christ.**

When One Member Suffers All Suffer

1 Cor. 12:26
And whether one member suffer, all the members suffer with it; or one member be honoured, all the members rejoice with it.

When a thorn punctures the foot, other members of the body respond in feeling. The back bends, the hands, stomach, and thighs are drawn together. The head drops, eyes squint, the brow is furrowed with sympathy for the wounded member. Hands of comfort approach the wounded part and proceed to extract the painful object and soothe the wound. Plato states: "When one's finger is hurt such is the fellow-feeling which spreads along the body to the soul until it reaches the ruling principle, that, the whole body sympathizes with the part afflicted. The man says not 'my finger is in pain,' but I have a pain in my finger."

-- From The Pulpit Commentary

What if the hands should wish to injure the feet, or the eyes the hands? As all the members agree together because it is the interest of the whole that each should be kept safe, so men spare their fellow men because we are born for heaven, and society cannot be saved except by the love and protection of its elements. We have been born for mutual help, like the feet, like the hands, like the eyes. To act in opposition to another is therefore contrary to nature.[4]

Unity is Essential for Victory on the Battlefield

The kingdom of satan is setting its battle in array against the mission of the church and every born-again believer. This is the same battle that has been waged through the centuries between right and wrong. However, the final battle between the forces of good and evil, will be even more violent because it is satan's final stand to destroy the purpose of God for the great end-time harvest of lost souls.

Rev. 12:12
Woe to the inhabiters of the earth and of the sea! for the devil is come down unto you, having great wrath, because he knoweth that he hath but a short time.

1 Peter 5:8
Be sober, be vigilant; because your adversary the devil, as a roaring lion, walketh about, seeking whom he may devour.

This evil, aggressive enemy is abusing, killing and committing unspeakable atrocities against innocent victims.

The Commitment of the Christian Soldier

We as Christian soldiers are called by our great Commander in Chief, Jesus Christ, to engage, defeat and bind the enemy -- bringing deliverance to those bound in prisons of sin, sickness and abuse. But we are also called to rally under one banner of truth and fight together in unity against the evil empire of satan. Our efforts to survive and successfully defeat the enemy are directly related to how we unselfishly work together with unity in the brotherhood for the greater cause.

- **May our loyalty and commitment to the brotherhood (our fellow soldiers), in our noble battle for the things of the eternal, exceed that of soldiers whose mission and goals are bounded by the horizon of the temporal.**

The Commitment of the Marine Soldier

A Marine states: "In a combat zone or on a critical mission we lose awareness of self as we become dependent on our unified team. The accomplishment of our mission and often our survival depends on teamwork."

"Semper Fidelis distinguishes the Marine Corps bond from any other. It goes beyond teamwork -- it is a **brotherhood** that can always be counted on. Latin for 'always faithful,' *Semper Fidelis* became the Marine Corps motto in 1883. It guides Marines to remain faithful

to the mission at hand, to each other, to the Corps and to country, no matter what. Becoming a Marine is a transformation that cannot be undone, and *Semper Fidelis* is a permanent reminder of that. Honor, courage and commitment, the core values of the Marines, define how every Marine in the Corps thinks, acts and fights."[5]

Biblical Example for Handling Conflict in the Church

In the early church many Jews embraced the faith of Christ, yet continued very zealously for the Law. They contended that the Gentile Christians must be circumcised and keep the ceremonial Law of Moses. Church leaders called a council meeting at Jerusalem to discuss this very delicate issue. This was a very volatile subject with *". . . much disputing" (Acts 15:7)*. However, a wonderful spirit of unity accompanied their conclusions:

Acts 15:28-31
*28 **For it seemed good to the Holy Ghost, and to us**, to lay upon you no greater burden than these necessary things;*
29 That ye abstain from meats offered to idols, and from blood, and from things strangled, and from fornication: from which if ye keep yourselves, ye shall do well. Fare ye well.
30 So when they were dismissed, they came to Antioch: and when they had gathered the multitude together, they delivered the epistle:
31 Which when they had read, they rejoiced for the consolation.

- **May we all work together, like the early church in the spirit of unity, to resolve any differences in our common efforts to spread the gospel of Jesus Christ. And may we always seek for what seems good to the Holy Ghost and to our brethren, and not just our own personal preference.**

Conclusion

- **There is an essential principle vital and mandatory for a revival that will reach our lost world in a significant way -- and that is *"one mind and one accord"* unity among the brotherhood.**

- **There is an essential requirement vital and mandatory for unity to operate in the church -- and that is genuine humility.**

- **There is an essential requirement vital and mandatory for genuine humility -- and that is "God's perfect love" flowing in the brotherhood.**

Chart H-1

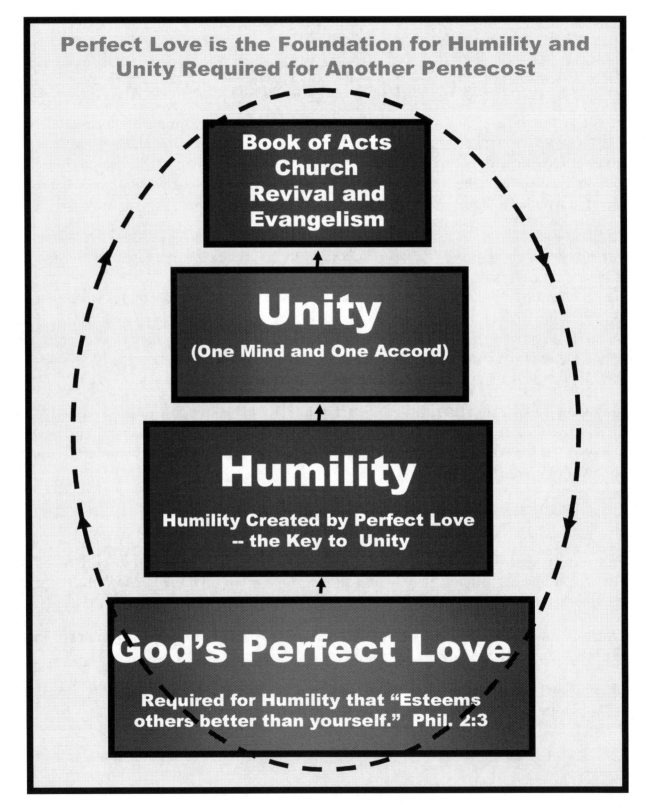

Perfect Love is the Foundation for Humility and Unity Required for Another Pentecost

Book of Acts Church Revival and Evangelism

Unity
(One Mind and One Accord)

Humility
Humility Created by Perfect Love -- the Key to Unity

God's Perfect Love
Required for Humility that "Esteems others better than yourself." Phil. 2:3

8. Prayer -- The Power Arm of the Christian and Church

Theme Summary and Key Scripture Text

Prayer

There is a law of God etched into the stone of eternity declaring that prayer stands alone at the very highest priority in God's economy and it has no rival -- everything else pales in comparison. All of our actions of compassion and care must start and end with effectual, fervent (powerful) prayer.

The prophecies concerning the restoration of the apostolic ministry of the early church will be realized as they are **prayed** into fruition through effectual, fervent (powerful) dominion prayers.

A balanced prayer life includes these three categories of prayer:

- **Relationship Prayers:** thanksgiving, praise, worship, petitions for needs.

- **Transformation Prayers:** *(change me)*. Repenting and emptying of self to be filled with more of God. Removing hindrances to the flow of His love and power through me. Less of my will, mind and emotions and more of God's.

  Renewal of the Holy Ghost: "Building up yourselves on your most holy faith, praying in the Holy Ghost." (Jude 20)

- **Dominion Prayers:** (Dominion over satan and sickness):

  Intercessory Prayer - standing between God and man; interceding for our lost neighbor, city and world.

  Spiritual Warfare - Standing between satan and man; binding the powers of satan that have bound and blinded people.

  Praying for wisdom and guidance to use the dominion and authority we have been given as a son of God.

Communion With God

- **King David's prayer for forgiveness and transformation**: Wash me thoroughly from mine iniquity, and cleanse me from my sin. Purge me with hyssop, and I shall be clean: wash me and I shall be whiter than snow. Create in me a clean heart, O God and renew a right spirit within me. Restore unto me the joy of thy salvation. Then will I teach transgressors thy ways; and sinners shall be converted unto thee. (Psalms 51:1-13)

- Let the words of my mouth, and the meditation of my heart, be acceptable in thy sight, O Lord, my strength, and my redeemer. (Psalms 19:14)

- But thou, when thou prayest, enter into thy closet, and when thou hast shut thy door, pray to thy Father which is in secret; and thy Father which seeth in secret shall reward thee openly. (Matt. 6:6)

- Pray without ceasing. (1 Thess. 5:17)

- Let us therefore come boldly unto the throne of grace, that we may obtain mercy, and find grace to help in time of need. (Heb. 4:16)

- The effectual fervent prayer of a righteous man availeth much. (James 5:16-18)

- But ye, beloved, building up yourselves on your most holy faith, praying in the Holy Ghost. (Jude 20)

If we follow in the footsteps of Jesus, there must be frequent times of solitude when we leave the hustle and bustle of life and commune with God alone in prayer:

- He went up into a mountain apart to pray: and when the evening was come, he was there alone. (Matt. 14:23)

- In the morning, rising up a great while before day, he went out, and departed into a solitary place, and there prayed. (Mark 1:34-35)

- And he withdrew himself into the wilderness, and prayed. (Luke 5:16)

Study References

Vol.	Book Name	Primary Study Section / Chapter	Elective Study
III	Spiritual Growth - Dominion Over Sin and Self	Sec. III	Sec. I / Ch. 1, Sec. II / Ch. 5
IV	Unlimited Partnership With a Supernatural God	Sec. III / Ch. 4	
VIII	Addendum Volume (PowerPoint Charts)	Charts at the end of this chapter	Charts E-1, 6, 8, 10, G-6, J-2, 5

The Prayer Ministry is not a department of the church. It is the power generator of the church! Prayer brings anointing (divine ability vs. human ability). All of our evangelism processes and efforts must be anointed of God to be effective.

The Prayer Ministry must not be perceived as just another ministry. It must be elevated and presented as:
- The most important ministry in the church.
  - The enabling power for effectiveness in all other ministries and departments.
    - A ministry in which everyone feels compelled to participate.

- **The prophecies concerning the restoration of the apostolic ministry of the early church in the last days will be realized as they are prayed into fruition through effectual, fervent (powerful) dominion prayers with fasting.**

The highest calling in the Kingdom of God is the call to prayer. Regardless of our assignment in the Kingdom of God, it will be ineffective without prayer. Answering the call to prayer is the best thing we can do for ourselves, our family, our church, and our relationship with God. So we must come back to it again and again and stoke the fire of effective and consistent:
- Prayer with our family at meals and in devotions,
- Prayer with our spouse,
- Prayer in our daily private devotion with God each day *(the highest priority)*,
- Prayer in small groups,
- Prayer in scheduled times at church,
- An attitude of prayer during our daily routine as we recognize our dependence on God.

Prayers are permanent and valuable assets: Prayers are not temporary; they are permanent assets stored somewhere in God's Kingdom until the end of time. The prayers of the saints live on, even after death. Many prayers of a mother for a lost child have been answered after her death. And her prayers have made the difference in the lives of a family for generations after her death.

God places such high value on our prayers that He has stored every sincere prayer that we have prayed in golden vials in heaven: *"And when he had taken the book the four and twenty elders fell down before the lamb, having every one of them harps, and golden vials full of odors, which are the prayers of the saint" (Rev. 5:8).* The prayers of the saints are precious to God. He records them and remembers them. Acts Chapter 10 records that the prayers of Cornelius came up as a memorial before God and an angel was dispatched from heaven with a message of salvation for him and his family.

Prayer fuels and keeps the relationship engine running. All of the aspects of our relationship with God are enabled and enhanced by communication with Him. Without prayer the relationship will stop growing and become stagnant, resulting in a lukewarm and distant relationship. Our long term relationship with God will not survive without talking to Him often and for quality periods of time in prayer. To know someone you have to spend time communicating with them. That is how two people bond together as one. This is true in our relationship with God. By talking to God in prayer we tune our spirit to hear His Voice. He desires to talk and commune with us: *"Behold, I stand at the door, and knock: if any man hear my voice, and open the door, I will come in to him, and will sup with him, and he with me" (Rev. 3:20).*

Prayer tunes our spiritual ears to hear God's Voice: God's communication to us is much more effective if we are consistently talking to Him. In an electronic communication device there is a **transmitter** and a **receiver**. Regardless how strong the transmitter is, the receiver must be turned on and tuned in to receive the message. The transmitter (God's Voice) has no weakness: *"For the word of God is quick, and powerful, and sharper than any twoedged sword, piercing even to the dividing asunder of soul and spirit" (Heb. 4:12).* *"Is not My word like fire?" declares the LORD, "and like a hammer which shatters a rock?" Jer. 23:29.*

But it takes prayer to tune our spiritual receiver to receive God's message to us. It takes prayer to open our spiritual ears to hear with clarity what God is speaking to us. Prayer opens up our spiritual ears and prepares our spirit to receive His Word. Seven times in the Gospels and eight times in the book of Revelation we are challenged by God to hear His Voice – His Word.

Matt. 11:15, 13:43; Mark 4:9, 23, 7:16; Luke 8:8, 14:35
He that hath ears to hear, let him hear.

Rev. 2:7, 11, 17, 29, 3:6, 13, 22, 13:9
He that hath an ear, let him hear what the Spirit saith unto the churches.

The devil will let you do anything but pray. He will let you go to church; he will let you teach Bible lessons; he will let you pay your tithes and be faithful in other ways. But he will challenge you every day at your prayer closet door, because he knows that is the key to a deeper relationship and power with God.

Martin Luther said: "If I fail to spend time in prayer each morning, the devil gets the victory through the day. I have so much business I cannot get on without spending time daily in prayer."

The story is told about Napoleon and his generals on one of their military expeditions. Having looked at the maps, they could not agree on their location. After a while Napoleon stood and said, "Gentlemen we have just marched off the maps. We are somewhere we have never been before, we are in uncharted territory."

It is time for us as Christians to leave the status quo and our comfort zones and "march off the maps" into places in the Kingdom of God where we have never been before. And that will happen through the power of prayer (relationship) followed by actions of care (dominion over satan and sickness). Prayer is the last frontier of a mature Christian. To experience new places in the Spirit, where we have never been before, there is only one door and one path, and that is through the door of consistent, persistent prayer.

The sands of time are quickly running out on this sin-cursed world. We're so near the end of the Church Age that we should be spending a significant amount of time each day in our personal devotion of prayer and the Word. We can live in an attitude of prayer on the highway or at the work place. However, our quality time in communion with God should be in a private place where we can shut out distractions and be alone with God: *When thou prayest, enter into thy closet, and when thou hast shut thy door, pray to thy father which is in secret; and thy father which seeth in secret shall reward thee openly" (Matt. 6:6).*

If you want to have God bear your burdens of the day, pray. This includes both physical burdens and spiritual burdens. We cast our cares upon Him through prayer; *"Casting all your care upon him; for he careth for you" (1 Peter 5:7).* Even during vacation and time of relaxation, if you want to maximize your joy for the day, put God first in prayer. Don't leave Him at home - take Him with you fishing, hiking, etc. That is what God spoke to me on vacation during a time of relaxation: "If you want to enjoy the day, pray."

We must learn anew the worth of prayer and enter anew the school of prayer. Only God can move mountains, but faith and prayer move God. Prayer can reach around the world. It can reach across time and distance. It can reach across nationality barriers. It can reach into the pit and prison of sin – bringing hope and deliverance. Prayer can reach any place that God can reach.

God demands that His house be kept clean and holy: The only time Jesus displayed anger in His ministry was in the temple where merchandising and socializing by "religious men" was the business of the day. He overturned their tables of money and merchandise and drove them out of the temple. His words are still applicable today as they were back then: ***"My house shall be called a house of prayer."***

We, by our fervent prayers and godly lifestyles, must be holy vessels that repel the world and its' culture from entering the church. We must pray dominion prayers to bind the powers of satan and hell that try to assault the church. The world has always tried to get into the church at many points in many ways. Like a ship on the ocean, the water is always trying to get in the old ship of Zion. Sin is always trying to seep in. It oozes in, it pours in. It comes in with brazen front or soft disguise. It comes in at the top, the bottom and the sides. It percolates through in hidden ways. Someone must pray for the church; and pray that we will keep the fire of God in our hearts to destroy the works of satan. Someone must be a part of the honor guard that protects God's church, God's ministers and God's people from satan's attacks.

God loves the persistent pleader: Jesus gave an example of this with the widow woman that kept coming back to the unjust judge. The unjust judge gave her what she requested because she wearied him with her continual coming and persistence: *"Yet because this widow troubleth me, I will avenge her, lest by her continual coming she weary me. And the Lord said, Hear what the unjust judge saith. And shall not God avenge his own elect, which cry day and night unto him, though he bear long with them? I tell you that he will avenge them speedily"* (Luke 18:5-8).

The New Testament stresses the intensity and violence of the Kingdom. We press our way into the Kingdom and defeat the enemy by fervent, intense dominion prayers:
- *The kingdom of God suffereth violence and the violent take it by force. (Matt. 11:12)*
- *The law and the prophets were until John: since that time the kingdom of God is preached, and every man presseth into it. (Luke 16:16)*
- *Put on the whole armour of God, that ye may be able to stand against the wiles of the devil. Wherefore take unto you the whole armour of God, that ye may be able to withstand in the evil day, and having done all, to stand. Praying always with all prayer and supplication in the Spirit, and watching thereunto with all perseverance and supplication for all saints. (Eph. 6:11, 13, 18)*

The need for intensity and violence in the Kingdom of God is accentuated by the fact that we are in a spiritual war against the kingdom of satan who is controlling much of America, "Christian America" and the world. Many are affected or bound by the evil and debauchery of satan's kingdom (drugs, alcohol, abortion, homosexuality, divorce and turmoil in the home, child abuse, pornography and godless behavior, etc.):
- **Alcoholics:** 18 million in the U.S. (affecting more than 28 million children).
- **Drugs:** Approximately 25 million in the U.S. use illicit drugs each year.
- **Abortions:** Approximately 57 million legal abortions in the last 40 years in the U.S. Approximately 205 million in the world each year (1.35 billion since 1980).
- **LGBT:** An estimated 20 - 30 million are living this lifestyle in America. An unprecedented and shocking decision by the U.S. Supreme Court has changed the law to support same sex marriage.

- **Divorce:** Statistics show if the current rate continues, 50% of marriages will end in divorce.

- **Violence:** Violent crime is on the rise in America and around the world. Horrendous and inconceivable atrocities are being committed in the name of religion around the world causing great upheaval and suffering of millions. World War III lies just ahead that is prophesied to kill one third of mankind.

- **Lawlessness:** Rebellion and hatred toward lawmen is rising at an unprecedented rate in our country. Lack of respect for authority in our homes, schools and universities is rising at an alarming rate.

The only hope for this hopeless end-time generation is the power of prayer and the gospel. May we be a part of the prayer force who sighs and cries for the abominations of our country and world: *"And the Lord said unto him, Go through the midst of the city, through the midst of Jerusalem, and set a mark upon the foreheads of the men that **sigh and that cry for all the abominations** that be done in the midst thereof" (Ezek. 9:4).*

Holy Writ identifies reaping with weeping: *"They that sow in tears shall reap in joy. He that goeth forth and weepeth, bearing precious seed, shall doubtless come again with rejoicing, bringing his sheaves with him" (Psalms 126:5-6). "And when he was come near, he beheld the city, and wept over it" (Luke 19:41).* Who is weeping over your city?

Heb. 5:7
Who in the days of his flesh, He [Jesus] *offered up prayers and supplications with strong crying and tears.*

-- From "Prayer" by E. M. Bounds

The crying evils of these times, maybe of all times is little or no praying. Of these two evils, perhaps little praying is worse than no praying. Little praying is a kind of a salve for the conscience. The prayers of God's saints are the capital stock in heaven by which Christ carries on His great work upon the earth. The earth is changed, revolutionized; angels move on more powerful, more rapid wings; and God's policy is shaped when the prayers of His people are more numerous and more efficient.

The most important lesson we can learn is how to pray. Indeed, we must pray so that our prayers take hold of God. The man who has done the most and the best praying is the most immortal, because prayers do not die. Perhaps the lips that uttered them are closed in death, or the heart that felt them may have ceased to beat, but the prayers live before God, and God's heart is set on them. Prayers outlive the lives of those who uttered them -- outlive a generation, outlive an age, and outlive a world. When God's house on the earth is a house of prayer, then God's house in heaven is busy and powerful in its plans and movements. *'For mine house shall be called an house of prayer for all people'* *(Isa. 56:7)*, says our God. Then, His earthly armies are clothed with the triumphs and spoils of victory, and His enemies are defeated on every hand. God shapes the world by prayer. The more praying there is in the world, the better the world will be and the mightier the forces against evil everywhere. The very life and prosperity of God's cause -- even its very existence -- depend on prayer.[1]

A challenge to improve your prayer life: If consistent prayer has been a struggle in your daily life, consider this six week challenge. You have nothing to lose; you have everything to gain -- physically, spiritually and mentally. It takes at least six weeks of concentrated effort to break old habits and develop new ones. You will most likely not experience the benefits and rewards until the new habit or initiative is consistently established in your life.

If a renowned, successful doctor gave us a six weeks prescription for a therapy (one hour a day, four days a week and some reference material to read) that would miraculously rejuvenate our body, soul and spirit -- we would all try it. The following is a prescription for a six week therapy from the Great Physician – the Doctor who has all wisdom and knows every detail of our lives:

1. Spend one hour a day, three to four days a week in your personal devotion (prayer and the Word). This considers that you will be going to church two days each week where prayer is included:
    - Praying focused prayers in your prayer closet (a place with no distractions).
    - Praying relationship, transformation and dominion prayers.
    - Praying for your burdens, the burdens of others and the burden of the Lord.
    - Praying and reading the Word (claiming the promises of God).

2. Read one to two good books on prayer, that describe the importance of prayer and the benefits experienced by the author and his peers.

3. Take notes on the preached Word so you won't forget the message and can meditate on it later. Then discuss the message with your family -- explaining the meaning and practical application to your children.

4. Focus on taking God with you 24 hours a day and staying away from activities that might grieve His spirit.

5. Have at least one or two extended, uninterrupted sessions in prayer and the Word of two hours or more.

6. Select one or two prayer partners for specific needs. You don't have to pray with them; just agree in the Spirit for the answer for your needs and the needs of others: *"If two of you shall agree on earth as touching anything that they shall ask, it shall be done for them of my Father which is in heaven"* (Matt. 18:19).

Spurgeon states: "One night alone in prayer, might make us new men, changed from poverty of soul to spiritual wealth, from trembling to triumph. Jacob wrestled all night in prayer and his name was changed because he now had power with God."

Examples of Prayer in the Old Testament

Jabez's Prayer: In 1 Chronicles Chapter 4, in the middle of the genealogies, Scripture pauses for two verses to mention a godly man named Jabez. It is the first and last time we ever hear of him. He is a virtual nobody in biblical history. But if you were going to get only a two sentence biography for your life's story, what would you want written of you? May it be like Jabez -- a life of prayer: *"And Jabez was more honorable than his brethren: and his mother called his name Jabez, saying, because I bare him with sorrow. And Jabez called on the God of Israel, saying, Oh that thou wouldest bless me indeed, and enlarge my coast, and that thine hand might be with me, and that thou wouldest keep me from evil, that it may not grieve me! And God granted him that which he requested"* (1 Chron. 4:9-10). That is all that is said about Jabez. He appears. He prays a fervent, effectual prayer. God grants his prayer. And that's all. And may we, like Jabez, be remembered for our fervent prayers that God answers because of our close and growing relationship with Him.

2 Chron. 7:12-15 (Solomon's prayer)
12 And the Lord appeared to Solomon by night, and said unto him, I have heard thy prayer, and have chosen this place to myself for an house of sacrifice.
13 If I shut up heaven that there be no rain, or if I command the locusts to devour the land, or if I send pestilence among my people;
14 If my people, which are called by my name, shall humble themselves, and pray, and seek my face, and turn from their wicked ways; then will I hear from heaven, and will forgive their sin, and will heal their land.
15 Now mine eyes shall be open, and mine ears attent unto the prayer that is made in this place.

1 Kings 18:24, 38-39 (Elijah's prayer brings revival to backslidden Israel)
24 And call ye on the name of your gods, and I will call on the name of the LORD: and the God that answereth by fire, let him be God. And all the people answered and said, It is well spoken.
38 Then the fire of the Lord fell, and consumed the burnt sacrifice, and the wood, and the stones, and the dust, and licked up the water that was in the trench.
39 And when all the people saw it, they fell on their faces: and they said, The Lord, he is the God; the Lord, he is the God.

Psalms 55:17 (David's prayer)
Evening, and morning, and at noon, will I pray, and cry aloud: and he shall hear my voice.

Dan. 6:10 (Daniel's prayer)
Now when Daniel knew that the writing was signed, he went into his house; and his windows being open in his chamber toward Jerusalem, he kneeled upon his knees three times a day, and prayed, and gave thanks before his God, as he did aforetime.

Examples of Prayer in the New Testament

Pentecost Was Born in a Prayer Meeting: The New Testament apostolic church, born on the Day of Pentecost, in a fervent and fiery prayer meeting still challenges us today. With the fire, the heat and the purity of its birth there came an energy that has been unequaled in almost twenty centuries. We see in the book of Acts the intensity of prayer and the resulting miracles and evangelism that shook cities and nations. An example of one of these prayer meetings is described in *Acts 4:31: "And when they had prayed, the place was shaken where they were assembled together; and they were all filled with the Holy Ghost, and they spake the word of God with boldness."*

The outpouring of the Holy Ghost in Topeka, Kansas, on January 1, 1901, was born in much prayer. This ignited the outpouring of the Holy Ghost and the birth of apostolic churches around the world. The Azusa Street revival a few years later was preceded by several months of prayer. Historians say that the Azusa Street revival played a major role in the development of a movement that changed the religious landscape and became the most vibrant force for world evangelization in the 20th century. Azusa Street became the most significant revival of the century in terms of global perspective, as people from all over the world came to experience their personal Pentecost. And may we follow the example of these early church leaders and saints that shook the world with the power that only comes when we connect with God on our knees.

Jesus Our Example -- Praying Alone in a Private Place

We see this exampled in the prayer life of Jesus when He often went to a private place to pray. We also see it in His instruction to His disciples: *"When thou prayest, enter into your prayer closet and shut the door, pray to thy Father which is in secret; and thy Father which seeth in secret shall reward thee openly" (Matt. 6:6).*

Matt. 14:22-23
22 And straightway Jesus constrained his disciples to get into a ship, and to go before him unto the other side, while he sent the multitudes away.
23 And when he had sent the multitudes away, he went up into a mountain apart to pray: and when the evening was come, he was there alone.

Matt. 26:39
And he went a little further, and fell on his face, and prayed, saying, O my Father, if it be possible, let this cup pass from me: nevertheless not as I will, but as thou wilt.

Mark 1:34-35
34 And he healed many that were sick of divers diseases, and cast out many devils; and suffered not the devils to speak, because they knew him.
35 And in the morning, rising up a great while before day, he went out, and departed into a

solitary place, and there prayed.

Mark 6:46
And when he had sent them away, he departed into a mountain to pray.

Luke 5:16
And he withdrew himself into the wilderness, and prayed.

Luke 6:12-13 (Before making an important decision, Jesus prayed all night)
12 And it came to pass in those days, that he went out into a mountain to pray, and continued all night in prayer to God.
13 And when it was day, he called unto him his disciples: and of them he chose twelve, whom also he named apostles;

Luke 9:28-29
28 And it came to pass about an eight days after these sayings, he took Peter and John and James, and went up into a mountain to pray.
29 And as he prayed, the fashion of his countenance was altered, and his raiment was white and glistering.

Luke 5:16
*And he withdrew himself into the wilderness, and **prayed.***

- **If we follow in the footsteps of Jesus, there must be frequent times of solitude when we leave the hustle and bustle of life and commune with God alone in prayer.**

Jesus Teaching His Disciples How to Pray

The disciples of Jesus asked Him to teach them to pray and He responded to their request: *"One of His disciples said unto Him, Lord, teach us to pray, as John also taught his disciples."*

Matt. 6:7-15
7 But when ye pray, use not vain repetitions, as the heathen do: for they think that they shall be heard for their much speaking.
8 Be not ye therefore like unto them: for your Father knoweth what things ye have need of, before ye ask him.
9 After this manner therefore pray ye: Our Father which art in heaven, Hallowed be thy name.
10 Thy kingdom come. Thy will be done in earth, as it is in heaven.
11 Give us this day our daily bread.
12 And forgive us our debts, as we forgive our debtors.
13 And lead us not into temptation, but deliver us from evil: For thine is the kingdom, and the power, and the glory, forever. Amen.
14 For if ye forgive men their trespasses, your heavenly Father will also forgive you:
15 But if ye forgive not men their trespasses, neither will your Father forgive your trespasses.

- **There is great value in teaching people to pray, particularly children, new converts and others who are struggling with their prayer life.**

Refer to the charts at the end of this chapter for types of prayer.

Prayer in the Book of Acts Church

The New Testament church was born on the Day of Pentecost in a 7-10 day prayer meeting

Acts 1:13-14
13 And when they were come in, they went up into an upper room, where abode both Peter, and James, and John, and Andrew, Philip, and Thomas, Bartholomew, and Matthew, James the son of Alphaeus, and Simon Zelotes, and Judas the brother of James.
14 These all continued with one accord in prayer and supplication, with the women, and Mary the mother of Jesus, and with his brethren.

The first recorded miracle, after the ascension of Jesus, was on the way to a prayer meeting

Acts 3:1, 6, 8
*1 Now Peter and John went up together into the temple at the **hour of prayer,** being the ninth hour.*
6 Then Peter said, Silver and gold have I none; but such as I have give I thee: In the name of Jesus Christ of Nazareth rise up and walk.
8 And he leaping up stood, and walked, and entered with them into the temple, walking, and leaping, and praising God.

The Gentiles were included in the plan of God because the one with the need of salvation and the one with the message of salvation prayed

Acts 10:2, 3, 5, 9, 19, 20, 44-48
2 A devout man, and one that feared God with all his house, which gave much alms to the people, and prayed to God always.
3 He saw in a vision evidently about the ninth hour of the day an angel of God coming in to him, and saying unto him, Cornelius.
5 And now send men to Joppa, and call for one Simon, whose surname is Peter:
9 On the morrow, as they went on their journey, and drew nigh unto the city, Peter went up upon the housetop to pray about the sixth hour:
20 Arise therefore, and get thee down, and go with them, doubting nothing: for I have sent them.
44 While Peter yet spake these words, the Holy Ghost fell on all them which heard the word.
45 And they of the circumcision which believed were astonished, as many as came with Peter, because that on the Gentiles also was poured out the gift of the Holy Ghost.

46 For they heard them speak with tongues, and magnify God. Then answered Peter,
47 Can any man forbid water, that these should not be baptized, which have received the Holy Ghost as well as we?
48 And he commanded them to be baptized in the name of the Lord.

Fervent prayer continues in the book of Acts church

Acts 4:31
And when they had prayed, the place was shaken where they were assembled together; and they were all filled with the Holy Ghost, and they spake the word of God with boldness.

Acts 6:4
But we will give ourselves continually to prayer, and to the ministry of the word.

Acts 9:40
But Peter put them all forth, and kneeled down, and prayed; and turning him to the body said, Tabitha, arise. And she opened her eyes: and when she saw Peter, she sat up.

Acts 12:5, 12
5 Peter therefore was kept in prison: but prayer was made without ceasing of the church unto God for him.
12 And when he had considered the thing, he came to the house of Mary the mother of John, whose surname was Mark; where many were gathered together praying.

Acts 14:23
And when they had ordained them elders in every church, and had prayed with fasting, they commended them to the Lord, on whom they believed.

Acts 16:25-26
25 And at midnight Paul and Silas prayed, and sang praises unto God: and the prisoners heard them.
26 And suddenly there was a great earthquake, so that the foundations of the prison were shaken: and immediately all the doors were opened, and every one's bands were loosed.

Additional Scriptures: Acts 13:3, 21:5, 22:17-18, 28:8.

Apostle Paul's and James' Admonition to Pray

1 Thess. 5:17
Pray without ceasing.

Heb. 4:16
Let us therefore come boldly unto the throne of grace, that we may obtain mercy, and find grace to help in time of need.

Rom. 12:12
Rejoicing in hope; patient in tribulation; continuing instant in prayer.

Col. 4:3
Withal praying also for us, that God would open unto us a door of utterance, to speak the mystery of Christ, for which I am also in bonds:

Eph. 6:17-18
17 And take the helmet of salvation, and the sword of the Spirit, which is the word of God:
18 Praying always with all prayer and supplication in the Spirit, and watching thereunto with all perseverance and supplication for all saints;

James 5:16-17
16 Confess your faults one to another, and pray one for another, that ye may be healed. The effectual fervent prayer [powerful and effective] of a righteous man availeth much.
17 Elias was a man subject to like passions as we are, and he prayed earnestly that it might not rain: and it rained not on the earth by the space of three years and six months.

Additional Scriptures: 1 Thess. 3:10, Col. 1:9, 2 Tim. 1:3.

Praying in the Spirit

We benefit greatly when we pray in the Spirit. It builds our faith and helps us at times when we don't know how to pray or what to say.

Jude 20
*But ye, beloved, **building up yourselves on your most holy faith**, praying in the Holy Ghost,*

Rom. 8:26-27
26 Likewise the Spirit also helpeth our infirmities: for we know not what we should pray for as we ought: but the Spirit itself maketh intercession for us with groanings which cannot be uttered.
27 And he that searcheth the hearts knoweth what is the mind of the Spirit, because he maketh intercession for the saints according to the will of God.

26 So too the [Holy] Spirit comes to our aid and bears us up in our weakness; for we do not know what prayer to offer nor how to offer it worthily as we ought, but the Spirit Himself goes to meet our supplication and pleads in our behalf with unspeakable yearnings and groanings too deep for utterance.
27 And He Who searches the hearts of men knows what is in the mind of the [Holy] Spirit [what His intent is], because the Spirit intercedes and pleads [before God] in behalf of the saints according to and in harmony with God's will. [Psalms 139:1-2] AMP

Your Prayer Life

What are you praying over and over in the name of Jesus that He will make of your life? What are you asking God to do through you during your time on this earth? What part of God's purpose and will has become a passion for you, so that you take hold of God day after day in prayer and ask Him to use you in it?

What prayer have you prayed most often over the last few years? What things do you want God to do so much that it is in your prayers every day? For many of us the answer to that would be: prayers that our children will be saved and walk in truth; that we would be protected from harm and danger and the needs of our family would be met.

There is nothing wrong with praying those kinds of prayers. They are needed and are good, but what about the bigger picture? God is the God of the whole earth and all of the nations and all of the cities are filled with people that do not know Him. Each of us was created to have a significant place in God's purpose and plan to seek and save the lost. What do you pray for every day about God's plan for your life?

We should pray that our life, our family and our church would accomplish something great for the Kingdom of Jesus Christ. May we read books about prayer, think about prayer and make plans for more consistent and fervent prayer.

So many of the best things in life are squeezed out, by many other good things, because we don't plan a time and a way to include them in our daily life. We should plan our day and select a time to talk to our heavenly Father. Select a private place for prayer and make it as sacredly consistent as a favorite meal.

Three Major Divisions of Prayer

As discussed in Chapter 1, "The Ecosystem of God's Kingdom", every living thing is defined and sustained by three functions: **input, process and output**. Likewise, the spiritual growth and maturity of a Christian revolves around these three processes or themes redefined as: **relationship, transformation, and dominion** (Chart E-1, in Chapter 1). Although there are many types of prayer, they will fit into one of these three categories. A balanced prayer life will include these three types of prayer:

1. **Relationship Prayers** (includes just God and me)
   Thanksgiving, praise, worship, and petitions for personal needs, etc.

2. **Transformation Prayers** (includes just God and me)
   Repenting and emptying of self to be filled with more of God.
   Asking God to change me:
   - Less of my will and more of His.

- Less of my mind and ways and more of His.
- Less of my limited human love and more His perfect love.

3. **Dominion Prayers** (involves praying for the needs of others):
    - Intercessory Prayer (intercession between friendly forces). Standing between God and man, interceding for our lost neighbor, city and world.
    - Spiritual Warfare (intercession between unfriendly forces). Standing between satan and man (binding the powers of satan that have bound and blinded them).
    - Praying for wisdom and understanding to use the apostolic authority we have been given, as a son of God, with dominion over satan and sickness.
    - Praying and fasting for God's anointing (divine ability) as we pursue God's will and purpose for our lives.
    - Praying into fulfillment the promises and prophecies in God's Word regarding restoration of apostolic power, dominion and authority.

These three types of prayer are also reflected in the three division of Moses' tabernacle (Chart T-1 in Chapter 3). Praying through the tabernacle:

1. Starts in the outer court with **transformation prayers** of repentance at the altar of sacrifice and purity at the brazen laver.

2. Continues to the inner court, the Holy Place, with **relationship prayers** of thanksgiving, praise and worship at the altar of incense.

3. Continues past the veil into the Most Holy Place with **dominion prayers** of power and authority over satan and sickness. This is the supernatural realm where the Gifts of the Spirit operate.

Refer to the following pages for the **"Prayer"** overview charts.

Chart P-1

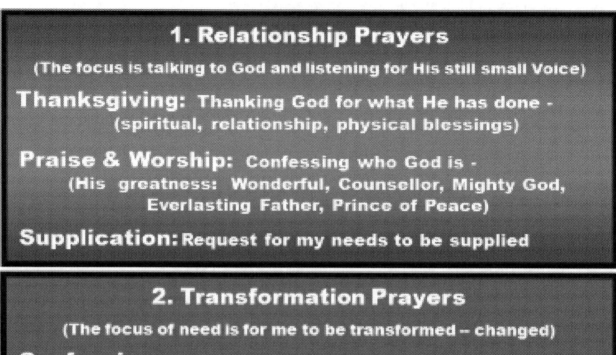

1. Relationship Prayers

(The focus is talking to God and listening for His still small Voice)

Thanksgiving: Thanking God for what He has done -
(spiritual, relationship, physical blessings)

Praise & Worship: Confessing who God is -
(His greatness: Wonderful, Counsellor, Mighty God,
Everlasting Father, Prince of Peace)

Supplication: Request for my needs to be supplied

2. Transformation Prayers

(The focus of need is for me to be transformed – changed)

Confession: Repentance of sin and self

Transformation: Change me prayers
- Less of my will and more of His
- Less of my thoughts and ways and more of His
- Less of my limited human love and more of His perfect love
- Ask God to help me identify and remove hindrances to the
  flow of His love and power through my life

3. Dominion Prayers

(The focus of need is for others)

Intercessory Prayers: Standing between God and man,
interceding for our lost neighbor, city and world

Intercessory Prayers (Spiritual Warfare): Standing between
Satan and man (binding the powers of Satan that have bound and
blinded them)

**Praying for God to help us walk in the dominion and authority
we have been given as a son of God**

Chart P-2

1. Relationship Prayers

The focus is talking to God and listening for His still small Voice

Thanksgiving:

Thanking God for His love and blessings:

- Spiritual Blessings

- Relationship Blessings (family and friends)

- Physical Blessings:

  Resources He has graciously given us to manage:

  Time (years of life).

  Health (strength to do His will).

  Wealth (finances and possessions).

- Protection Blessings (harm, danger, sickness, disease)

Praise & Worship:

Confessing who God is:

- His greatness: Wonderful, Counsellor, Mighty God, Everlasting Father, Prince of Peace

- His goodness (loving, merciful, gracious, kind, omnipotent, omniscient, omnipresent . . .)

Supplication:

Request for my needs to be supplied.

2. Transformation Prayers

- ## The focus of need is for me to be transformed -- continuously changed

"To grow in the grace and knowledge of our Lord and Savior Jesus Christ"

Confession & Repentance

- A plea for cleansing and forgiveness (Psalms 51)

- Repentance of sin and self

- Repentance for any pride or self-righteousness

Transformation (Change me prayers)

- Less of my will and more of His

- Less of my mind and ways and more of His

- Less of my limited love and more of His agape love

- Asking God to help me to identify and remove any hindrances to the flow of His love and power through my life

- Renewal of the Holy Ghost *(Building up yourselves on your most holy faith, praying in the Holy Ghost. Jude 20)*

He must increase and I must decrease !

Chart P-4

3. Dominion Prayers

- ## The focus of need is for others (people in need)

Intercessory Prayer (friendly forces):

Standing between God and man and interceding for our lost neighbor, city and world.

Intercessory Prayer (unfriendly forces):

Spiritual Warfare -- Standing between Satan and man and binding the powers of Satan that have bound and blinded them from coming to the light and knowledge of Jesus Christ.

God's Direction and Wisdom:

Praying for God wisdom and direction to know how to operate in the dominion and authority that we have been given as a son of God.

Praying Prophecies into Fulfillment

Praying into fulfillment the promises and prophecies in God's word regarding restoration of apostolic power, dominion and authority.

Chart P-5

LEVELS OF BURDEN, PRAYER & ANOINTING

LEVELS OF BURDEN (VISION)	LEVELS OF PRAYER	LEVELS OF ANOINTING (DIVINE ABILITY)
0. NO BURDEN / VISION	0. PRAYERLESSNESS	0. NO ANOINTING
1. BURDEN FOR SELF (PERSONAL) (MY KINGDOM)	1. SURVIVAL PRAYER - SEEKING THE HANDS OF GOD - MAINTENANCE PRAYER (Maintaining Our Own Salvation)	1. PERSONAL ANOINTING BEGINS HERE
2. BURDEN FOR OTHERS (HIS KINGDOM)	2. REVIVAL PRAYER - SEEKING THE FACE OF GOD (Favor & Relationship) - RELATIONSHIP PRAYER - TRANSFORMATION PRAYER - DOMINION PRAYER	2. PUBLIC ANOINTING SOUL WINNING MINISTRY BEGINS & INCREASES HERE
3. BURDEN OF THE LORD (Restoration of the Church to the book of Acts & beyond) (HIS KINGDOM)	3. REVIVAL PRAYER - SEEKING THE HEART OF GOD (Consumed with His Purpose) - RELATIONSHIP PRAYER - TRANSFORMATION PRAYER - DOMINION PRAYER	3. PRIESTLY ANOINTING (DOUBLE PORTION) - INTENSE SOUL WINNING CONCERN & MINISTRY - USED IN THE GIFTS OF THE SPIRIT

Note: The above is a draft model to be used for teaching prayer and related concepts. The horizontal lines in the above table are not meant to depict a precise concept.

Chart P-6

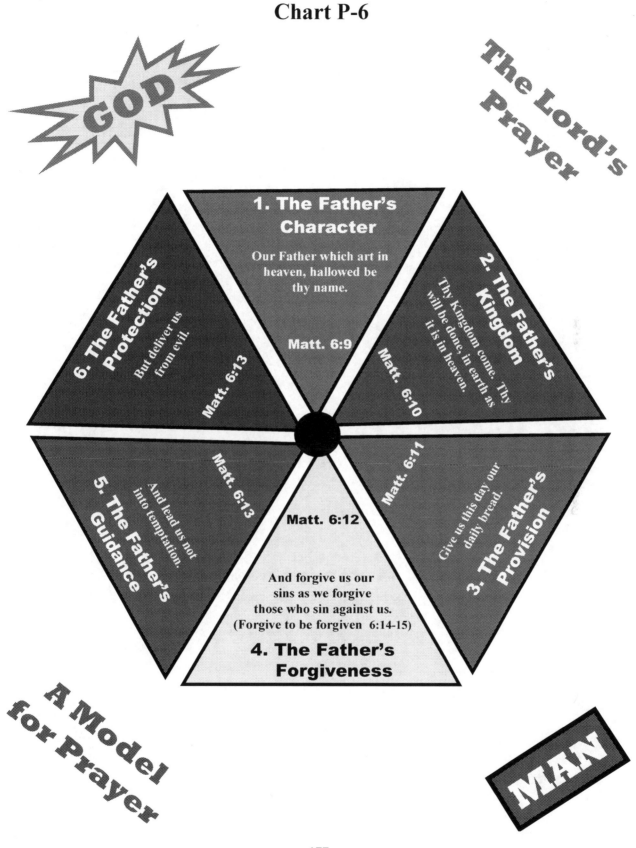

GOD

The Lord's Prayer

A Model for Prayer

MAN

1. The Father's Character

Our Father which art in heaven, hallowed be thy name.

Matt. 6:9

2. The Father's Kingdom

Thy Kingdom come. Thy will be done, in earth as it is in heaven.

Matt. 6:10

3. The Father's Provision

Give us this day our daily bread.

Matt. 6:11

4. The Father's Forgiveness

And forgive us our sins as we forgive those who sin against us. (Forgive to be forgiven 6:14-15)

Matt. 6:12

5. The Father's Guidance

And lead us not into temptation.

Matt. 6:13

6. The Father's Protection

But deliver us from evil.

Matt. 6:13

9. Fasting Intensifies the Power of Prayer

Fasting

Fasting is decreasing our focus for physical food and increasing our desire for spiritual food -- the bread of life and the water of life.

Fasting is much easier when we become hungrier for God and His perfect will than we are for food. Fasting is taking food from the carnal man and giving it to the spiritual man.

A properly conducted fast will:

1. Make us spiritually stronger and produces a more healthy spiritual man.

2. Make us physically stronger and produces a more healthy natural man.

3. Weaken the carnal man and strengthen the spiritual man.

A truth taught in Isaiah Chapter 58 is, that no mere outward expressions of penitence, such as fasting, will be accepted by God without first an inward cleansing of the heart.

Jesus imparted the timeless truth to His disciples in Mark Chapter 9: "There are obstacles and circumstances that will not yield to prayer alone – but require prayer and fasting."

Prayer With Fasting Brings Restoration

- Turn ye even to me with all your heart, and with **fasting**, and with weeping. Sanctify a **fast**. Let the priests, the ministers of the LORD, weep between the porch and the altar. Then I will restore **to** you the years that the locust hath eaten. And it shall come to pass afterward, that I will pour out my spirit upon all flesh. (Joel 2:12, 15, 17, 25, 28)

- Then there came some that told Jehoshaphat, saying, There cometh a great multitude against thee from beyond the sea on this side of Syria . . . And Jehoshaphat feared, and set himself to seek the Lord, and proclaimed a **fast** throughout all Judah . . . Then came the Spirit of the Lord in the midst of the congregation and said Thus saith the Lord unto you, Be not afraid nor dismayed by reason of this great multitude; for the battle is not yours, but God's . . . Ye shall not need to fight in this battle: stand ye still, and see the salvation of the Lord. (2 Chron. 20:2-3, 15, 17)

- This is the kind of **fasting** I have chosen: Loosen the chains of wickedness, untie the straps of the yoke, let the oppressed go free, and break every yoke. Share your food with the hungry, take the poor and homeless into your house, and cover them with clothes when you see them naked. Don't refuse to help your relatives. Then your light will break through like the dawn, and you will heal quickly. Your righteousness will go ahead of you, and the glory of the Lord will guard you from behind. Then you will call, and the Lord will answer. You will cry for help, and he will say, "Here I am!" (Isa. 58:6-9) GWT

- And he said unto them, This kind can come forth by nothing, but by **prayer and fasting.** (Mark 9:29)

	Study References		
Vol.	**Book Name**	**Primary Study Section / Chapter**	**Elective Study**
III	Spiritual Growth - Dominion Over Sin and Self	Sec. I / Ch. 1, Sec. II / Ch. 5	
IV	Unlimited Partnership With a Supernatural God	Sec. III / Ch. 4	
VIII	Addendum Volume (PowerPoint Charts)	Charts at the end of this chapter	Charts B-1a, C-9, 13, 21, G-3, 13

There is an appetite that satisfies the natural man (son of man); it is driven by a hunger for things in our kingdom. However, the appetite that satisfies the spiritual man (son of God) is fueled by a hunger for things in the Kingdom of God. To be filled with His Kingdom, we must take away or fast from things in our kingdom.

Appetite for the things of God can be energized by prayer with fasting that says to God: "I want the things of Your Kingdom more than anything in my kingdom." Eating is one of the most essential needs and strongest cravings. To forsake food and seek God emphasizes His superior importance in our lives.

- **Fasting is decreasing our focus for physical food and increasing our desire for spiritual food -- the bread of life and the water of life.**

John 6:35
*Jesus said unto them, I am the **bread of life**: he that cometh to me shall never hunger; and he that believeth on me shall never thirst.*

Rev. 21:6
*I will give unto him that is athirst of the fountain of the **water of life** freely.*

Isa. 55:1
Ho, every one that thirsteth, come ye to the waters, and he that hath no money; come ye, buy, and eat; yea, come, buy wine and milk without money and without price.

Fasting with the right motive intensifies prayer. Fasting and prayer lead us into a God-consciousness that opens the supernatural realm. Prayer and fasting increase the dimension of charity (love in action to those in need) where the supernatural Gifts of the Spirit operate: *"This kind can come forth by nothing, but by prayer and fasting"* (Mark 9:29).

A properly conducted fast will:

1. Make you spiritually stronger and produces a more healthy spiritual man.

There is nothing like fasting, with prayer that will remove barriers and distractions from our spirits and produce a cleansing of the inner man. We can then hear with more clarity what the Spirit is saying to the church and to us as individuals. We can then receive more revelation about His ways, His Word and His will for our lives.

2. Make you physically stronger and produces a more healthy natural man.

There is nothing like fasting to allow the body to rid itself of toxins, cleanse the liver, kidneys, and colon and purify the blood. Fasting allows the organs to rest, facilitates healing, reverses the aging process and promotes a longer and healthier life.

-- From Prescription for Nutritional Healing

Fasting rids the body of toxins, cleansing the liver, kidneys, and colon while purifying the blood. Fasting allows the organs to rest, facilitates healing, reverses the aging process, and promotes a longer and healthier life. Physical benefits of fasting include lower blood pressure and cholesterol level, resting the digestive system, allowing the body time to cleanse itself, relieves nervousness and tension, allows better sleep, and sharpens mental processes.[1]

3. Weaken the carnal man and strengthen the spiritual man.

Fasting is denying the carnal man his craving for natural food to satisfy the spiritual man's craving for spiritual food.

-- From "A Hunger for God" by John Piper

Our appetites dictate the direction of our lives – whether it be the cravings of our stomachs, the passionate desire for possessions or power, the insatiable appetite for entertainment and pleasure or the longings of our spirits for God. For the Christian, the hunger for anything besides God can be our enemy, while our hunger for God -- and Him alone -- is the only thing that will bring fullness, satisfaction and victory.

Do you have that hunger for Him? Do you have that thirst for Him? If we don't feel strong desires for the manifestation of the glory of God in our lives, it is because we have not drunk deeply from His fountain. It is because we have nibbled so long at the table of the world. Our soul is stuffed with small things, and there is no room for the great.

If we are full of what the world offers, then perhaps a fast might express, or even increase, our soul's appetite for God. Between the dangers of self-denial and self-indulgence is this path of pleasant pain called fasting. For when God is the supreme hunger of your heart, He will be supreme in everything. And when you are most satisfied in Him, He will be most glorified in you.[2]

- **When we control our physical appetite, we develop strength to control our spiritual appetite.**

Fasting Should Lead to Service

After we have fasted, we must go to work for Jesus Christ. The proof of our fasting is measured by the energy of our service afterward. It is one thing to withhold food from oneself; it is another thing to give oneself in dedicated service. Fasting should lead to ministering to the needs of others. How we are affecting the lost in our personal harvest field (our circle of influence) is a good measure of the work of the Holy Ghost in our life. D. L. Moody said, "Every Bible should be bound in shoe leather. We show our love to God, not by empty words, but by willing works."

Types of Fasts

The following are some suggestions for ways to fast:

1. No Food: Never without water. Usually 1 - 3 days.

2. Juice Fast: (3-40 days): Liquids only, no solid food or milk. Fresh fruit and vegetable juices, vegetable broth (vegetables boiled and drink the water). You will need a quality juicer to get the nutritional benefits of juicing raw fruits and vegetables. Search the internet for: "Bill Bright 40 day juice fast" for a description of this fast.

Bill Bright, founder of Campus Crusade for Christ, author of "The Four Spiritual Laws" and the visionary behind the "Jesus" film, realized that even our most ambitious evangelism efforts were not turning the tide for Christ in our world. So each year Rev. Bright fasted for 40 days, drinking only water and juice. Another recommended book of Bill Bright is: "The Coming Revival, America's Call to Fast, Pray, and Seek God's Face." Refer to Appendix 2 for an interview with Bill Bright regarding his ministry of fasting.

3. Daniel's Fast: Two types (21 days)

There are two references to fasting in the book of Daniel from which the "Daniel Fast" is drawn. Daniel Chapter 1, describes how Daniel and his three friends ate only vegetables and drank only water. At the end of a 10-day trial period, Daniel and his friends appeared healthier than their peers who ate the rich foods from the royal table. In Daniel Chapter 10, Daniel fasts for 21 days, abstaining from pleasant food (e.g. desserts), meat and wine.

    a. No meats, no sweets, no strong drinks (e.g. caffeine).

    b. More restrictive, eating only raw fruits, vegetables, nuts, seeds, etc.

For more information search the internet for "Daniel's fast."

Examples of combining a juice fast with a Daniel's fast:

    (1) 3-7 day Daniel's fast, 3-7 day liquids only fast, 3-7 day Daniel's fast

    (2) 7-10 day Daniel's fast, 7-10 day liquids only fast, 7-10 day Daniel's fast

Examples in the Bible of God's Call and Response to Fasting and Prayer

Much of the call to fasting in the Old Testament was related to the restoration of Israel to their homeland from exile in Babylon, or the return of God's favor because of their sin.

God's call and response to fasting and prayer are still applicable to us today as we seek for and reach for total restoration of the apostolic power and authority of the first church in the book of Acts: *"And they went forth, and preached everywhere, the Lord working with them, and confirming the word with signs following" (Mark 16:20).*

Isaiah describes God's requirements for a fast that He will recognize and bless: First turning from sin, doing good deeds, then He will provide bountiful blessings. The truth taught here is, that no mere outward expressions of penitence will be acceptable to God, without first an inward cleansing of the heart. (Isa. 58:1-13)

(1) Repentance required before sacrifice in fasting is accepted (v. 1-5):
The Lord says, Shout as loud as you can! Tell my people Israel about their sins! They worship me every day, claiming that they are eager to know my ways and obey my laws. . . The people ask, "Why should we fast if the Lord never notices? Why should we go without food if he pays no attention?" The Lord says to them, "The truth is that at the same time you fast, you pursue your own interests. When you fast, you make yourselves suffer; you bow your heads low like a blade of grass and spread out sackcloth and ashes to lie on. Is that what you call fasting? Do you think I will be pleased with that?" GNT

(2) God's requirements (v. 6-7):
The kind of fasting I want is this: *Remove the chains of oppression and the yoke of injustice, and let the oppressed go free. Share your food with the hungry and open your homes to the homeless poor. Give clothes to those who have nothing to wear, and do not refuse to help your own relatives.*

(3) God's promise of blessings (v. 8-9):
Then my favor will shine on you like the morning sun, and your wounds will be quickly healed. I will always be with you to save you; my presence will protect you on every side. When you pray, I will answer you. When you call to me, I will respond.

(4) God's requirements (v. 9-10):
If you put an end to oppression, to every gesture of contempt, and to every evil word; if you give food to the hungry and satisfy those who are in need . . .

(5) God's promise of blessings (v. 10-12):
Then the darkness around you will turn to the brightness of noon. And I will always guide you and satisfy you with good things. I will keep you strong and well. You will be like a garden that has plenty of water, like a spring of water that never goes dry. Your people will rebuild what

has long been in ruins, building again on the old foundations. You will be known as the people who rebuilt the walls, who restored the ruined houses.

(6) God's requirements (v. 13):

The Lord says, If you treat the Sabbath as sacred and do not pursue your own interests on that day; if you value my holy day and honor it by not traveling, working, or talking idly on that day . . .

(7) God's promise of blessings (v. 13):

Then you will find the joy that comes from serving me. I will make you honored all over the world, and you will enjoy the land I gave to your ancestor, Jacob. I, the Lord, have spoken.

-- From Barnes' Notes

[Is not this the fast that I have chosen?] Fasting is right and proper; but that which God approves will prompt to, and will be followed by, deeds of justice, kindness, charity. The prophet proceeds to specify very particularly what God required, and when the observance of seasons of fasting would be acceptable to him.[3]

God honors Daniel and the three Hebrew children with wisdom and understanding when they refused to defile themselves with the king's meat and wine.

Then said Daniel to Melzar, whom the prince of the eunuchs had set over Daniel, Hananiah, Mishael, and Azariah, Prove thy servants, I beseech thee, ten days; and let them give us pulse to eat, and water to drink. And at the end of ten days their countenances appeared fairer and fatter in flesh than all the children which did eat the portion of the king's meat . . . **God gave them knowledge and skill in all learning and wisdom**: *and Daniel had understanding in all visions and dreams . . . And in all matters of wisdom and understanding, that the king inquired of them,* **he found them ten times better** *than all the magicians and astrologers that were in all his realm. (Dan. 1:11-12, 15-20)*

Daniel's prayer, fasting and repentance for the nation of Israel sets in motion the wheels of prophecy for the restoration of the Jews back to their homeland.

In the first year of his reign I Daniel understood by books the number of the years, whereof the word of the Lord came to Jeremiah the prophet, that he would accomplish seventy years in the desolations of Jerusalem. And I set my face unto the Lord God, to seek by prayer and supplication, with fasting, and sackcloth, and ashes. (Dan. 9:2-3)

Daniel's prayer and fasting sets in motion the actions of the archangels, Gabriel and Michael, breaking through the powers of satan, to bring him a message from God.

In those days I Daniel was mourning three full weeks. I **ate no pleasant bread, neither came flesh nor wine in my mouth,** *neither did I anoint myself at all,* **till three whole weeks were fulfilled.** *And, behold, an hand touched me, which set me upon my knees and upon the palms* *of my hands. And he said unto me, O Daniel, a man greatly beloved, understand the words that I speak unto thee, and stand upright: for unto thee am I now sent. Then said he unto me, Fear not, Daniel: for from the first day that thou didst set thine heart to understand, and to chasten thyself before thy God, thy words were heard, and I am come for thy words. But the prince of the kingdom of Persia withstood me one and twenty days: but, lo, Michael, one of the chief princes, came to help me; and I remained there with the kings of Persia. Now I am come to make thee understand what shall befall thy people in the latter days. (Dan. 10:2-3, 10-14)*

God's promises of blessings and restoration for His people, when they answer His call to prayers of repentance with fasting.

Therefore also now, saith the LORD, turn ye even to me with all your heart, and with fasting, and with weeping, and with mourning: And rend your heart, and not your garments, and turn unto the LORD your God: for he is gracious and merciful, slow to anger, and of great kindness . . . Blow the trumpet in Zion, sanctify a fast, call a solemn assembly . . . Let the priests, the ministers of the LORD, weep between the porch and the altar . . . Let them say, Fear not, O land; be glad and rejoice: for the LORD will do great things . . . Rejoice in the LORD your God: for he hath given you the former rain moderately, and he will cause to come down for you the rain, the former rain, and the latter rain in the first month. And the floors shall be full of wheat, and the fats shall overflow with wine and oil. And I will restore to you the years that the locust hath eaten, the cankerworm, and the caterpillar, and the palmerworm, my great army which I sent among you. And ye shall eat in plenty, and be satisfied, and praise the name of the LORD your God . . . And it shall come to pass afterward, that I will pour out my spirit upon all flesh; and your sons and your daughters shall prophesy, your old men shall dream dreams, your young men shall see visions: And also upon the servants and upon the handmaids in those days will I pour out my spirit. (Joel 2:12-17, 21-29)

Fasting and prayer for God's protection on their journey as Ezra and a remnant of the Jews are returning from exile in Babylon to restoration in their homeland.

Then I proclaimed a fast there, at the river of Ahava, that we might afflict ourselves before our God, to seek of him a right way for us, and for our little ones, and for all our substance. For I was ashamed to require of the king a band of soldiers and horsemen to help us against the enemy in the way: because we had spoken unto the king, saying, The hand of our God is upon all them for good that seek him; but his power and his wrath is against all them that forsake him. So we fasted and besought our God for this: and he was intreated of us. (Ezra 8:21-23)

God's miraculous deliverance when Queen Esther and the Jews fasted and prayed to be spared from annihilation by an evil plot by their enemies.

And in every province, whithersoever the king's commandment and his decree came, there was great mourning among the Jews, and fasting, and weeping, and wailing; and many lay in sackcloth and ashes. Then Mordecai commanded to answer Esther, Think not with thyself that thou shalt escape in the king's house, more than all the Jews. For if thou altogether holdest thy peace at this time, then shall there enlargement and deliverance arise to the Jews from another place; but thou and thy father's house shall be destroyed: and who knoweth whether thou art come to the kingdom for such a time as this? Then Esther bade them return Mordecai this answer, Go, gather together all the Jews that are present in Shushan, and fast ye for me, and neither eat nor drink three days, night or day: I also and my maidens will fast likewise; and so will I go in unto the king, which is not according to the law: and if I perish, I perish. (Esther 4:3, 13-16)

God's decision to destroy the city of Nineveh is reversed to one of mercy in response to the people of Nineveh fasting and praying to be spared the judgment of God.

The people of Nineveh believed God's message, and from the greatest to the least, they declared a fast and put on burlap to show their sorrow. When the king of Nineveh heard what Jonah was saying, he stepped down from his throne and took off his royal robes. He dressed himself in burlap and sat on a heap of ashes. Then the king and his nobles sent this decree throughout the city: "No one, not even the animals from your herds and flocks, may eat or drink anything at all. People and animals alike must wear garments of mourning, and everyone must pray earnestly to God. They must turn from their evil ways and stop all their violence." (Jonah 3:5-8) NLT

Jesus taught in the Sermon on the Mount that we should fast, as He declared: "When ye fast", not "if ye fast". He ended His sermon with a warning: *"He that doeth not these sayings of mine is like a foolish man that build his house on the sand."*

Moreover when ye fast, be not, as the hypocrites, of a sad countenance: for they disfigure their faces, that they may appear unto men to fast. Verily I say unto you, They have their reward. But thou, when thou fastest, anoint thine head, and wash thy face; That thou appear not unto men to fast, but unto thy Father which is in secret: and thy Father, which seeth in secret, shall reward thee openly. (Matt. 6:16-18)

When the disciples could not cast the devil out of a boy, Jesus told them: *"This kind can come forth by nothing, but by prayer and fasting."*

*Lord, have mercy on my son: for he is lunatick, and sore vexed: for ofttimes he falleth into the fire, and oft into the water. And I brought him to thy disciples, and they could not cure him. Then came the disciples to Jesus apart, and said, Why could not we cast him out? And Jesus said unto them, Because of your unbelief: for verily I say unto you, If ye have faith as a grain of mustard seed, ye shall say unto this mountain, Remove hence to yonder place; and it shall remove; and nothing shall be impossible unto you. **Howbeit this kind goeth not out but by prayer and fasting**. (Matt. 17:15-16, 19-21)*

The Gentiles were included in the New Testament plan of salvation in response to the prayers and fasting of Cornelius.

And Cornelius said, Four days ago I was fasting until this hour; and at the ninth hour I prayed in my house, and, behold, a man stood before me in bright clothing. And said, Cornelius, thy prayer is heard, and thine alms are had in remembrance in the sight of God. Send therefore to Joppa, and call hither Simon, whose surname is Peter; he is lodged in the house of one Simon a tanner by the sea side: who, when he cometh, shall speak unto thee . . . While Peter yet spake these words, the Holy Ghost fell on all them which heard the word. And they of the circumcision which believed were astonished, as many as came with Peter, because that on the Gentiles also was poured out the gift of the Holy Ghost. For they heard them speak with tongues, and magnify God. Then answered Peter, Can any man forbid water, that these should not be baptized, which have received the Holy Ghost as well as we? And he commanded them to be baptized in the name of the Lord. (Acts 10:30-32, 44-48)

Fasting and prayer accompanied the ordination of elders in the early church.

Confirming the souls of the disciples, and exhorting them to continue in the faith, and that we must through much tribulation enter into the kingdom of God. And when they had ordained them elders in every church, and had prayed with fasting, they commended them to the Lord, on whom they believed. (Acts 14:22-23)

After many days in a storm on the Mediterranean Sea, when all hope was gone that they would survive, the angel of the Lord appeared to Paul after a long fast.

*And when neither sun nor stars in many days appeared, and no small tempest lay on us, all hope that we should be saved was then taken away . . . And now I exhort you to be of good cheer: for there shall be no loss of any man's life among you, but of the ship . . . For there stood by me this night the angel of God, whose I am, and whom I serve . . . Wherefore, sirs, be of good cheer: for I believe God, that it shall be even as it was told me . . . And while the day was coming on, Paul besought them all to take meat, saying, This day is the **fourteenth day that ye have tarried and continued fasting**, having taken nothing . . . Wherefore I pray you to take some meat: for this is for your health: for there shall not an hair fall from the head of any of you. (Acts 27:20-34)*

Jesus, at the age of 30, fasted 40 days in the wilderness before He began His ministry. He went into the wilderness full of the Spirit, encountered and defeated satan and came out of the wilderness in the power of the Spirit, then His miracle ministry began.

*And Jesus **being full of the Holy Ghost** returned from Jordan, and was led by the Spirit into the wilderness. Being forty days tempted of the devil. And in those days he did eat nothing: and when they were ended, he afterward hungered. And when the devil had ended all the* *temptation, he departed from him for a season. And **Jesus returned in the power of the Spirit into Galilee: and there went out a fame of him through all the region round about.** (Luke 4:1-2, 13-14)*

Jesus' Encounter With the Devil

When Jesus reached 30, the age of maturity for the culture of that day, He began His public ministry -- a ministry of miracles.

- He was first baptized by John in the Jordan River.

- He then went into the wilderness, fasted for 40 days and had an encounter and clash with satan.

- He defeated satan, departed the wilderness in the **power of the Spirit** and immediately His miracle ministry began.

Luke records the formula for release of power for the supernatural:

1. **Impartation** - Jesus went into the wilderness **full of the Spirit.**

2. **Encounter and Engagement** - Jesus experienced conflict with the evil forces of satan.

3. **Release of Supernatural Power** - When Jesus defeated satan, He came out of the wilderness in the power **of the Spirit**, and His miracle ministry began.

The power, resident in Jesus, was released in that initial battle with satan, however, His ministry was simply a continued encounter and engagement in battle with the kingdom of darkness. Every time this occurred, power was released that defeated satan and brought miracles of deliverance and healing.

**Impartation + Encounter and Engagement
= Release of Power for Miracles**

The twofold mission of Jesus is still the mission of His church today:

- Destroy the works of the devil, 1 John 3:8.
- Seek and save the lost, Luke 19:10.

We will accomplish this mission only as we use the power imparted to us by the Word and the Spirit (prayer and fasting) to encounter and engage the kingdom of satan in spiritual warfare.

Refer to Chart F-1, "Encounter and Engagement Releases Supernatural Power", at the end of this chapter.

Power in the Words of Jesus

Luke 4:32-33, 35-37
*32 And they were **astonished at his doctrine: for his word was with power.***
33 And in the synagogue there was a man, which had a spirit of an unclean devil, and cried out with a loud voice,

35 And Jesus rebuked him, saying, Hold thy peace, and come out of him. And when the devil had thrown him in the midst, he came out of him, and hurt him not.
*36 And they were all amazed, and spake among themselves, saying, What a word is this! **for with authority and power he commandeth the unclean spirits,** and they come out.*
37 And the fame of him went out into every place of the country round about.

- **Jesus' words had power because they were confirmed with a demonstration of the miraculous.**

It is the will of God for every born-again believer to enter the dimension of apostolic dominion, power and authority where their words of spreading the gospel have power -- confirmed by signs following.

Mark 16:20
*And they went forth, and preached everywhere, the Lord working with them, and **confirming the word with signs following.***

Charles Stanley said: "Fasting brings about a supernatural work in our lives. God will not entrust **supernatural power** to those whose lives are not under total control of the Holy Spirit."

Wesley Duewel said: "Fasting is still God's chosen way to deepen and strengthen prayer. You will be the poorer spiritually and your prayer life will never be what God wants it to be until you practice the privilege of fasting. Our ability to perceive God's direction in life is directly related to our ability to sense the inner promptings of His Spirit. God provides a specific activity to assist us in doing this. Men through whom God has worked greatly, have emphasized the significance of prayer with fasting."

- **There is great value in teaching and encouraging every born-again believer to fast, particularly new converts and those who are struggling with significant physical or spiritual issues in their lives.**

Chart F-1

Impartation + Encounter and Engagement with the Forces of Satan and Sickness Releases Supernatural Power!

GOD

You become more Christlike **with more Christlike actions!**

- Partakers of His divine nature.
- Power to become a son of God.
- Freely you have received, **freely give.**

Passion for God

Flow

3. Releases Supernatural Power

Signs and Miracles Following the Believer.
Mark 16:17-18

Operating as a son of God

1. Impartation
(Revival)
Being Full of the Spirit

Flow

Compassion for the lost

Flow

2. Encounter & Engagement

With the Opposing Forces of Satan and Sickness

(Evangelism)

Jesus came out of the wilderness in the power of the Spirit and His miracle ministry began.
Luke 4:14

Jesus went into the wilderness full of the Spirit.
Luke 4:1

Man in Need

Ministering to someone in need blesses them – and in turn blesses you.

10. The Urgency of the Father's Business

Urgency of the Father's Business

The prophetic events unfolding in our world today (particularly those concerning Israel and their surrounding enemy nations) scream out the message that we are living at the very end of the Church Age, just before the coming of Jesus Christ.

Endtime prophecy is a tremendous tool to warn, stir and mobilize the church for the endtime harvest and soon coming of Jesus Christ. Only as the church is stirred and awakened to the urgency of the times can it then sound the warning to the world.

Satan is aware of the shortness of time and is increasing his evil influence and power in the world. May every born-again believer respond with increased dominion and authority over this evil power of the Antichrist rapidly rising in the world today.

We should pray for God to help us to align our lives with His purpose and will; help us to align our time clock with His prophetic time clock -- managing our priorities and activities consistent with our knowledge of the times.

Understanding the times and knowing what to do:

- And of Issachar, men who had understanding of the times to know what Israel ought to do. (1 Chron. 12:32) AMP

- Jesus said unto them when it is evening, ye say, It will be fair weather: for the sky is red. And in the morning, It will be foul weather today: for the sky is red and lowering. O ye hypocrites, ye can discern the face of the sky; but **can ye not discern the signs of the times**? (Matt. 16:2-3)

- But the natural man receiveth not the things of the Spirit of God: for they are foolishness unto him: neither can he know them, because they are **spiritually discerned**. (1 Cor. 2:14)

- And that, knowing the time, that now it is high time to awake out of sleep: for now is our salvation nearer than when we believed. The night is far spent, the day is at hand: let us therefore cast off the works of darkness, and let us put on the armour of light. (Rom. 13:11-12)

- All of us must quickly carry out the tasks assigned us by the one who sent me, for there is little time left before the night fall and all work comes to an end. (John 9:4) TLB

- Making the very most of the time, because the days are evil. Therefore do not be vague and thoughtless and foolish, but understanding and firmly grasping what the will of the Lord is. (Eph. 5:16-17) AMP

- Woe to you, O earth and sea, for the devil has come down to you in fierce anger (fury), because he knows that he has a short time! (Rev. 12:12) AMP

Study References

Vol.	Book Name	Primary Study Section / Chapter	Elective Study
I	God's Purpose for Man - Relationship - Dominion		Sec. II / Ch. 4
II	Dominion - Doing God's Will and Work		Sec. IV
IV	Unlimited Partnership With a Supernatural God	Sec. II / Ch. 4	
V	Revival & Evangelism - Passion for God - Passion for Souls	Sec. II / Ch. 8	
VIII	Addendum Volume (PowerPoint Charts)	Charts at the end of this chapter	

Today many end-time prophetic events are converging and pointing to the midnight hour. Three great witnesses to the endtime are the calendar, the world news and the prophetic time clock of God's Word. All these are now in alignment much like a total solar eclipse. They signify the end of the Church Age and the soon coming of Jesus Christ.

Events in the Middle East are unfolding as the prelude to the Battle of Armageddon with the nations of the earth turning against Israel. May we recognize the approaching midnight hour and understand the urgency of the Father's business.

One of the most notable end-time prophetic signs is the nation of Israel. The central focus of the Old Testament is Israel, a physical kingdom of God's chosen people. The church, a spiritual Kingdom of God's chosen people, is the focus of the New Testament. Events in church history have tracked the history of Israel throughout the past 2,000 years with:

- The dispersion of the Jews by the end of the first century.

- The Dark Ages for the Jewish people, with terrible persecution and worldwide suffering.

- The beginning of restoration in the early 1900s with the Balfour Declaration favoring the establishment of a Jewish national homeland in Palestine.

- The miraculous survival against overwhelming odds with victory in numerous wars.

- Israel's desert has blossomed like a rose.

- Israel is now a powerful nation that continues to thrive in a hostile environment.

Refer to Chart U-1, "Restoration -- The History of the Church", at the end of this chapter.

God's divine plan has restored Israel to its current status as a powerful nation. And it is His will to restore the church to the power and evangelism of the first century church -- and beyond. The complete fulfillment of these two events will very soon usher in the second coming of Jesus Christ.

Examining what is happening in Israel will disclose what should be happening in the church during a particular time period. In the nation of Israel today, there is a high alert and readiness to deploy military offensives to protect their nation and to destroy the enemy. That is what the true church should do in response to the all-out attack by satan: *"Be careful -- watch out for attacks from satan, your great enemy. He prowls around like a hungry, roaring lion, looking for some victim to tear apart" (1 Peter 5:8). TLB*

As satan launches his all-out offensive attack against the church, we must launch a counter-offensive against him. Too long the church has been in a defensive position.
  - Although the apostolic doctrine has been restored to the church, total restoration of the apostolic power, authority and dominion of the first century church is not complete. Rev. Jeff Arnold asserts that: "Doctrine without demonstration is frustration."
  - We must not allow religious traditions to hinder the restoration of apostolic ministry and prevent us from stepping into the eternal purpose and will of God for our lives.

There will be a great harvest before the Rapture of the church. This will be unlike any other revival because it will be driven by apostolic ministry with aggressive evangelism and miracles. It will involve duplicating the mission and ministry that Jesus exampled for us:
  - To seek and save the lost.
  - To destroy the works of the devil.

Are we polishing our ticket to heaven by validating it every Sunday with a religious routine or are we sharpening our sword for the battle and our sickle for the harvest? The pertinent message for the saints is not to prepare for the Rapture, but prepare for the battle and harvest. Because, if we are involved in the battle and harvest, we will be ready for the Rapture.

The first battle is not against demons and the kingdom of satan -- it is against carnality, apathy and self:
  - Self-will vs. God's will.
  - Our mind vs. the mind of Christ.
  - Our limited human love vs. Christ's agape love and compassion for a lost world.

We must win the battle over carnality and self. As we decrease and He increases in our lives, we will then be empowered to defeat the kingdom of satan and rescue lost souls. This is a sifting and testing time, when everything that can be shaken will be shaken. The Word of God warns that the love of many will become cold. Apostle Paul declares that before the coming of Jesus Christ there would be a great falling away: *"Let no man deceive you by any means:*

*for that day shall not come, except there come a **falling away** first, and that man of sin be revealed, the son of perdition" (2 Thess. 2:3).*

In the Olivet discourse recorded in Matthew 24, Jesus answered His disciples' question: *"What shall be the sign of thy coming, and of the end of the world?"* The last sign that Jesus gave was the sign of, "love growing cold": *"Because iniquity shall abound, **the love of many shall wax cold.**"* This is speaking of Christians, because for love to grow cold, it must have been hot at a prior time. This was discussed in Chapter 6.

Never has there been a greater urgency in all of church history. The age of the Gentiles is almost over; the midnight hour is approaching. We should be feeling the tug of the Spirit that is soon to rapture the church, but first that **intense tug of the Spirit will draw us deeper into the harvest field and the battlefield.** The gathering place for the Rapture will be the harvest field. Refer to Chart U-3 at the end of this chapter.

- **The key message is: If we are not ready, we must get ready. If we are ready, help someone else get ready, because it will keep us ready.**

We will be tested and tried before we step into the New Jerusalem. The world could not distinguish between the house built on the rock and the one built on the sand until the storm came. God will always manifest His people to the world through testing. The nation of Israel has been tested like no other nation and they are currently under great pressure.

Breakthrough revival will require breakthrough change. It will require a paradigm shift in our thinking, prayer and actions. It will require, "God doing a new thing" -- working in unfamiliar ways. It will mean relying on God's supernatural ability instead of our limited natural abilities.

For many years in teaching and preaching, I did not spend much time studying end-time prophecy. I felt the most important issue was to help people get ready for the Rapture, regardless of how prophetic events played out in the endtime. However, for the last ten years I have felt the need for a better understanding of prophecy -- particularly current events that are significant prophetic sign posts, warning us of the soon coming of Jesus Christ.

End-time prophecy is a tremendous tool to warn, stir and mobilize the church for the end-time harvest and soon coming of Jesus Christ. First, the church must recognize the final prophetic end-time events that are now converging, pointing to the end of the age and the eminent coming of Jesus Christ. When the church is stirred and awakened to the urgency of the times, it can then sound the alert and warning to the world.

Luke 21:34
Watch out! Don't let my sudden coming catch you unawares; don't let me find you living in careless ease, and occupied with the problems of this life, like all the rest of the world. TLB

Time -- Our Most Precious Resource

Time is man's most valuable God-given resource. Even corporations stress time management. Since it is also a most precious resource in the church, should we not teach time management as it applies to God's Kingdom and His will for our lives?

Every day God deposits 1,440 minutes into our account and we are accountable for their use. Wasted time is like water spilled on the ground; it is lost forever. God will forgive us of sin, but He may not give us back lost time.

Our greatest responsibility is to wisely manage our time (our most precious resource) with godly activities that add value to our life and others.

Scripture teaches that time is valuable and should be used wisely. King David, King Solomon, and Job address the brevity and frailty of life:

Psalms 39:4
LORD, make me to know mine end, and the measure of my days, what it is; that I may know how frail I am.

Eccl. 12:5-7
5 Because man goeth to his long home, and the mourners go about the streets:
*6 Or ever the **silver cord be loosed**, or the **golden bowl be broken**, or the **pitcher be broken** at the fountain, or the **wheel broken** at the cistern.*
7 Then shall the dust return to the earth as it was: and the spirit shall return unto God who gave it.

Job 7:6, 22
*6 My days **are swifter** than a weaver's shuttle.*
*22 When a **few years** are come, then I shall go the way whence I shall not return.*

Psalms 90:12
So teach us to number our days, that we may apply our hearts unto wisdom -- [Wisdom to use our precious allotted time wisely -- considering His Kingdom vs. our kingdom].

Life is fragile and our time on earth is fleeting. The most sobering question that a patient will ask his doctor is, **"How much time do I have left?"** Likewise, we need to ask Doctor Jesus, **"How much time do we have left?"**

Most of us are very optimistic about our longevity and we behave as though we will live forever on this earth. The length of our lives is important and an issue for every individual. However, our focus should not be our personal time clocks, as they relate to the end of our natural lives:

   - Many of us will be alive at the Rapture of the church.
   - We must not make future plans based on our natural time clock, but God's time clock.
   The 20 year old possibly does not have more time than many who are 60 years old.

-- From "Life is a Vapor"

Life is brief, a vapor that appeareth for a little while and then vanisheth away, a passing shadow, just one thin footprint upon a sea-lashed shore. We think of how God gives the rocks a million years, the trees a thousand years, the elephant a hundred years, and a man, only threescore and ten. Then we see that a man's life is a handbreadth.

'Tis a tale; 'tis a vessel under sail.

'Tis an eagle on its way, darting down upon its prey.

'Tis an arrow in its flight, mocking the pursuing sight.

'Tis a short life, fading flower; 'tis a rainbow on a shower.

'Tis a momentary ray, smiling on a winter's day.

'Tis a torrent's rapid stream; 'tis a shadow, 'tis a dream.

'Tis the closing watch of night, dying at the rising light.

'Tis a bubble; 'tis a sigh. Be prepared, oh man, to die.[2]

- **Don't make the mistake that many have made by misjudging the brevity of life and the length of eternity.**

The Four Questions of Time

There are four questions that we must answer as we approach the end of the age and set the priorities for our most precious resource -- time:

1. **Where** are we on God's prophetic time clock?
2. **How** much time do we have left?
3. **What** should we do with our remaining days?
4. **When** will we make the changes demanded by these momentous times?

The answer to the first two questions can be found through our understanding of the end-time prophetic events that are occurring in our world today.

Approximately every 2,000 years a major event in the plan of God for the human race takes place. Sometime near 4,000 B.C., Adam and Eve were created. Around 2,000 B.C., Abraham was born. He became the father of the physical nation Israel – God's chosen people. Two-thousand years later, Jesus Christ was born. Through His death, burial and resurrection the church, a spiritual nation, was born.

We now live at the end of the Church Age and another 2,000 year milestone. This historic point in time is the most important since the beginning of the human race. The prophetic fulfillments that we are presently witnessing point to the second coming of Jesus to establish

His 1,000 year reign of peace here on earth. Refer to Chart U-2, "Prophetic Time Clocks", at the end of this chapter.

God has always warned His people of impending danger and judgment. God is warning this generation of the end-time season and His very soon coming. May we give strict attention to recognize each prophetic sign and be prayerfully cautious in these momentous times. May the priorities and actions of our lives be in alignment with this knowledge.

The World-wide Empires of Daniel's Image

Approximately 600 years before Christ, King Nebuchadnezzar, king of Babylon, dreamed about a great image that Daniel interpreted. This dramatic prophecy described five world-ruling empires:

- Babylon (gold head).
- Media-Persia (silver chest).
- Greece (brass stomach and thighs).
- Rome (iron legs).
- Future world government (combination iron and clay feet).

Four of these world empires have risen and fallen; the last being the Roman Empire over 1,500 years ago. Since then we have not had a world empire or a one world ruler.

The fifth worldwide kingdom prophesied just before the second coming of Christ is now rising and being assembled. Components of this world government being assembled include:

- Redesigned United Nations for world government.
- World court system.
- World religious system. "The United Religions Organization will be an international, inter-religious organization modeled after and affiliated with the United Nations, according to its literature," states W.B. Howard of Despatch Ministries
- Worldwide numbering system of everyone on earth (current legislation in Congress as the Real ID Act). Many nations already have implemented a national ID.
- World army (UN peacekeeping force).
- World communication system (satellites, World Wide Web).
- Proposed world tax.
- Increased pressure from the proponents of globalism to manage the shared global resources of clean air, water, etc. This agenda is being labeled, "climate change", but has little to do with climate issues. Rather, it involves world government control and advancing the socialistic agenda of wealth distribution.

Prophecies of Christ's First and Second Coming

With 100 prophecies concerning Christ's first coming, the religious world missed it because they did not know the prophecies. There are hundreds of prophesies concerning Christ's second coming. Many, including Christians, are overlooking the end-time prophecies being fulfilled before their eyes. Could it be that many may miss the second coming of Jesus Christ because they do not know the prophecies?

The period in history most like ours was the time of Noah because the world and all of the unrighteous were destroyed. The similarities include:
- Great wickedness.
- Total destruction of the wicked -- the entire world.
- One way to escape the wrath of God -- by getting into the **ark of safety.**

Luke 17:26-27
*26 As it was in the **days of Noah, so shall it be also in the days of the son of man.***
27 They did eat, they drank, they married wives, and they were given in marriage, until the day that Noe entered into the ark, and the flood came, and destroyed them all.

God destroyed that generation after many warnings from Noah, and one final sign -- the most miraculous sign of all millennia past.

- **The most spectacular warning sign God has given to any generation was when His Spirit caused the animals to methodically and orderly march into the ark.**

Vicious and carnivorous animals evidently became docile. It would have been impossible for Noah to capture every animal -- seven pairs (male and female) of the clean and one pair of the unclean. God's last warning sign to that wicked generation was when He directed thousands of animals to travel methodically from every direction, entering orderly into the ark, day after day, before He closed the door.

Despite this miraculous sign, not one soul perceived what was about to happen, not one person made a change. They watched as the last few animals trudged up the gangplank to board the ark. They listened as Noah warned, "There are 7, 6, 5, 4, 3, 2, 1 day left to enter the ark" and yet not one person moved toward the open door of safety.

Noah was 600 years old when God instructed him to enter the ark. The world was destroyed by water at the end of the 6th day of Noah's life. We are at the end of the 6th day of man's history -- 6,000 years from Adam. Ironically, in the seventh chapter of Genesis (six chapters had expired) the flood came and God gave Noah a seven day warning: *"For yet seven days, and I will cause it to rain upon the earth forty days and forty nights; and every living substance that I have made will I destroy from off the face of the earth" (Gen 7:4).* In past dispensations, God sent warning signs that the end was near and judgment eminent; He is doing the same today.

- **Like the last few animals standing on the gangplank to board Noah's ark, the last few end-time prophecies are on the doorstep, in our daily news headlines and in current peace negotiations.**

What Should We Do With Our Remaining Days?

Along with the question, "Lord, how much time do we have left", we should also ask, "**Lord, what would You have me to do with this time?**" Apostle Paul asked this question when he was knocked down on the road to Damascus: *"Lord, what would You have me to do?"*

Like the children of Issachar, we should pray for an understanding of the times and **to know what we ought to do**: *"And of the children of Issachar, which were men that had understanding of the times, to know what Israel ought to do" (1 Chron. 12:32).*

Another probing question is, "Am I currently doing all I should do in the Father's business?" This may best be answered by rolling the clock ahead a few days to the end of our life. Looking back from that perspective what would we want to have accomplished in the Father's business?

While ministering to a number of terminally ill people over the last few years, their perspectives were revealed. When they realized their days were numbered, only one issue was paramount in their minds -- their relationship with God and their work accomplished in the Father's business.

What are your dreams? What are your plans and goals for the Father's business? We must maintain sight of the goal and our great heavenly reward that cannot be measured in earthly riches. As Moses did, let us look beyond the hardships in the battlefield and harvest field and compare the great reward: *"It was by faith that Moses, when he grew up, refused to be called the son of Pharaoh's daughter. He chose to share the oppression of God's people instead of enjoying the fleeting pleasures of sin. He thought it was better to suffer for the sake of Christ than to own the treasures of Egypt, for he was looking ahead to **his great reward"** (Heb. 11:24-27). NLT*

Let us heed the Father's voice urging late evening workers to work a little longer because He is coming soon -- bringing a rich reward: ***"Behold, I am coming soon! My reward is with me**, and I will give to everyone according to what he has done. I am the Alpha and the Omega, the First and the Last, the Beginning and the End" (Rev. 22:12-13). NIV*

*"All of us must **quickly carry out the tasks assigned us** by the one who sent me, for there is little time left before the night falls and all work comes to an end" (John 9:4). TLB*

When Will We Make the Changes Demanded by These Momentous Times?

When there is a warning of an approaching category 5 hurricane, people take action when they believe the reports of the seriousness and closeness of the storm:
  - When a hurricane is a few weeks away, no action is taken.
  - When it is just one day or a few hours away, action is taken by some.
  - When it is 30 minutes away, it is too late for action.

Likewise, we will make changes when we recognize and heed the prophetic warnings that are screaming out the message of the coming end-time storm. The long shadows of 6,000 years of man's day are reminders that we are in the closing days of time. The 2,000 years that have transpired since Christ's first coming, declare that the Church Age is ending and Christ's second coming is eminent. God's prophetic time clock is pointing to the midnight hour. This era of time is like none other with the convergence of many signs and prophetic events. Let us pray daily for God to help us recognize every warning sign and to take the appropriate actions.

-- From "Time of the Signs"

This generation of passengers on Planet Earth is passing through a corridor John the apostle and prophet called "the last time" (1 John 2:18). More to the point, we are somewhere near the very end of that corridor, and signs the size of billboards are on either side of the broad way that leads the world's inhabitants toward Armageddon. The only way to miss those gargantuan signs, for the true child of God, is to deliberately ignore them, choosing instead to focus on things of this world that perspective hides in the distant blackness.

We are in the **time of the signs**. They are signs so dramatic, so blatant, that the whinnying and violent snorting of the four horses of the apocalypse can almost be heard as they angrily paw the earth with rage, straining to burst to full gallop, determined to carry their death-dealing riders on their missions of globe-shattering devastation.[3]

How close is it? Are our actions consistent with this knowledge? Time is quickly running out for this sin-cursed world. The end-time prophecies of God's Word are almost all fulfilled:

- God's Word is warning us of His soon coming.
- The world news is heralding the message of His coming.
- The calendar is pointing to His soon coming.

Rom. 13:11-12
11 And that, knowing the time, that now it is high time to awake out of sleep: for now is our salvation nearer than when we believed.
12 The night is far spent, the day is at hand: let us therefore cast off the works of darkness, and let us put on the armour of light.

Let us not live in denial of His soon coming!
- Let us be vigilant!
- Let us be busy working in the Father's business!
- Let us be ready for the Rapture of the church!

The Challenge of the Unfinished Task

- **The Race** - This is the last and final lap of the Christian race and we are the last runners in the relay. The torch of truth has been passed to us to reach the last generation before the coming of Jesus Christ.

- **The Clock** - The prophetic time clock of the Ages points to midnight, we are almost out of time. Much work remains with billions desperately in need of a Savior. We are racing against the clock. We are racing the sunset.

This is the anchor leg of a relay race where truth has been passed down from generation to generation for the past 2,000 years of the New Testament church. The fastest and most skilled runner is always placed in the strategic position on the anchor leg of the race. We must run harder and with more determination than ever before. We are running for the gold -- a place where the streets are paved with gold. We are at the end of the Christian race. Heaven's city limit is now in view; eternal life is within our grasp.

We must take no risk on this lap because there is too much at stake. Everything we have lived for, worked for, and stood for, is depending on our actions in the next few days, just before the coming of Jesus Christ. "Dear heavenly Father, please reveal anything that is a weight or distraction in our lives hindering us from doing our best in Your Kingdom business."

Heb. 12:1-2
*1 Wherefore seeing we also are compassed about with so great a cloud of witnesses, let us **lay aside every weight, and the sin which doth so easily beset us**, and let us **run** with patience **the race** that is set before us,*
2 Looking unto Jesus the author and finisher of our faith;

We must lay aside, not just sin, but every weight, every distraction and anything that would hinder our spiritual progress. We must get our second wind in the Spirit and sprint to the finish line. The momentous times in which we live demand our best for the Father's business. We should strive to cross the finish line of this Christian race, running more determined than ever before, because we are running for our lives, the lives of our family and the lives of souls in our harvest field.

The night cometh: Man's day is almost over. The sun is quickly setting on this dispensation. What do you plan to do in these final closing days of time? What are your plans for the Father's business before the final rays of the light of the gospel have faded on the harvest field?

John 9:4
*4 I must work the works of him that sent me, while it is day: **the night cometh**, when no man can work.*

*4 All of us must quickly carry out the tasks assigned us by the one who sent me, because there is **little time left before the night falls** and all work comes to an end.   NLT*

When time has almost expired and there is still much work to do, our priorities and plans must be rearranged and realigned with the Father's business priorities. The devil, aware of the shortness of time remaining, is stepping up his activity and war against the Kingdom of God. Every born-again believer must respond with their actions of prayer and care to defeat the enemy and bring deliverance to those held captive by the god of this world.

> ### An urgent call is being made by our heavenly Father for soldiers, intercessors, caregivers and harvesters.

The Great Commander is Calling His Soldiers to Arms

The forces of evil are set in array against the purpose and mission of the church. This is the last opportunity to volunteer as a soldier for the Great Commander's army with the forces of good against the forces of evil. The kingdom of satan has issued its challenge to the church. What will be our response?

- Will it be like that of King David as he faced the giant that defied his God: ***"Is there not a cause?"*** -- a cause worth fighting and dying for?

- Will it be that of Mordecai's challenge to Queen Esther when the slaughter of the Jews was decreed: ***"Thou art come to the kingdom for such a time as this."***

The Great High Priest is Calling for Intercessors

Our heavenly Father is seeking for two things:
- **Worshippers** (involves our relationship with Him).
- **Intercessors** (involves our dominion role of doing His will and work).

An intercessor is a "go between", standing between two forces or causes:

- If the **forces are unfriendly**, there will be a **clash**. Standing between satan and man in need is often referred to as spiritual warfare, but it is also a form of intercessory prayer. *"For this purpose the Son of God was manifested, that he might destroy the works of the devil" (1 John 3:8).*

- If the **forces are friendly**, there will be a **pleading** to the one in position of power for the one in need. This is standing between God and man in need. It is intercessory prayer like Abraham pleading for Sodom and Gomorrah to be spared. It is Moses standing between God and Israel, interceding with God for a nation to be spared.

One of the greatest needs and challenges of our time is for every Christian to step into the dominion role and fulfill the call for intercessors.

Ezek. 22:30
*And I **sought for a man among them, that should make up the hedge, and stand in the gap** before me for the land, that I should not destroy it: **but I found none.***

The Great Physician is Calling for Caregivers

No other generation since the beginning of time has experienced so much suffering from physical, mental, emotional, and spiritual sickness. Jesus, the Master Physician who heals those with broken bodies, hearts and spirits, has left this work in our hands. He is depending on us; our lost world is depending on us. They are crying for someone to care for them and minister to:

- Their physical needs.
   - Their emotional and mental needs.
      - Their spiritual needs.

The world is full of people dying from disease and sin, crying out in their despair and hopelessness, desperately in need of a remedy -- the balm of Gilead, and the healing power of the Great Physician.

Jer. 8:20-22
20 "The harvest is finished, and the summer is gone," the people cry, "yet we are not saved!"
21 I weep for the hurt of my people. I am stunned and silent, mute with grief.
*22 **Is there no medicine in Gilead**? **Is there no physician** there? Why is there no healing for the wounds of my people? NLT*

The Lord of the Harvest is Calling for Harvesters

The Father's harvest business is labor intensive; it depends on laborers. He has chosen to do nothing on earth except through man. He is depending on you -- He is depending on me.

The only prayer request of Jesus, the Lord of the Harvest, is still calling and pleading for every believer to come to His help just before the sun sets forever on the harvest field. For every believer that doesn't get involved in the harvest, there will be souls not saved.

Luke 10:2
*Therefore said he unto them, The harvest truly is great, but the labourers are few: **pray ye therefore the Lord of the harvest, that he would send forth labourers into his harvest.***

John 4:35
*Say not ye, There are yet four months, and then cometh harvest? behold, I say unto you, Lift up your eyes, and **look on the fields; for they are white already to harvest.***

Prayer for: Understanding of the times and to know what we ought to do. Wisdom to align our priorities and actions with the demand of the times.

"Dear God, don't let me be satisfied with what and where I am in Your Kingdom. Let there always be a hunger and thirst for more of Your righteousness. Don't let me be satisfied with an outer circle of relationship, but help me to always be reaching for that inner circle, closer to You.

Give me the grace to embrace the cross when that is Your plan for my life. Change me to enable Your resurrection power to work in me and through me. Help me to endure the Refiner's fire when it is needed to reveal and burn out the impurities in my life. Let the veil of self be torn away. Let there be less of my will, mind and limited human love and more of your will, mind and agape love. Let me pursue an encounter of the changing kind that will not only affect me but my desperately lost world. Let me be more like You, with a mind that believes for the impossible; eyes that see the invisible; and ears that hear the inaudible (the cries of lost souls).

Help me to submit every area of my life to Your authority, allowing You to reign as Lord in my life. Help me to set the right priorities and be disciplined to live by them. Don't let me be satisfied with the usual, the routine, or the status quo. Help me reach for a frontier in Your Kingdom where I have never been before. Help me discover new heights and depths in the Spirit and a greater revelation of You and Your ways.

Thank you for the great privilege to be called Your son and to be chosen to work in Your business. I want to be a good son and carry on Your business in a way that You exampled for me as You walked the shores of Galilee. Thank you for Your many blessings; they are more than I deserve. But more than Your blessings, I now desire Your favor. Thank you for including me in Your plan and in Your Kingdom business here on earth.

Dear Jesus, forgive me for not being all that I should have been in the harvest seasons of yesteryear. Let me see Your lost world and Your ripe harvest field like You see it. Let Your burden become my burden, and Your vision become my vision. Let me see the awful reality of sin, abuse and hopelessness in the desperately lost world for which You suffered and died.

Help me to align my spiritual compass with Your mission and purpose and will. Help me to align my time clock with the prophetic time clock of Your Kingdom -- managing my priorities and activities consistent with the urgency of the times.

I intend by Your help and grace, that when the last rays of light have faded on this final generation and Your great time clock of the ages has expired, You will find me working in Your business with a **sword** in one hand and a **sickle** in the other -- fighting in Your **battle** and working in Your **harvest**."

Refer to the following pages for the "**Urgency of the Father's Business**" overview charts.

Chart U-1

RESTORATION - THE HISTORY OF THE CHURCH

**It is God's will for history to repeat itself – for us to go back (full circle)
to the original pattern of the first church in the Book of Acts!**

"The glory of this latter house shall be greater than the former"

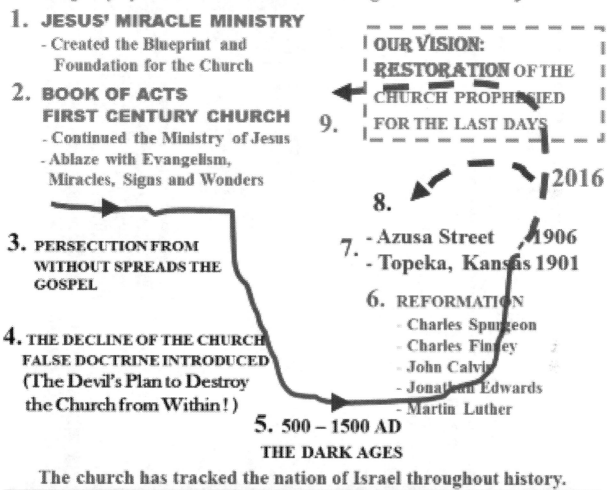

1. JESUS' MIRACLE MINISTRY
   - Created the Blueprint and
     Foundation for the Church

**2. BOOK OF ACTS
   FIRST CENTURY CHURCH**
   - Continued the Ministry of Jesus
   - Ablaze with Evangelism,
     Miracles, Signs and Wonders

**3. PERSECUTION FROM
   WITHOUT SPREADS THE
   GOSPEL**

**4. THE DECLINE OF THE CHURCH
   FALSE DOCTRINE INTRODUCED
   (The Devil's Plan to Destroy
   the Church from Within!)**

**5. 500 – 1500 AD
   THE DARK AGES**

**OUR VISION:
RESTORATION OF THE
CHURCH PROPHESIED
FOR THE LAST DAYS**

9.

8.

2016

7. - Azusa Street 1906
   - Topeka, Kansas 1901

6. REFORMATION
   - Charles Spurgeon
   - Charles Finney
   - John Calvin
   - Jonathan Edwards
   - Martin Luther

The church has tracked the nation of Israel throughout history.

OUR CHOICE – Today at the beginning of the 3rd Millennia:

8. TAKE A SHORT CUT? – Be part of the falling away (II Thess. 2:3)
(Deception – The devil's plan to destroy the Church from within).

9. PAY THE PRICE FOR RESTORATION? (A Deeper Relationship with Him)
We must not look at Restoration as a heaven or hell issue for us:
It is a heaven or hell issue for our Harvest Field! If we fall short of
Restoration, there will be many SOULS that will be LOST!

Chart U-2

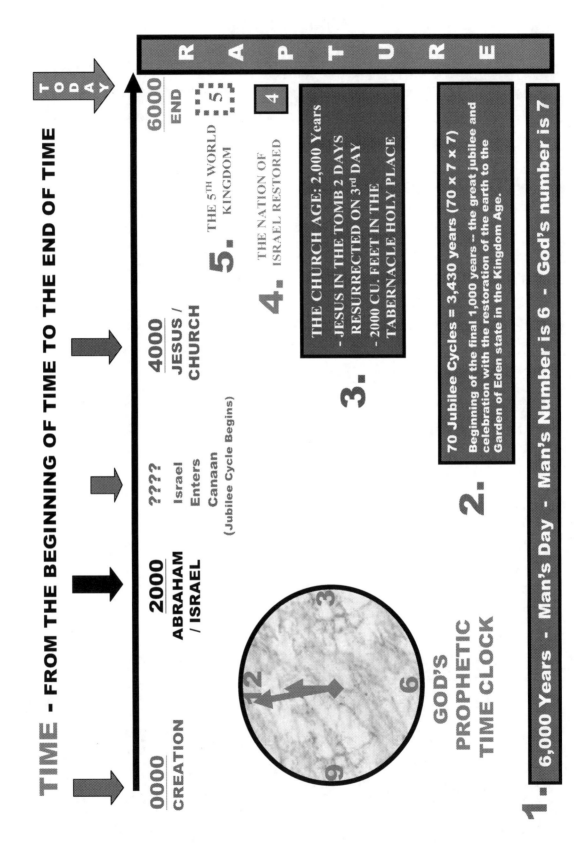

TIME - FROM THE BEGINNING OF TIME TO THE END OF TIME

0000	2000	????	4000	6000
CREATION	ABRAHAM / ISRAEL	Israel Enters Canaan (Jubilee Cycle Begins)	JESUS / CHURCH	END

TODAY

RAPTURE

5. THE 5TH WORLD KINGDOM

4. THE NATION OF ISRAEL RESTORED

3. THE CHURCH AGE: 2,000 Years
- JESUS IN THE TOMB 2 DAYS RESURRECTED ON 3rd DAY
- 2000 CU. FEET IN THE TABERNACLE HOLY PLACE

2. 70 Jubilee Cycles = 3,430 years (70 x 7 x 7)
Beginning of the final 1,000 years -- the great jubilee and celebration with the restoration of the earth to the Garden of Eden state in the Kingdom Age.

GOD'S PROPHETIC TIME CLOCK

1. 6,000 Years - Man's Day - Man's Number is 6 - God's number is 7

Chart U-3

REAPING YOUR PERSONAL HARVEST FIELD
WHEN WE DO OUR PART – GOD WILL BACK US UP & DO HIS PART

STIR UP THE GIFT THAT IS IN YOU !
- Exercising Faith - Repetition
- Experiencing His Will & Work
- Believing that God Needs You
- Feeling His Passion - Compassion
- Envisioning a Mega Harvest
- Claiming a Double Portion
- Partnering with God to do His Work
- Following Jesus' Example and
  Approach to Soul Winning

THERE IS ANGELIC HELP IN REAPING THE HARVEST! Heb. 1:14

Soul Winning is a Spiritual Process - Led by the Spirit:
- The deeper our relationship with God, the greater our depth and effectiveness in soul winning will be
- The foundational principles can be taught, but it is more than duplicating what someone else does

**LET YOUR LIGHT SO SHINE -
In Every Dark Place:**
- You are the lamp
- He is the source of all light
- Walk in the light as He is in the light and it will shine thru you

LIGHT OF REVELATION TO US:
- God's will for our life
- As a son of God our purpose is to duplicate the ministry of Jesus, that He exampled to us on earth as the Son of God

**HIS LIGHT SHINING THRU US -
To a Dark & Hurting World:**
His light will direct you to those that shall be heirs of salvation:
- They will be changed
- You will be changed

GOD'S GLORY & LIGHT

LED BY THE SPIRIT INTO THE HARVEST FIELD!

The wise men were led by a light to Jesus.
Abraham's servant was led by God to find a bride for Isaac.
As many as are led by the Spirit, they are the sons of God.
The Spirit will lead and guide us into His will and work in the harvest.

His light will direct our steps in the harvest field !

The Center
of God's Will
is the
Harvest Field

The meeting place for the rapture is the harvest field !

... the Harvest ... The Plowman Overtaking the Reaper !
... Believer Experiencing the ... of Apostolic Ministry
... in the harvest field !

Appendices

Appendix 1

Soul Winning and Breaking Bread Experiences

The following is a brief summary of people we have been blessed to meet and become a part of their conversion experience. It was by accident that we came to minister first to physical needs before addressing spiritual needs. Before we learned this concept in a training setting, we discovered that fellowship (friendship and food) in a home setting was the same powerful concept that Jesus used as He dined and visited with sinners.

My wife and I have hosted many fellowship events in our home. Our home became dedicated as a house of God. We experienced special blessings on our family similar to Obed-edom when the Ark of the Covenant was in his home for three months. This special Obed-edom blessing is for anyone who will dedicate their home as the house of God -- sharing food and fellowship with people in need.

An amazing bond of friendship results when we invest our time ministering to the needs of people that are reaching for God. There is nothing more rewarding and fulfilling as ministering to people in need of God's healing and saving touch -- an eternal investment.

The names of the people in this chapter are changed to protect their identity and privacy.

1. **(Richard and June)** Richard would attend church occasionally with his wife, but was very guarded when we approached him. In every meeting in our home with fellowship and food, we included them and made them feel special. Richard's poem that he wrote to us a few years later acknowledged, "I was won to the Lord through the Twentier's barbecue and wiener roasts."

Richard is now a minister and travels to Mexico often to preach and help build churches. They are a very intricate part of our church today and are some of our dearest friends.

2. **(Jack)** We were shopping in Office Depot when my wife stopped to assist an elderly man find an item. We found out that he operated a lawn mower shop at his home. He lived alone and was very lonely. We took him a plate of cookies and an old lawn mower for repair (for an excuse to get to know him). Through this connection, we developed a friendship and conducted Bible studies in his home a number of times. He started coming to church with us. When we gave him a birthday party with some of our friends, he exclaimed, "No one has ever treated me this special."

3. **(John)** I was teaching a Soul Winning Seminar in another city. One Saturday I told my wife, "We need to go win a soul." We went to Burger King for a biscuit and coffee and noticed an elderly man sitting alone. My wife said, "Let's go talk to him." I said, "No, if he's the one, he'll come to us."

A few minutes later, John got up to leave and stopped by our table. He greeted us and we invited him to sit down. He began telling his life story. He was very lonely since his wife recently passed away and his only daughter lived 500 miles away and had multiple sclerosis. He immediately became comfortable and told us things about his life that one should not tell a stranger. I did not identify myself to be a preacher and did not mention church. I was trying to emulate Jesus - sitting down to eat with people in need.

An hour later, when he finished talking, I acknowledged, "We enjoyed visiting with you." He responded that he had, too. He did most of the talking, unburdening his soul to a sympathetic listening ear -- the first key to soul winning. Like Jesus inviting himself to lunch at Zaccaheus' house, I said, "My wife will make cookies and, if you make the coffee, we will come to your home tomorrow." He responded, "Yes, I would really like that."

In his home the next day, he treated us like his own children, showing us around and giving us bags of shelled pecans from his freezer. Before we left, we prayed with him, for his daughter and other needs.   Tears welled up in his eyes as we prayed the peace and blessing of God on his home.

We thanked him for his hospitality. I complimented his coffee and he responded that he really liked our cookies. We said: "Let's do this again the day after tomorrow." He replied, "That sounds good; I will make another pot of coffee."

After our next visit he asked, "What church do you attend." We had never mentioned church, that I was a preacher, or any religious subject to him. He accompanied us to church the next few weeks and we continued to correspond when we returned to our home in Houston.

4. **(Elizabeth)** My wife met Elizabeth at Taco Bell in another city where we were ministering. After a short conversation, she mentioned end-time prophecy. My wife told her that I studied prophecy and offered to come to her home for a Bible study.

We took her a plate of fresh home-baked cookies. When we arrived at her apartment, there was no furniture -- nothing but a mattress on the floor. She had an 18 month old baby. We sat on the floor, held her baby and talked and prayed with her. She had just gotten a job but had not yet been paid. I gave her $20 that she reluctantly accepted. Afterwards, we stopped by a Salvation Army store and bought her an inexpensive, nice, used sofa and chair and delivered it to her apartment. She started attending church with us and brought four children and a friend.

5. **(Melvin and Brenda)** We were in another city holding a series of meetings. While taking our daily walk, we met Melvin pushing his wife in her wheelchair into their home. When I greeted him, he began a conversation, telling us why he moved to this city, and other details about his life. A few days later, my wife went to their home, knocked on their door, handed them a plate of home-baked cookies, saying, "We are praying for you." He thanked her for the cookies and said: "My wife is ill and we are not accepting company today."

My wife was out walking the next week when Melvin ran out of his house across the street, "Are you the lady who brought us cookies? After we ate them, we asked each other, "Was that an angel who delivered these cookies?" He invited us into their home, assuring that we were welcome anytime. We prayed for his wife and he pledged, "When my wife gets stabilized, I'm coming to your church."

6. **(Jeff and Sandra)** The first time Sandra walked into our church, she felt the presence of God so strongly, she immediately began crying and couldn't stop. She didn't know why she was crying. We talked with her and began to build a relationship. Her husband Jeff, who attended with her occasionally, said his Sunday morning church was, "saint mattress." We taught them a Home Bible Study series and over the months developed a close friendship. We were in each other's home many times. They were surprised that you could feel God's presence in your home the same as in the church.

These good friends are active in the church today and we honor their birthdays, anniversaries and children's activities. We also taught Bible studies to her parents and uncle and had food and fellowship in both our homes. Her parents came to church and were baptized.

7. **(Mike and Cindy)** For two years, we had been teaching two families having very difficult problems. Like an emotional roller-coaster ride, one wife would call at 3 A.M. crying, asking us to pray for her husband, who had not come home. With another family, their children were calling 911 to report their parents fighting. In both situations, the small children were emotionally disturbed by unfaithfulness, drugs and sin in the home.

My wife prayed, "Lord, this may be a selfish prayer, but would You please send us some normal people to reach with the Gospel; someone who has a clean house and loves each another!" God answered her prayer. Mike and Cindy visited our church for the first time and soon we began teaching them a Bible study series in their home. They lived conveniently close to our home, had a clean house, and adored each other and their infant son. They visited our home a number of times over the next few months; it was so refreshing to go to theirs. A vital part of our church now, they are some of our best friends. You never know when the ones you reach will become your treasured friends.

8. **(Rick and Tina)** A friend asked me to teach a Home Bible Study series to his friends. Rick and Tina brought a tape recorder and a notebook to every lesson. This appeared to be a hard case because Rick loved our church and worship, but Tina was reared much differently. Over the months, we shared fellowship and food while teaching and praying with them. They both received an outstanding conversion experience and remain a vital part of the church today. They said their goal was to be godly parents to their children as we were to ours.

Appendix 2

Interview with Rev. Bill Bright regarding Fasting[1]

Bill Bright, founder of Campus Crusade for Christ, author of The Four Spiritual Laws and the visionary behind the "Jesus" film, realized that even our most ambitious evangelism efforts were not turning the tide for Christ in our world. So each year Rev. Bright fasted for 40 days, drinking only water and juice.

Evangel: Why has there been such an emphasis on fasting in your life in the last few years?

Bright: In 1994, God led me for my first 40-day fast. I've had seven since, one each year, to intercede for revival. I would say it was God's timing. I've fasted and prayed shorter periods for years. I simply obeyed what He called me to do. He impressed me to write a book on prayer and fasting, "The Coming Revival, America's Call To Fast, Pray, and Seek God's Face". He called me to invite Christian leaders to come and pray with me in Orlando in December 1994. That was the beginning of a movement worldwide. There is a deep sense of the tragic disintegration of the morals of America and that is what prompted me to seek God's face. I realized that all the things we're doing are not enough. God doesn't have to help; but, for those who humble themselves and cry out to God to be merciful to them, as sinners, God hears. I've seen the dramatic results in pastors and individuals; ministries and churches have been revolutionized.

Evangel: What is the relationship between fasting and global evangelism?

Bright: Fasting is preparing your heart for greater intimacy with God. You don't earn brownie points. We already have the unlimited and inexhaustible love and favor of God. When we seek His face — as it says in 2 Chronicles 7:14, "If my people, who are called by my name, will humble themselves and pray and seek my face and turn from their wicked ways, then will I hear from heaven and will forgive their sin and will heal their land" (NIV) — we develop an intimacy we don't experience any other way. God hears our prayers like He heard Jesus' prayers. The disciples couldn't cast out demons. Jesus said it comes by prayer and fasting. Jesus fasted 40 days. He gave the Great Commission: "Teach what I taught you."
I strongly admonish every young pastor, seminarian and leader to fast at least one 40-day period of their lives.

Evangel: How does this apply to the individual believer?

Bright: It sharpens the believer to be salt and light in a way that he or she may not be if everything was business as usual. It gives one a greater sensitivity to God, to His Word and for lost souls.

Evangel: What do you say to the person who struggles to maintain a fast?

Bright: Just fast one moment at a time. Remember, you're fasting to seek God's face. Humble yourself. I encourage an individual to realize Jesus not only did it Himself, but also commanded us to do what He did.

Fasting is good for your physical body. Fasting is a marvelous way of bringing healing to your body. When satan seeks to discourage and frustrate you, just fast and pray — the Lord Jesus will help you. I recommend water and fruit and vegetable juices without added sugar. I wouldn't recommend water only without medical attention.

Evangel: Did you experience healing in your body during one of these fasts?

Bright: I wasn't sick to my knowledge; but, as the 40 days progressed, I became aware that little arthritic pains in my hands had lessened. So my physical body benefited from the fast. I wasn't even hungry for the 40 days.

Sometimes satan makes you feel it's a great sacrifice, but it's really a great blessing. When my wife and I fasted together, our relationship with our Lord was enhanced and our relationship with each other was enhanced. You never lose.

Evangel: What sins should the American church be repenting from as it fasts?

Bright: The sins of gross disobedience; of insulting God by removing the Bible and prayer from schools, the way our founding fathers established it. Christ was Lord of Harvard, Princeton and Yale — all the major universities. God was expelled from schools in the '60s; by the '70s we were legalizing the murder of unborn babies. That continual posture has brought great dishonor to our Lord and our nation.

Evangel: Do you see hope for the church in this new millennium?

Bright: I see great hope. The situation is very dark now, but there are glimmers of light. I am optimistic we'll see revival.

Evangel: What is your bottom line on prayer and fasting?

Bright: The final word: Every believer should take seriously the admonition to fast and pray. Again, Jesus commands us to do what He did, and that included a 40-day fast. God would never command you to do anything without His blessing and ability. I would strongly admonish anyone who is able-bodied — not diabetic or hypoglycemic — to one 40-day fast for the advancement of the Great Commission and revival.

Appendix 3

Refer to the following page for a cross reference of the major subjects addressed in this book to the other seven books in the series, **"I Must Be About My Father's Business."**

"I Must Be About My Father's Business" Book Series Subject Cross Reference

<-------------------- Section and Chapter Numbers -------------------->

Vol.	Volume Name	Relationship With God	Transformation (Spiritual Growth)	Dominion	Perfect Love	Humility and Unity	Prayer and Fasting	Urgency of the Father's Business
I	God's Purpose for Man • Relationship • Dominion	Sec. I, II		Sec. I / Ch. 1 Sec. III	Sec. II / Ch. 2-4			Sec. II / Ch. 4
II	Dominion Doing God's Will & Work			Sec. I, II, III				Sec. IV / Ch. 1
III	Spiritual Growth Dominion Over Sin and Self		Sec. I, II				Sec. III	
IV	Unlimited Partnership With a Supernatural God		Sec. I, II, III	Sec. I, II, III	Sec. III / Ch. 1, 6			
V	Revival & Evangelism • Passion for God • Compassion for Souls						Sec. III / Ch. 3	Sec. II / Ch. 8
VI	Perfect Love The Highest Law and Strongest Force	Sec. I / Ch. 4			Sec. I	Sec. I / Ch. 6, 7		
VIII	Addendum PowerPoint Charts (for all volumes)	A-1 - A-12	C-1 - C-21 D-1 - D-7	B-1 - B-9 F-1 - F-10 G-1 - G-27 J-1 - J-35 L-1 - L-5	N-1 - N-15	N-4	E-1 - E-7	L-1

Appendix 4

Summary of "My Father's Business" Book Series

Refer to the following pages for a brief description of this project. These eight volumes are shown here to:

- Briefly describe the complete scope of this project.
- Define the purpose and scope of each volume and where each one fits in this progressive series.

Volume I

God's Purpose for Man
Relationship and Dominion

Volume I sets forth God's purpose for man -- relationship and dominion. It addresses in more depth man's **relationship** with God and God's desire to have a close and growing relationship with man.

This book discusses man sharing a mutual relationship of love, communication, and trust with God -- as a son of God, a friend of God, a servant of God and as the bride of Christ. It also describes the God and man relationship roles: Father / Child, Groom / Bride, Friend / Friend, Master / Servant (love slave). It emphasizes God's **love** for man and man's love for God by loving his fellow man.

Volume II

Dominion
Doing God's Will and Work

This volume emphasizes the importance of **dominion**, since we often lead people to a relationship with God, but sometimes fail to help them take the next important step -- exercising dominion in the Kingdom of God. Dominion involves God sharing His authority and power with man in a partnership to fulfill His purpose and work on earth. The two concepts of relationship and dominion working together in a believer's life will bring balance, spiritual growth and fulfillment.

Love for God is the foundation for obedience that includes not just saying "no" to satan and sin, but "yes" to God's perfect will for our lives.

This book addresses the subject of dominion and why we need to be involved in the mission and work of the Father's business. It includes many examples from both the Old and New Testaments of God's plan to work through man to accomplish His will on earth. It also describes God and man dominion roles: Great Physician / physician; Great High Priest / priest; Great Commander / soldier; King of Kings / prince; Lord of the Harvest / harvester.

Volume III

Spiritual Growth – Passion for God
• Dominion Over Sin and Self

This book addresses **what** actions are required to become more effective in the Father's business. This encompasses foundational principles of spiritual growth that will prepare individuals to be more fruitful Christians. The primary emphasis is transformation: dominion over self (the will, the mind and the emotions) vs. dominion over sin.

Transformation is a continuous process of: less of my will and more of His, less of my thoughts and more of His, less of my limited human love and more of **God's perfect love**. Spiritual growth results from a hunger and a passion for the things of God -- "Loving God with all of our heart, soul and mind." The will of God will always lead us to greater spiritual growth.

Spiritual growth at the individual level will result in church growth at the corporate level.

Volume IV

Unlimited Partnership
With a Supernatural God

The greatest reason for God's creation of man was that He might obtain sons to carry out His will and work on earth. He desired to reproduce His image in a creature.

The greatest reason for God's new creation of man (through a new birth, a spiritual birth) first recorded in the book of Acts, was that He might obtain **sons to carry out the supernatural work of His Kingdom**. True son-ship is an obligation to live out, or put in practice, the Father's nature. It is the Father's will for us as sons of God, to become, *"Partakers of His divine nature"*, His supernatural nature -- partnering with Him in His business. As a partaker of the Father's divine nature we must grow in our **love** for God that will be manifested by our **love** and loving actions for man.

Volume V
Revival and Evangelism
- ### Passion for God
- ### Compassion for the Lost

The key to soul winning is **love** and compassion while exercising **dominion** in the harvest field. This book describes some of the biblical foundational principles of revival and evangelism. Discussed in more detail is the "**how to**" of putting the evangelism principles into practice through the two arms of the church:

- The **Prayer Ministry** -- reaching for Him.

- The **Compassion and Care Ministry** (attracting, winning and retaining) -- reaching for them with God's **perfect love**.

Volume VI
Perfect Love
The Highest Law and Strongest Force

If we had only one word to describe God, it would be "**l-o-v-e.**" If we had only one word to describe the entire Bible, it would be "**l-o-v-e**" -- a love story of God's love for mankind, a love letter to mankind.

- Love is the only motive accepted by God for working in His Kingdom. *"Though I have all spiritual gifts . . . give all my goods to the poor . . . give my body to be burned, and have not love, it is nothing" (1 Cor. 13:1-3).*

- It is the foundation and driving force for everything that is meaningful and lasting in the Kingdom of God. It is the currency of God's Kingdom.

- It is the key element required to produce revival and evangelism with miracles, signs, and church growth like the first century church in the book of Acts that shook their known world.

In this study we will discuss some hindrances that obstruct the growth and flow of God's love in our lives. We will also discuss some of the principles that promote and increase the growth of God's love in our lives.

Some of the amazing benefits and results of the **perfect love** of God flowing and working in our lives include: humility, unity, forgiveness, reconciliation of relationships, intensified revival and evangelism, love for our neighbor and enemy and especially the brotherhood (the body of Christ). Loving God and loving our brother are completely and indivisibly linked, because we are members of one body. Our love for God (the invisible) is manifest by our love for our brother (the visible): *"He who does not love his brother, whom he has seen, cannot love God, whom he has not seen" (1 John 4:20).*

Volume VII

Deeper Life Spiritual Growth Cycle

Relationship, Transformation and Dominion Working in the Love of God

The primary purpose and scope of the lesson series in this book is directed and driven by the greatest need and challenge for the born-again believer in these momentous days of the endtime. And that is to attain the spiritual maturity required to operate in the apostolic power, dominion and authority demonstrated in the book of Acts. Only this course of action will combat and overcome the evil and vicious spirit of the Antichrist rapidly rising in the world today and empower us to effectively reap the end-time harvest.

The seemingly impossible task to reach the lost of this godless, hopeless generation, with time running out, sets the stage for God to do a new thing -- a supernatural thing.

Our great omnipotent, omniscient, omnipresent God is calling every born-again believer to partner with Him at the supernatural level as a son of God -- fighting in His battle and working in His harvest with dominion and authority over satan and sickness:

The key spiritual growth cycle concepts discussed in this book include: Relationship, Transformation and Dominion, all working in the love of God.

Volume VIII

Addendum Volume

PowerPoint Charts for all Volumes

The Addendum Volume contains the 8.5 X 11 copies of the PowerPoint charts supporting the themes and concepts presented in the seven volume series entitled, *"I Must Be About My Father's Business."*

The purpose of these charts is to, the extent possibly, provide a graphic image of a concept as a strawman to initiate and facilitate understanding and discussion of biblical concepts.

The full color charts are available on CD in Adobe Acrobat and PowerPoint formats. For group teaching, these can be printed on printer transparencies for presentation on an overhead projector or with a computer and multi-media projector.

How to purchase copies of these books:

The E-copy of these books can be purchased from web sites: My-Fathers-Business.net (English) and Negocios-De-Me-Padre.net (Spanish). Hard copies and E-copies may be purchased by contacting the author by email: jtwentier@peoplepc.com.

Appendix 5

Refer to the following pages for the high level table of contents for each book in the series **"I Must Be About Father's Business":**

Volume	Title of Book
I	God's Purpose for Man -- Relationship and Dominion
II	Dominion -- Doing God's Will and Work
III	Spiritual Growth -- Dominion Over Sin and Self
IV	Unlimited Partnership With a Supernatural God
V	Revival and Evangelism -- Passion for God / Compassion for the Lost
VI	Perfect Love -- The Highest Law and Strongest Force
VII	Deeper Life Spiritual Growth Cycle (refer to pages 3-5)
VIII	Addendum - PowerPoint Charts for the all volumes

Volume I
God's Purpose for Man
Relationship and Dominion

Volume II
Dominion - Doing God's Will & Work

Volume III
Spiritual Growth
Dominion Over Sin and Self

Volume IV
Partnership With a Supernatural God

Volume V
Revival and Evangelism
Passion for God and Passions for Souls

Volume VI
Perfect Love the Highest Law and Strongest Force in the Kingdom

Volume VIII
Addendum Volume
PowerPoint Charts

Appendix 6

Notes

Introduction

(1) The Pulpit Commentary, Electronic Database. Copyright © 2001, 2003, 2005, 2006 by Biblesoft, Inc. All rights reserved

(2) Barnes' Notes, Electronic Database, Copyright © 1997, 2003, 2005, 2006 by Biblesoft, Inc. All rights reserved.

Chapter 1

(1) Pond Ecosystem in Science, russell.kyschools.us

Chapter 2

(1) Jamieson, Fausset, and Brown Commentary, Electronic Database, Copyright © 1997, 2003, 2005, 2006 by Biblesoft, Inc. All rights reserved.

Chapter 3

(1) Thayer's Greek Lexicon, Electronic Database, Copyright © 2006 by Biblesoft, Inc. All rights reserved.

(2) Webster's New World College Dictionary, Fourth Edition, Copyright © 2002, by Wiley Publishing, Inc., Cleveland, Ohio, p. 569.

(3) Watchman Nee, *The Spiritual Man*, Copyright © 1968, by Christian Fellowship Publishers, Inc., New York, NY, Volume 1, Chapters 1, 3.

(4) Watchman Nee, *The Spiritual Man*, Copyright © 1968, by Christian Fellowship Publishers, Inc., New York, NY, Volume 1, Chapter 1.

(5) Stan Shockley, song: *Change Me, Lord*.

Chapter 5

(1) *Effective Evangelism*, J. Smith, http://powertochange.com/itv/spirituality/evangelism-is-listening/

Chapter 6

(1) *Four Types of Love*, www.paxvobisca.tripod.com/literature /fourloves.html.

(2) *The Apostle John,* BiblePath.Com.

(3) Biblesoft's New Exhaustive Strong's Numbers and Concordance with Expanded Greek-Hebrew Dictionary. Copyright © 1994, 2003 Biblesoft, Inc. and International Bible Translators, Inc.

Chapter 7

(1) *Humility,* Andrew Murray, Chapter 1, pg. 2, 7, Chapter 7, pg. 25, www.faculty.gordon.edu/hu/bi/ted_hildebrandt/spiritualformation/texts/murray_humility/murray_humility.pdf, Originally published in New York: Anson D. F. Randolph & Co. 895, Currently in the public domain.

(2) *The Spirit of Prayer, Part II,* pg. 73, Edition of Moreton, Canterbury, 1893.

(3) The Teacher's Commentary, Copyright © 1987 by Chariot Victor Publishing. All rights reserved.

(4) The Pulpit Commentary, Electronic Database, Copyright © 2001, 2003 by Biblesoft, Inc. All rights reserved.

(5) *Marine Principles and Values*, www.marines.com/history-heritage/principles-values.

Chapter 9

(1) James F. Balch, M.D., Phyllis A. Balch, C.N.C., *Prescription for Nutritional Healing*, Second Edition, p. 548, copyright information unknown.

(2) John Piper, *A Hunger for God,* Copyright © 1997 by Crossway Books, Wheaton Illinois, p. 242. All rights reserved.

(3) Barnes' Notes, Electronic Database Copyright © 1997, 2003, 2005, 2006 by Biblesoft, Inc. All rights reserved.

Chapter 10

(1) Author Unknown. poem: *Life is a Vapor.*

(2) *Time of the Signs,* www.raptureready.com.

Appendix

(1) Bill Bright, www.pe.ag.org/conversations2001/4531_bright.cfm.

Appendix 7

Author's Note

The project of writing this eight volume progressive series of books was very challenging in both scope and content.

The first edition of this book series is a work in progress and is by no means a complete exegesis on the subjects discussed. It is only a summary of themes that God has dealt with me regarding these inexhaustible subjects. It is my thesis and collection of findings at this point in my Christian experience from:

- Several thousand hours studying various themes and subjects related to God's purpose and will for man, the restoration of the Church (partnering with God in the supernatural), passion for God (revival), compassion for the lost (evangelism), the end-time harvest (urgency of the times).

- A theme that began as a slice of bread from the Word of God, the Bread of Life. As my studies continued, it became a loaf of bread, and another, and another. As many of these themes came together, it became a bread truck, an overwhelming burden driving through my spirit, soul and mind that had to be delivered.

- Many years of trying to apply these principles in my life and ministry. I have not attained all that I should in His work and Kingdom, but I am reaching and striving for more.

- A direction and burden from God accompanied by an urgency to complete this project. This is comparable to the burden of a message waiting to be preached. However, this feeling has persisted throughout many years of study and preparation.

The Word of God is like a hammer -- one that has worn out many anvils throughout time without becoming weakened or diminished in its effectiveness. I pray that God will hammer these messages and themes into your spirit like He has mine.

"Is not my word like as a fire? saith the LORD; and like a hammer that breaketh the rock in pieces?" Jer. 23:29

This book series is a product of hearing several thousand messages, studying the greatest Book, the Bible, and from many other sources of great writers over the past 50 years. I have tried to give proper credit to sources. If I have overlooked someone or something, it is unintentional and only an indication that their individual work has blended into the larger themes of this ten year, 10,000 hour, 2,200 published page project.

Your comments for changes and additions to the content of these books are welcomed and will be considered for future revisions. God bless and multiply your harvest as we labor together with Him.

Note:
The 13 lessons in this book serve as the foundational curriculum for teaching in Global Missions Bible Schools. Each student is given an E-copy of this book and the other seven volumes in the series, "I Must Be About My Father's Business."